Value by Design with Microsoft Copilot Studio

Designing Strategic Agents with Microsoft's AI Tools

Steve Jeffery

Foreword by Ruby Bedford

Apress®

Value By Design with Microsoft Copilot Studio: Designing Strategic Agents with Microsoft's AI Tools

Steve Jeffery
Cambridge, UK

ISBN-13 (pbk): 979-8-8688-2612-2   ISBN-13 (electronic): 979-8-8688-2613-9
https://doi.org/10.1007/979-8-8688-2613-9

Managing Director, Apress Media LLC: Welmoed Spahr
Acquisitions Editor: Smriti Srivastava
Editorial Assistant: Marina Engler

Cover designed by eStudioCalamar

Cover image designed by pikisuperstar on Freepik

Distributed to the book trade worldwide by Springer Science+Business Media New York, 1 New York Plaza, New York, NY 10004. Phone 1-800-SPRINGER, fax (201) 348-4505, e-mail orders-ny@springer-sbm.com, or visit www.springeronline.com. Apress Media, LLC is a Delaware LLC and the sole member (owner) is Springer Science + Business Media Finance Inc (SSBM Finance Inc). SSBM Finance Inc is a **Delaware** corporation.

For information on translations, please e-mail booktranslations@springernature.com; for reprint, paperback, or audio rights, please e-mail bookpermissions@springernature.com.

Apress titles may be purchased in bulk for academic, corporate, or promotional use. eBook versions and licenses are also available for most titles. For more information, reference our Print and eBook Bulk Sales web page at http://www.apress.com/bulk-sales.

Any source code or other supplementary material referenced by the author in this book is available to readers on GitHub. For more detailed information, please visit https://www.apress.com/gp/services/source-code.

If disposing of this product, please recycle the paper

For my wife and our children.

Table of Contents

About the Author

Steve Jeffery is a Principal Program Manager at Microsoft, where he works with organizations around the world to unlock business value through AI-powered platforms and low-code innovation. His work sits at the intersection of strategy, design, and delivery, helping teams move beyond experimentation to sustained, measurable impact.

At the forefront of Microsoft's AI and low-code adoption efforts, Steve has partnered with hundreds of customers to design, govern, and scale intelligent solutions across Microsoft Power Platform and Microsoft Copilot Studio. His experience spans enterprise transformation, agent-based system design, and the establishment of value-driven Centers of Excellence that enable organizations to translate ambition into execution.

Steve is known for his practical, design-led approach. He has developed widely used frameworks for agent selection, value measurement, risk assessment, and stakeholder alignment, tools that help teams reason clearly about *why* a solution exists, *who* it serves, and *how* value is realized over time.

Through his workshops, writing, and open source contribution, Steve focuses on equipping practitioners to design solutions that augment human capability, accelerate time-to-value, and ensure technology investments remain grounded in real business outcomes.

About the Technical Reviewer

Ruby Bedford is a Cloud Solution Architect at Microsoft, where she has worked since September 2016. She has spent the majority of her career specializing in the Power Platform, more recently focusing on Copilot Studio and the role of agents in driving meaningful business outcomes. Through her work, Ruby has partnered with customers across a wide range of industries, helping organizations design, build, and govern scalable low-code and AI-powered solutions.

Outside of work, Ruby is based in the South East of England. She enjoys traveling and spending time with friends and family.

Acknowledgments

This book was written for the practitioners, leaders, and makers who are navigating the practical realities of designing and delivering AI-enabled solutions inside real organizations.

I am grateful to the many teams and communities across Microsoft who have shaped my thinking through collaboration, challenge, and shared learning. Working alongside customers and partners over the years has provided the real-world context that underpins every framework and example in this book.

Thank you to Ruby, who challenged assumptions, asked difficult questions, and pushed for greater clarity and precision. Her feedback significantly strengthened the final manuscript.

My approach has been influenced by disciplines well beyond technology alone, including service design, systems thinking, organizational change, and product strategy. These perspectives have deeply informed how value, responsibility, and impact are treated throughout the book.

Finally, I am deeply thankful to my family for their encouragement, patience, and support throughout the writing process.

Introduction

Artificial intelligence has moved from promise to practice. Across industries, teams are now building AI-powered agents that answer questions, coordinate work, automate decisions, and support people in their day-to-day roles. The tools are increasingly accessible, experimentation is encouraged, and progress is visible.

Yet, for many organizations, a familiar gap remains.

While agents are being built, their value is often unclear. Success is measured by activity rather than impact. Pilots struggle to scale. Governance is bolted on late, and teams find it difficult to explain, clearly and confidently, why a solution matters, who it serves, and how it contributes to meaningful business outcomes.

This book exists to address that gap.

Value by Design with Microsoft Copilot Studio is not a guide to building agents faster, nor a catalog of features or technical patterns. It is a practical framework for designing AI-powered agents with intent, grounded in strategy, shaped around people, and measured through outcomes rather than outputs. The focus throughout is on helping teams move from experimentation to execution and from isolated use case to sustained value.

Who This Book Is For

This book is written for practitioners and leaders responsible for shaping, delivering, or governing AI-enabled solutions. That includes product owners, architects, business analysts, makers, administrators, strategists, and Center of Excellence leads who are navigating the realities of introducing agents into live organizations.

It assumes some familiarity with modern platforms and AI concepts, but it does not require deep technical expertise. The emphasis is on decision-making, design choices, and trade-offs rather than implementation detail.

What This Book Covers

The chapters are organized into four stages, reflecting how value emerges over time:

- **Opportunity framing** focuses on aligning agent initiatives to strategic goals and defining success before anything is built.

- **Value foundations** explores agent types, design decisions, and the human considerations that shape adoption and trust.

- **Solution shaping** addresses time-to-value, telemetry, and the practical mechanics of measuring and communicating impact.

- **Value in motion** looks ahead to operating models, governance, responsibility, and the evolving relationship between people and intelligent systems.

Each chapter builds on the last, but the book is also designed to be used selectively. Readers may choose to focus on specific stages depending on their role, maturity, or immediate challenge.

How to Use This Book

This is a design-led book. You will find frameworks, questions, examples, and patterns intended to be applied, not just read. Some readers will work through it end-to-end. Others will dip in as new agent initiatives arise. Both approaches are valid.

The goal is not to prescribe a single "right" way to build agents but to help you reason clearly about value, responsibility, and impact – so that the systems you design serve both organizational goals and the people who rely on them.

Foreword

I started my career as an apprentice, primarily learning on the job, asking a lot of questions, and figuring things out as I went. That shaped how I think about technology to this day. It has always needed to be practical, useful, and tied to a real outcome rather than something abstract.

I ramped up into the Power Platform when it was still finding its feet. Back then it felt full of potential but also full of unknowns. As the platform evolved, new capabilities emerged and products like Power Virtual Agents came onto the scene, later transforming into Copilot Studio as we know it today. With that evolution came a shift in expectations. It was no longer enough to build something clever; customers wanted to understand the value, what problem does this solve, and what return can we expect.

That is where the need for strong business value conversations really came into focus. Power Platform was new and exciting, but excitement alone does not secure long-term success. This book does a great job of addressing that challenge head on. It introduces a clear and practical framework to help you move beyond building agents, toward realizing and articulating the full business value of Copilot Studio.

Inside, you will learn how to identify the right opportunities or hot spots within your organization, how to bring stakeholders with you on the journey, and how different types of agents naturally lend themselves to different value conversations. Importantly, this is not theoretical; scattered throughout the book are thought-provoking and actionable activities that encourage you to pause, reflect, and apply what you are learning in a way that is relevant to your own context.

—Ruby Bedford

Introduction: The Value Imperative

AI-powered agents are quickly becoming part of everyday business. They assist employees, improve customer experiences, and connect systems in ways that once took months of engineering effort. From automated workflows to intelligent copilots, the landscape is evolving fast – and with it, **expectations for what these systems can deliver**.

Speed rarely equals impact. In many cases, agents may appear successful on the surface but struggle to deliver meaningful business value. They generate activity but not always outcomes. They solve visible problems but don't always advance strategic priorities. So, what separates agents that truly deliver from those that simply perform?

Research reveals just how widespread this problem has become:

According to a Gartner[1] forecast released in June 2025, over 40% of agentic AI projects (systems designed to autonomously pursue goals) are expected to be canceled by the end of 2027, largely due to rising costs, ill-defined business value, and insufficient risk controls.

- AI is not inherently transformative. Without clear purpose and disciplined value measurement, even advanced systems flounder.

- Many projects today are driven more by buzz than impact – a dangerous tendency Gartner labels *"agent washing,"* where superficial capabilities are misrepresented as true AI autonomy.

- Yet, there is long-term promise. Gartner predicts that by 2028, 15% of routine work decisions will be handled autonomously by agentic AI, and one-third of enterprise software will embed these capabilities – up from virtually none in 2024.

---

[1] https://www.gartner.com/en/newsroom/press-releases/2025-06-25-gartner-predicts-over-40-percent-of-agentic-ai-projects-will-be-canceled-by-end-of-2027

The Emergence of Frontier Firms

The trajectory toward what many call "frontier firms" reflects a fundamental shift in how work is organized and executed.

In these organizations, agents evolve from personal assistants into business partners and, in some cases, autonomous operators, reshaping how decisions are made, how work flows, and how outcomes are delivered.

Frontier firms are structured around intelligence on demand, powered by hybrid teams of humans and agents, and they scale rapidly, operate[2] faster than traditional organizational models can match.

This vision is compelling – agents that gradually assume greater responsibility, eventually managing entire business functions with human oversight rather than human direction. The progression from helper, to employee, to manager requires increasingly sophisticated foundations that most organizations haven't yet built.

Without strategic alignment, stakeholder value clarity, and robust governance frameworks, the leap from simple automation to autonomous business operations becomes a risky experiment rather than a competitive advantage.

The potential for meaningful impact, however, is very real. Organizations using Microsoft Copilot Studio report significant results,[3] 25% reduction in time for key processes, substantial employee time savings, and $15.4 million in additional revenue over three years. However, these outcomes don't happen automatically or accidentally; they require intentional design focused on delivering specific, measurable value.

The three phases of frontier firm evolution:

1. **Phase one: personal assistants:** Agents augment individual productivity, handling routine tasks and information retrieval. Success depends on user adoption and immediate efficiency gains.

---

[2] https://www.microsoft.com/en-us/worklab/work-trend-index/2025-the-year-the-frontier-firm-is-born

[3] https://www.microsoft.com/en-us/power-platform/blog/2024/09/03/reduce-development-times-and-increase-roi-with-microsoft-power-platform/?utm_source=chatgpt.com

2. **Phase two: business partners:** Agents coordinate across teams and systems, supporting decision-making and orchestrating workflows. Success requires process integration and organizational trust.

3. **Phase three: autonomous operators:** Agents independently manage business functions within defined parameters, with human oversight focused on exceptions and strategic direction. Success demands comprehensive governance, measurement frameworks, and cultural readiness.

Each phase builds upon the previous one, and critically, each requires different approaches to value definition, measurement, and governance. Organizations that rush to Phase three capabilities without establishing phase one foundations experience the cancellations and failures Gartner forecasts.

How Value by Design Enables the Frontier Firm Journey

The journey to becoming a frontier firm isn't primarily a technology challenge; it's an organizational one. As Microsoft's research[4] makes clear: "If you have a people problem, you will have an AI problem." The main barrier is the challenge of imagining a totally new way to work and structure organizations, then figuring out how to execute that transformation.[5]

---

[4] https://www.microsoft.com/en-us/worklab/work-trend-index/2025-the-year-the-frontier-firm-is-born

[5] https://www.microsoft.com/en-us/worklab/the-ceo-guide-to-building-a-frontier-firm

Organizations attempting this transformation face several critical gaps:

The capacity paradox: Microsoft identifies what it calls "infinite workday"; 58% of leaders say productivity must increase, but 81% of the workforce says they lack enough time or energy to do their work.[6] Without a systematic approach to identifying where agents can genuinely expand capacity versus where they simply add complexity, organizations struggle to move beyond pilots.

The measurement void: As AI adoption moves from implementation to deployment, companies are questioning the Return On Investment (ROI) they receive on their investment. Frontier firm employees are more than twice as likely to say their companies are thriving, but organizations can't replicate that success without understanding what outcomes drive it and how to measure progress toward them.

The phase progression trap: Organizations commonly attempt to jump directly to phase three autonomous operations without establishing phase one and two foundations. Only a fraction have modernized the infrastructure and established the measurement frameworks needed to support this shift. Without systematic methods for assessing organizational readiness and sequencing capabilities appropriately, ambitious agents fail while simpler implementations languish unused.

The alignment crisis: Companies that already know how to enable their human workforce will succeed; breaking down silos, fostering collaboration, and ensuring the entire organization works toward common goals. So, how do you ensure agents align with strategic priorities when those priorities aren't clearly articulated or connected to measurable outcomes?

---

[6] https://www.uctoday.com/unified-communications/breaking-the-infinite-workday-why-microsoft-says-ai-agents-are-key-to-becoming-a-frontier-firm/

What's actually required?

The frontier firm research reveals what needs to happen, but organizations need something more fundamental: a systematic method for making the hundreds of decisions that transform vision into reality.

Consider what's required at each decision point:

> **When identifying opportunities**: How do you distinguish agents that genuinely expand capacity from those that simply automate the wrong things faster? How do you connect opportunities to strategic objectives rather than just solving visible problems? How do you sequence capabilities to build organizational readiness progressively?

> **When defining solutions**: How do you match agent complexity to organizational readiness? How do you know when governance frameworks are too restrictive (blocking value) or too permissive (creating risk)? How do you design for adoption across diverse user groups with different needs and concerns?

> **When proving value**: How do you communicate impact in ways that resonate with executives, process owners, and daily users? How do you maintain stakeholder confidence during the months *before* strategic value becomes visible? How do you know when results justify progressing to more autonomous agent types?

Microsoft emphasizes[7] that organizations need to "get to broad scale, fast" because "the time for copilots alone has passed." Scaling still requires being able to answer these questions consistently across tens or hundreds of agent opportunities. Without a systematic approach, each opportunity becomes a custom debate, progress stalls, and organizations will fall into the 40% of agentic AI projects that Gartner predicts will be cancelled by 2027.

---

[7] https://www.adamsstreetpartners.com/insights/the-next-frontier-the-rise-of-agentic-ai/

What's needed is a design discipline: a structured approach that ensures every agent opportunity

- **Connects explicitly to strategic objectives** rather than just solving interesting problems

- **Defines success in measurable terms** before building begins

- **Matches solution complexity** to organizational readiness

- **Establishes governance frameworks** appropriate for the agent's autonomy level

- **Maintains stakeholder alignment** throughout the development and evolution

Without this discipline, organizations experience exactly what the research predicts: enthusiasm for AI that doesn't translate into measurable business impact, pilot projects that never scale, and investments that fail to deliver promised ROI.[8]

This book provides that missing discipline. It presents a systematic framework: **Value by Design**, that gives organizations the structured approach needed to navigate the frontier firm journey successfully. Rather than making each agent opportunity a custom debate, the framework provides repeatable methods for the critical decisions that determine whether agents deliver lasting value or become expensive experiments.

Before we introduce that framework, however, one more reality check is essential: understanding exactly why so many agent initiatives fail to deliver value and what that reveals about the discipline required for success.

The AI Gold Rush

The gaps between vision and execution manifest in predictable patterns across every industry. Every leadership team faces the same questions: "What's our AI strategy?". Most have an answer. Some point to their frontier firm aspirations. Others reference their roadmap of planned agents. A few showcase impressive pilot projects.

---

[8] https://www.uctoday.com/unified-communications/breaking-the-infinite-workday-why-microsoft-says-ai-agents-are-key-to-becoming-a-frontier-firm/

Far fewer can answer the harder questions:

- "Which of these initiatives will genuinely advance our strategic objectives?"

- "How will we know if they're working?"

- "What makes this agent opportunity more valuable than the fifty others we could pursue?"

- "Are we building the right capabilities for our current organizational readiness?"

The gap between having an AI strategy and executing it effectively is where most organizations currently find themselves. They understand the destination, becoming a frontier firm with human–agent teams operating at scale. They recognize the importance of the journey, progressing thoughtfully through the three phases to becoming frontier; but they lack the systematic method for making the hundreds of decisions required to get there.

The result? Activity without impact.
In many cases, organizations are doing something. Hackathons and "promptathons" to spin up Copilot Studio agents and small proofs-of-concept. Innovation labs build impressive demos. Teams experiment with agent capabilities, but one uncomfortable question lingers:

Is any of this actually delivering value?
When teams rush to explore what's possible, they lose sight of what matters. They build agents because the technology is available, not because the opportunity is strategically aligned. They define success as "we built it, and people are using it" rather than establishing measurable business outcomes. They jump directly to autonomous capabilities without establishing the foundational measurement and governance frameworks that Phases one and two require.

AI promises increased efficiency and better decisions, but unless those promises are tied to specific, measurable outcomes that advance organizational priorities, they risk becoming tactical distractions. The potential is real, but so is the risk of wasted effort.

According to Gartner research,[9] only 49% of surveyed data and analytics leaders have established business outcome-driven metrics that allow stakeholders to track AI value, with 34% having no outcome metrics at all. Without these metrics, how do organizations know whether they're progressing toward becoming frontier firms or simply accumulating disconnected agents?

This book starts with value, because value is what makes the effort worthwhile. Value ensures work aligns with organizational needs.

Value takes many forms: saving time, reducing risk, improving quality, or enabling people to do things they couldn't before. Without intention, these outcomes rarely materialize.

A **value-first** mindset means designing with a clear purpose and a shared understanding of what good looks like before anything is built. And in this book, that principle becomes a **framework**; a value by design approach; a repeatable way to design, build, and scale AI agents so that value stays at the center of every decision, whether you're building phase one productivity enhancers or phase three autonomous operators.

The Role of Agents in Delivering Value

Microsoft Copilot Studio represents a fundamental shift in how organizations build intelligent automation. Unlike traditional chatbots that follow rigid scripts, Copilot Studio enables agents that sense context, decide on actions, and adapt to changing conditions while staying aligned to defined business purposes.

But what exactly is an agent? An agent is a self-contained capability that operates with a degree of autonomy. Rules, instructions, and prompts guide it toward achieving a specific outcome.

This distinction matters. Traditional applications deliver value indirectly by providing tools. Agents, by contrast, are built with an embedded role in the workflow: they act on behalf of a person, team, or organization. We measure their success *through the outcomes they enable.*

---

[9] https://www.gartner.com/en/newsroom/press-releases/2024-04-29-gartner-finds-61-percent-of-organizations-are-evolving-their-data-and-analytics-operating-model-because-of-ai-technologies

An agent might

- *Find and deliver relevant information* to the right person at the right time, reducing search effort and speeding up decisions

- *Work alongside people or systems* to complete a task, supporting smooth handoffs and coordination

- *Coordinate activities* across multiple steps, teams, or systems so that processes run consistently end-to-end

- *Offer insights, guidance, or recommendations* that help people make better-informed decisions

- *Assist in completing a specific task* by guiding the user through the necessary steps or actions

- *Take direct action automatically* when certain conditions are met, removing the need for manual intervention

These capabilities mean agents can occupy **many positions in the value chain**. They can be the *first point of contact* in a customer journey, the *silent optimizer* in a back-office process, or the *bridge* between disconnected systems. Each follows common patterns in how they create and deliver value.

Because of this versatility, agents can be designed to create value at different levels:

- **Operational**: Streamlining high-volume, repeatable tasks

- **Strategic**: Enabling better decisions or ensuring consistent compliance

- **Transformational:** Changing the way people work or collaborate, opening up possibilities that didn't exist before

These three value levels, and how they emerge over time, form a central lens throughout this book for assessing agent opportunities and measuring their impact. The value by design framework ensures your agents deliver the right type of value for your organization's current needs while building toward more ambitious outcomes over time.

What unites all effective agents is that they are *designed with intent*. This means starting from a **clear understanding of the outcome they are meant to achieve and the audience they are meant to serve**. By thinking of agents as value-delivery mechanisms, rather than generic "AI features," we can ensure that each one has a clear purpose, measurable success criteria, and a roadmap for growth.

What Do We Mean by Value?

In everyday language, *value* is one of those terms that seems self-explanatory – until you try to measure it.

When teams say: "we want to deliver value with AI," the intent is pretty clear, but the specifics are often left to interpretation. That ambiguity becomes a problem once work begins. Without a shared, transparent, and well-understood definition, it becomes difficult to evaluate trade-offs, prioritize work, or articulate success.

Defining value is not an abstract exercise – it has to be anchored in the organization's direction of travel. Put simply, we need to understand how agents will evidently move the needle in the directions the organization cares about.

AI agents can serve two strategic roles: and here they can **accelerate progress** toward existing goals, or they can make possible entirely **new capabilities** that were impractical or uneconomical before. In the first case, AI acts as an enabler, helping the organization reach its objectives faster, with fewer resources, or with greater precision. In the second, it becomes a catalyst for strategic evolution, enabling new services, business models, or ways of working.

Getting this right shapes everything that follows, because understanding which role an agent is meant to play determines how we design it, how we measure its success, and how we communicate its impact. Agents designed to accelerate progress for existing objectives tend to focus on efficiency, integration with existing systems, speed, and accuracy. Agents designed to enable new capabilities emphasize exploration, flexibility, and the ability to handle novel scenarios. These different priorities drive fundamentally different design decisions, from user experiences to system architecture and success metrics.

The recognition that value and strategy are connected is the first step. The next challenge is defining what value actually means for your specific context. This section establishes that definition, creating a structured view of impact that can guide decisions from initial design through ongoing measurement.

Value without strategic connection risks becoming activity without impact.

Value Is Diverse and Context-Specific

Before we talk about value in concrete terms, it helps to acknowledge that value itself is not singular or stable. Figure 1 illustrates the four dimensions that shape how value is perceived and judged: role, perspective, priority, and timing; and how they intersect to form very different definitions of success.

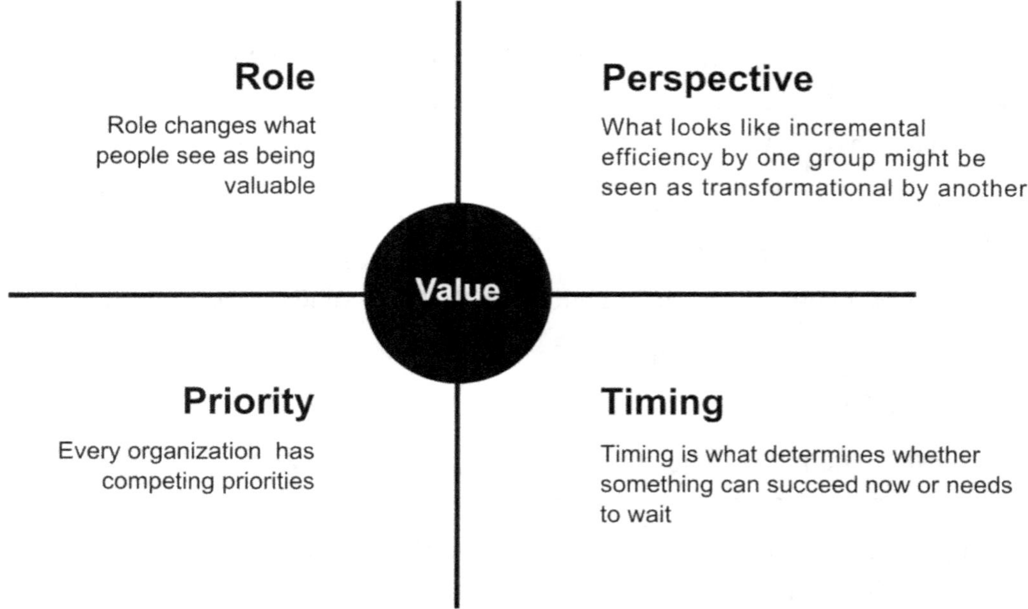

Figure 1. *How role, perspective, priority, and timing influence value*

What matters to one person may not register for another. Sometimes because their work is measured differently, sometimes because they are solving a different set of problems.

For example:

- A **frontline worker** may see value in fewer manual steps.

- A **team lead** may see value in better visibility of performance.

- An **executive** may see value in improved compliance or reduced risk exposure.

These are **not** competing definitions of value; they are different lenses on the same solution. The same agent could be seen as

- A *time-saver* by those using it daily

- A *quality improver* by those managing the output

- A *risk reducer* by those accountable for governance

Every agent has more than one audience. There are the direct users – the people who interact with it day to day. There are also **indirect users** who feel its impact through changes in processes, data quality, or decision-making; and there are **sponsors and decision-makers** who support its adoption and judge its success.

Quick recap – value across perspectives

- Value is context-specific: It depends on role, timing, and priorities.

- The same agent can mean different things to different stakeholders.

- Every agent has direct, indirect, and sponsor audiences.

Taking the time to identify and understand these different groups early allows us to design with greater clarity – ensuring the solution creates value in ways that are meaningful across roles, levels, and moments in time.

Value is also about **direction**. Agents can accelerate **progress toward goals** an organization already cares about, or they can reveal **entirely new possibilities** that weren't achievable before. This is why clarity on strategic context matters early. If you know what the organization is trying to achieve, you can assess whether an agent contributes to that path or risks pulling attention away from it. In other words: value is meaningful only when it helps the business move closer to where it intends to go.

More Than Just Time Saved

It's tempting to equate value with time saved or tasks automated. These are often the easiest things to measure, and they're a natural first focus when exploring agents, but the real potential goes further.

When designed well, they can also

- *Improve* the quality and consistency of decisions

- *Reduce* friction in customer or employee experiences

- *Unlock* access to knowledge or support in moments where it previously didn't exist

- *Strengthen compliance* or reduce operational risk

- *Accelerate* learning, onboarding, or productivity across teams

This is where the design conversation begins to mature. Time saved is part of the picture – but if we stop there, we miss the broader opportunities for agents to shift how work gets done and how outcomes are achieved.

While every agent is unique, they tend to fall into a small number of common patterns in how they deliver value. Some act as **retrievers**, surfacing information at the right moment. Others work as **assistants** or **collaborators**, helping people complete tasks more quickly and consistently. Some take on a bigger roles as **orchestrators**, coordinating steps across teams and systems. Others act as **advisors**, guiding decisions with insights and recommendations. And some are true **performers**, carrying out actions end-to-end with no human intervention.

Each of these patterns comes with its own typical value profile – the kinds of tangible and intangible benefits they are most likely to produce. For example:

- An "assistant" agent often delivers immediate, measurable time savings.

- A "performer" agent might primarily reduce risk exposure.

- An "advisor" agent may improve decision quality in ways that have a long-term strategic payoff.

We'll explore these patterns in detail later, but even now, recognizing that different agent types tend to deliver different mixes of value can help you frame more realistic expectations from the start.

Regardless of type, it's important to understand not just *what* value an agent delivers but *how* that value shows up in practice. Some benefits are easy to measure in hard numbers; others are less visible but just as important for long-term success. Thinking about **tangible** and **intangible** value helps ensure we capture the full impact an agent can have.

Tangible value is straightforward to quantify. It often appears in metrics you can track on a dashboard or in a report – hours saved, errors reduced, costs avoided, revenue generated. Because it is measurable, tangible value is easier to use when making a business case or reporting results.

Intangible value is harder to pin down in numbers but no less real. It includes changes in behavior, culture, and perception – improved employee morale, greater trust in data, stronger collaboration across teams. These benefits can influence an organization's ability to innovate, retain talent, or respond to change, even if they don't appear directly on a quarterly report.

When defining an agent's intended impact, it helps to consider value along two axes:

	Immediate	Long term
Tangible	Measurable and quickly visible: reduced call handling time, fewer manual approvals, lower error rates.	Measurable but realized over time: reduced staff turnover, lower costs of compliance, sustained revenue growth.
Intangible	Felt quickly but not easily measured: improved onboarding experience, higher customer confidence, better cross-team communication.	Cultural or behavioral shifts: stronger innovation culture, sustained adoption of new ways of working, improved organizational agility.

Taken together, these distinctions can be difficult to hold in your head at once. Figure 2 brings them together, showing how value can be understood across both time horizon and tangibility.

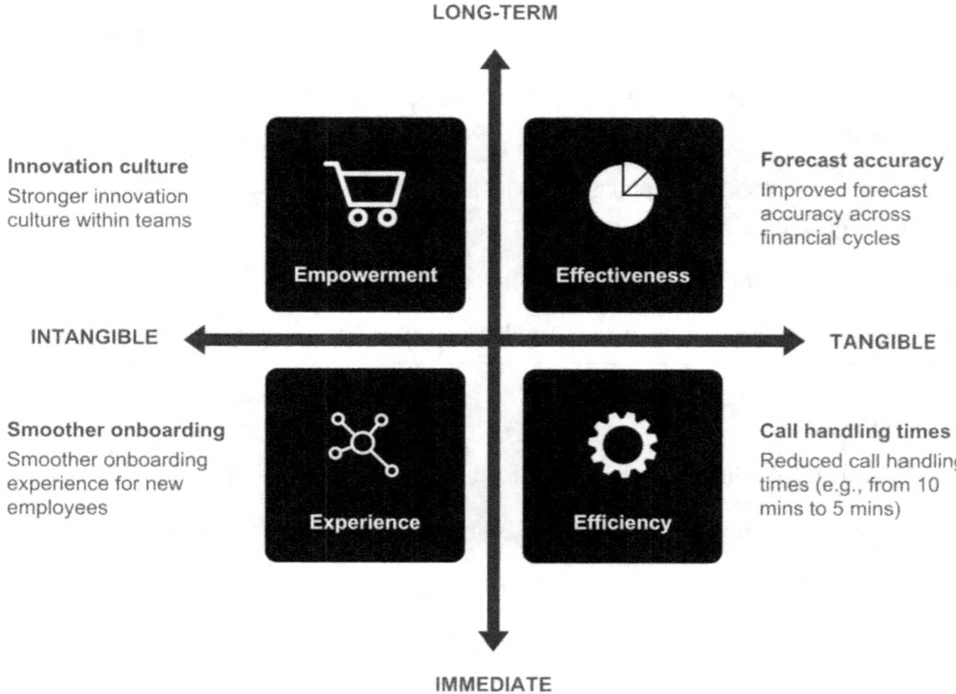

Figure 2. *A framework for classifying value by tangibility and time horizon*

By mapping benefits into these categories, you create a more complete picture of what the agent is meant to achieve. It also makes it easier to balance early operational wins with deeper, strategic outcomes that may take months or years to emerge.

Mental exercise: mapping the value

Imagine your organization has just launched a customer feedback analysis agent. Its role is to scan survey responses, flag urgent issues, and summarize trends for the product team.

For each of the following outcomes, decide if it is

- Tangible – immediate

- Tangible – long term

- Intangible – immediate

- Intangible – long term

Outcome	Your classification
Reduction in the time it takes to compile a weekly feedback report from two days to two hours	
Improved customer perception of responsiveness, based on post-interaction surveys	
A gradual drop in customer churn rates over 18 months	
A stronger culture of using customer insights in decision-making	

Answer guide:

- Report compilation time reduction: *tangible, immediate*

- Improved perception of responsiveness: *intangible, immediate*

- Reduced customer churn over 18 months: *tangible, long term*

- Culture of using insights: *intangible, long term*

Finished? Let's continue.

Recognizing whether a benefit is tangible or intangible, immediate or long term is the first step, but it's not enough on its own. Knowing what outcomes matter, and how they might show up over time gives you **clarity**. To consistently design agents that deliver that value, and keep doing so as needs evolve, you need more than insight.

You need a method.

Value by Design is the method we use to turn insight into structure. It provides the tools, questions, and framing techniques needed to keep outcomes at the center of every decision, from discovery through delivery. It helps you identify the people who matter, the kind of value that matters to them, the conditions required to realize that value, and the way to sustain progress over time.

Let's unpack the framework.

The Value by Design Framework

Before diving into agent types and technical patterns, we need to establish a foundation. We need a clear reason for building in the first place. We need a design principle that shapes how solutions are framed, built, and delivered.

That's the role of the **Value by Design** framework.

Value by Design is a practical, repeatable method for envisioning and delivering agents that are anchored in purpose, aligned with strategy, and measured by outcomes. It helps you make better decisions at every stage of the solution life cycle, from identifying the right opportunities to communicating the value delivered.

Figure 3 introduces the Value by Design framework, which brings together these ideas into a single, coherent approach:

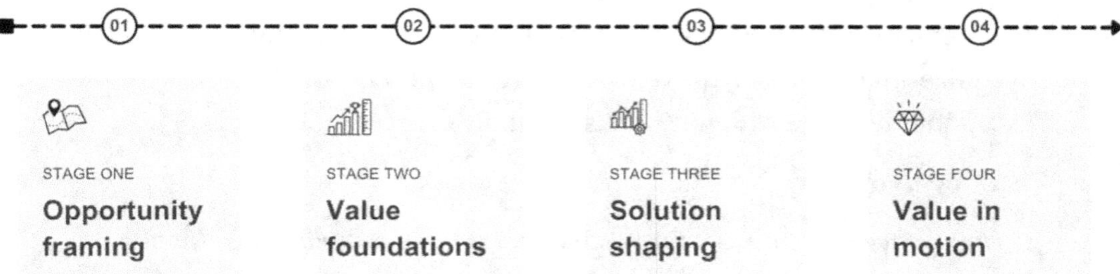

Figure 3. *The Value by Design framework*

1. **Opportunity framing**

    Where should we focus?

    This stage helps you identify the use cases worth solving. It starts by connecting to organizational goals, then narrows in on value hotspots – the areas in your organization where agents can move the needle. From there, it guides you to assess fit (what kind of agent is needed?) and apply decision filters to prioritize what to build first.

2. **Value foundations**

    What does value mean in this context – and to whom?

    Here, you define what success looks like. You'll map out the different people and teams who experience value, apply structured lenses to clarify the kind of value that matters, and explore what needs to be true (behaviorally and contextually) for that value to be realized.

3. **Solution shaping**

How do we design the right agent for the job?

This stage brings value into the design process. It guides you in understanding user needs and contexts, establishing agent identity and behavioral foundations through agent instructions, designing capability portfolios (knowledge sources, tools, topics, and prompts), and validating orchestration decisions through systematic evaluation. This stage is about making intentional choices that reinforce the desired outcomes and ensure capabilities align with how users naturally express their needs.

4. **Value in motion**

How do we measure, communicate, and evolve the value over time?

Agents don't stop evolving once they go live. This final stage focuses on tracking adoption, gathering real-world feedback, and iterating with purpose. It also equips you to tell the story of success – using metrics, telemetry, and storytelling techniques that resonate with different stakeholders.

Together, these stages form a design discipline: a way to connect ambition with action, strategy with delivery, and effort with measurable impact.

You don't need to apply every tool at once. But by working through these stages in a deliberate way, you give each agent a stronger chance of succeeding – not just technically but in the ways that matter the most.

This is a book about **decisions** – the kind that shape whether an agent stays an experiment or becomes an enduring source of value. Decisions about what problems are worth solving, whose outcomes matter, how responsibility is shared, and how success is measured over time.

Let's begin where every successful solution should: with a clear understanding of what value really is, and why it must guide everything we design.

Opportunity Framing

Organizations are full of ideas: backlog items, pain points, and exploratory pilots. Some are clearly valuable. Others are urgent but tactical. A few might be transformational. Without a clear way to assess them, it's easy to default to who's loudest or what's easiest to build.

This is where *opportunity framing* comes in.

Opportunity framing is the first stage of the Value by Design method. It helps you zoom in and identify the places where agents can deliver meaningful impact. It ensures those opportunities are worth the time and resources it takes to build and scale them.

The goal isn't to capture every idea. It's to focus your efforts where there is the highest chance of realizing value.

This stage sets the directions. It ensures that everything that follows – design, delivery, and governance – is aligned from the start.

CHAPTER 1

Strategic Alignment

This chapter connects the dots between the big-picture strategy and practical opportunities for agents. We'll use a structured approach that works horizontally across the organization: identifying departments with clear strategic direction, engaging the right stakeholders within those areas, and pinpointing high-potential hotspots where agents can deliver measurable impact.

From there, we'll break each hotspot into specific opportunities, assess them against clear criteria, and use a framework to filter and prioritize. The goal is to build a portfolio of strategically grounded opportunities that can be objectively compared and prioritized. We ensure every potential initiative is anchored in strategy, supported by evidence, and positioned to deliver measurable value – then use consistent frameworks to assess and rank them for maximum organizational impact.

The diagram in Figure 1-1 illustrates the journey from strategy to opportunity: a chain of alignment that connects vision and goals to real agent use cases.

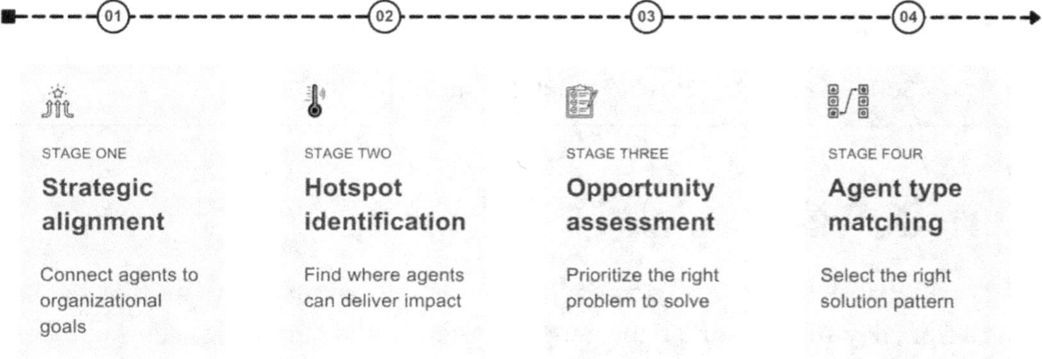

Figure 1-1. *From strategy to prioritized opportunities*

Strategic alignment is the discipline of ensuring that every initiative, from a quick proof of concept to a scaled enterprise rollout, contributes to the direction your organization is already trying to move in.

© Steve Jeffery 2026

S. Jeffery, *Value by Design with Microsoft Copilot Studio*, https://doi.org/10.1007/979-8-8688-2613-9_1

We're making sure the ideas and use cases you have or discover aren't just good; we're making sure those ideas **matter.**

Before building anything, we need to answer three simple, but essential questions:

1. **Why are we doing this?** – What problem are we solving, and why does it matter?

2. **How does it help us achieve our objectives?** – Which goals will it advance, and by what mechanism?

3. **How will we know if it's working?** – What metrics will prove success in business terms?

Getting clear, actionable answers to these questions depends on engaging the right stakeholders. Many alignment efforts fail because they're having strategic conversations with people who lack strategic context, or business conversations with people who don't understand operational realities.

Quick recap   Why strategic alignment goes wrong:

- Having strategic conversations with people who lack strategic context

- Focusing on features before understanding business outcomes

- Skipping measurement discussions until after launch

- Assuming alignment exists when it's never been tested

Where Do You Begin?

Strategies often live in high-level documents, or transformation roadmaps that feel far removed from day-to-day work. If the people designing and deploying agents can't see those objectives, or don't understand what they mean in practice, they can't align their work to them.

I[1] saw it time and time again: strategic direction existed, but it was scattered across different teams, tools, and formats. For anyone trying to build agents, this creates a real barrier; if the big picture is fragmented, it's hard to know where to begin.

Strategic alignment works best when you start in parts of the business where the connection between strategy and operations is already visible. This doesn't mean perfect alignment already exists, but it does mean the building blocks are in place: clear objectives, measurable outcomes, and leadership that can articulate what success looks like.

Think of this as choosing the right soil for planting; starting where conditions already support growth, rather than forcing change in ground that isn't ready. The three types of stakeholders you need – strategy holders, process owners, and decision makers – exist in every department. But in some places, they're easier to identify, more willing to engage, and better positioned to act on what you discover together.

What makes a good starting point?

You're looking for a department, business unit, or program that meets at least two of the following in Figure 1-2:

---

[1] https://learn.microsoft.com/en-us/power-platform/guidance/coe/business-value-toolkit

Visible strategic pressure

"A business unit or team with clear goals or challenges"

Active transformation or modernization

"Teams involved in automation, system changeovers, re-orgs, pilots or innovation labs"

Operational complexity

"Functions with lots of manual effort, coordination, or inconsistent processes"

Supportive leadership

"A manager or sponsor open to digital change and willing to share context"

Figure 1-2. *What makes a good starting point?*

Where NOT to start?

Avoid functions where

- Strategy is unclear and no one is willing to explain it

- Innovation is seen as risk or noise

- There are no measurable KPIs or transformation efforts to connect with

- Leadership is disengaged or defensive

You do not need a flawless environment, but you do need a foundation; enough clarity, sponsorship, and access to make progress real.

Once you've identified a promising department or function, your next step is to locate the specific individuals who can provide strategic, operational, and decision-making perspectives. This is where the **three-filter approach** becomes practical: it helps you systematically identify the right conversation partners within your chosen domain.

The three filters – accountability, proximity, and influence – are your method for finding the strategy holders, process owners, and decision-makers who can make strategic alignment real. Use department selection to choose where to focus, then use the three filters to identify who to engage. The three-filter approach is illustrated in Figure 1-3.

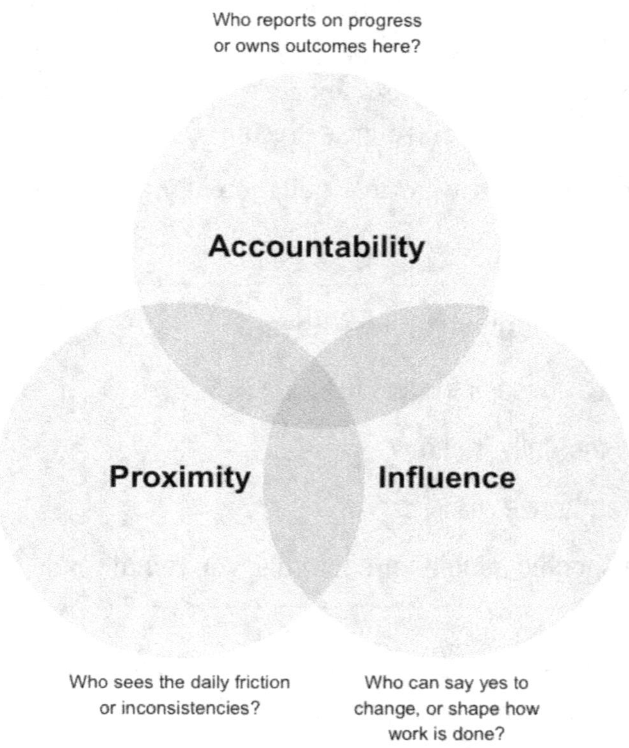

Figure 1-3. *Identifying effective conversation partners*

This guides you to the right people *within that domain* – so you can start surfacing real goals and pain points.

Example:

Imagine you're looking at the customer support function.

- Accountability sits with the head of customer experience, who reports on satisfaction scores and escalation rates.

- Proximity is the frontline (human) agents who see the daily friction customers face and where processes break down.

- Influence comes from the operations manager, who can decide to change workflows or introduce new tools.

- This example illustrates how the three filters help you to identify specific individuals who embody the stakeholder roles you need. The head of customer experience is your strategy holder – they understand what success means and how it's measured. The frontline agents are your process owners – they see where the current system breaks down. The operations manager is your decision-maker – they can authorize changes and allocate resources.

You need all three perspectives to create alignment that's both strategically sound and operationally viable.

Quick reality check – can you answer these?

- Who measures success for this function?

- Who sees the daily friction?

- Who can authorize changes?

If you can't name specific people for each role, you're not ready to proceed.

In some organizations, these three perspectives operate in isolation. Strategy holders set direction without understanding operational constraints. Process owners identify problems but lack strategic context to prioritize solutions. Decision-makers allocate resources without complete visibility into either strategic goals or operational realities.

To summarize, strategic alignment is about making impact **visible** and **defensible** at **every level**.

Identifying the stakeholders is only the first step. Once you've located your strategy holders, process owners, and decision-makers, the challenge shifts to bringing them together for conversations that actually produce actionable insights rather than drifting into abstract discussions or technical debates.

How Do You Keep These Conversations Focused?

Once you've identified your strategy holders, process owners, and decision-makers, the next step is bringing them together for focused strategic alignment conversations. These discussions work best when structured around specific prompts that keep everyone anchored to business outcomes rather than drifting into technical debates or wish lists. These questions help you unpack strategy, surface blockers, and capture outcomes in a way that makes sense to both business and technical audiences.

The framework below shows how to engage all three stakeholder types through a sequence of targeted questions. Each prompt is designed to extract specific insights while building toward actionable outcomes. Figure 1-4 shows how these conversations can be structured to surface the insights that matter most:

Figure 1-4. *Using structured prompts to focus stakeholder conversations*

The four prompts below form a conversation sequence that keeps strategic alignment discussions productive. Use them in order, allowing each question to build on the previous answers:

Prompt question	Action	Why it matters
"What does success look like here?"	Ask stakeholders what "success" looks like in practical terms.	High-level goals don't help unless they're made actionable
"How are we measuring progress today?"	Pinpoint how the business is tracking progress on those goals	You need measurable signals to guide agent design
"What's slowing us down?"	Surface current blockers, friction points, gaps	This starts to reveal hotspots – but we're not collecting use cases yet
"If we could change one thing…"	Capture desired outcomes in a clear, plain language	This becomes the raw materials for the next stage

Handling Conflicting Perspectives

Don't expect perfect agreement across stakeholder types. In fact, the most heated disagreements often signal the highest-value opportunities. Remember, value is a mix of perspective, role, priority, and timing.

When stakeholders are passionate about different aspects of a problem – whether it's strategic objectives, operational constraints, or resource allocation – that passion usually indicates pain points where solutions can create significant impact.

When perspectives conflict, dig deeper: *"Help me understand why you see this differently."* The intensity behind disagreements often reveals where current processes are failing people most acutely. A strategy holder frustrated by missed targets, a process owner dealing with daily inefficiencies, and a decision-maker concerned about resource allocation are all highlighting different facets of the same underlying problem.

These passionate disagreements become your roadmap for agent design. The friction points that generate the strongest reactions are where thoughtful automation or augmentation can deliver the most value.

What to Capture from These Conversations

Each strategic alignment conversation should produce three concrete outputs:

1. **Strategic context statement**: A clear articulation of what success means in this domain and how it connects to broader organizational objectives. This becomes your north star for agent design.

2. **Current friction inventory**: Specific pain points, bottlenecks, and inefficiencies that stakeholders experience today. Document both the operational impact and the business consequences.

3. **Success measures**: Concrete metrics that would demonstrate improvement. These should be things the organization already tracks or could easily implement.

Use the strategic alignment interview guide template to structure these conversations systematically. The template ensures you capture consistent insights across all stakeholder discussions while maintaining focus on business outcomes rather than technical possibilities.

Download the strategic alignment interview guide template from

```
https://github.com/Apress/Value-By-Design-with-Microsoft-
Copilot-Studio
```

Document your findings using the template structure shown in the HR example in Figure 1-5.

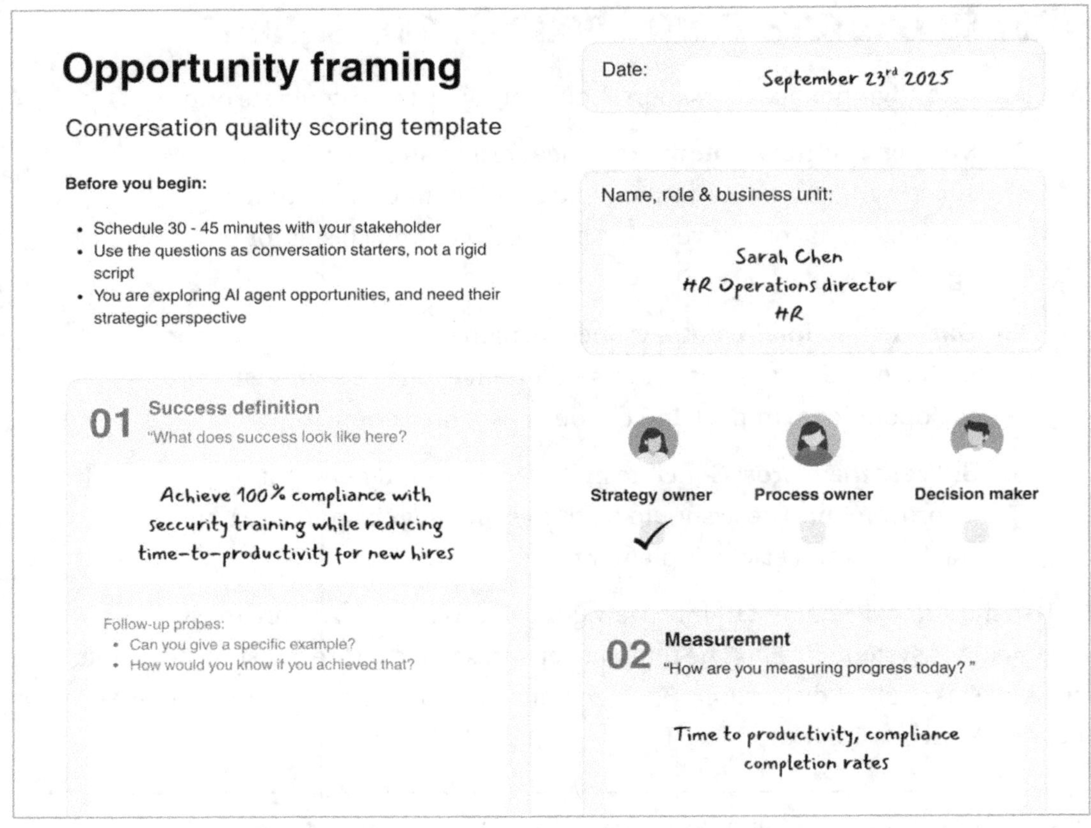

Figure 1-5. *Opportunity framing – conversation scoring template*

Once you've worked through these alignment conversations and captured the passionate disagreements that reveal high-value friction points, you have the raw material for identifying agent opportunities.

Some stakeholder discussions will have revealed clear strategic direction, measurable pain points, and genuine appetite for change. Others may have surfaced vague aspirations, unmeasurable problems, or organizational resistance. The quality of your strategic alignment conversations directly determines the strength of the opportunities you can build on them.

Stop and reassess if you hear

- "We just need to be more efficient"
- "Success is hard to define"
- "We don't really measure that"
- "Everyone knows what the problem is"

These responses signal weak foundations for agent development.

Before moving on to identify specific opportunities, you need to assess which conversations provided the strongest foundation for agent development. The scoring framework below helps you evaluate your alignment discussions consistently, ensuring you focus your efforts on departments where agents are most likely to succeed.

Scoring Conversation Quality

The stakeholder conversation scoring template gives you comparable data across departments. The scoring framework helps you evaluate that data consistently. For each strategic alignment conversation, assess three dimensions:

- **Clarity**: Did stakeholders articulate success in terms that are specific and actionable? (0–5 scale)

- **Evidence**: Were measurable signals identified, or did discussion stay high-level? (0–5 scale)

- **Energy**: Was there appetite for change, visible sponsorship, or enthusiasm from frontline voices? (0–5 scale)

Score	Clarity	Evidence	Energy
5 – Very high	Directly advances a flagship initiative or core strategic goal; visible priority for leadership	Quantifiable improvement >40% in key metric, or major cost/time savings (>$1M or >10K hrs/year)	Widespread buy-in; team eager to adopt; resources and skills already in place

(continued)

Score	Clarity	Evidence	Energy
4 – High	Strong alignment to a departmental or cross-functional goal	Significant improvement (20–40%) in a key metric, or moderate cost/time savings ($250k–$1M or 2k–10k hrs/year)	Clear interest from most stakeholders; some resources and skills available
3 – Moderate	Contributes to an operational or secondary strategic goal	Noticeable improvement (10–20%) in a key metric, or moderate cost/time savings ($50k–$250k or 500–2k hrs/year)	Mixed interest; may require training or modest investment to proceed
2 – Low	Marginal relevance to stated goals	Small improvement (<10%) in a niche metric; minor cost/time savings (<$50k or <500 hrs/year)	Limited interest; significant upskilling or process change required
1 – Very low	Weak or indirect link to organizational priorities	Minimal measurable change; benefit hard to quantify	Stakeholder resistance; major investment or policy changes needed
0 – None	No link to strategic objectives	No measurable improvement	No willingness or ability to adopt

The scoring connects directly to your conversation outputs: Clarity comes from how well stakeholders articulated success definitions; evidence emerges from the specific friction points and measures they provided; and energy reflects their engagement and authority during your discussions.

Figure 1-6 below shows how Sarah Chen's conversation as Operations Director would be scored across all three dimensions, demonstrating strong clarity and evidence with moderate evidence.

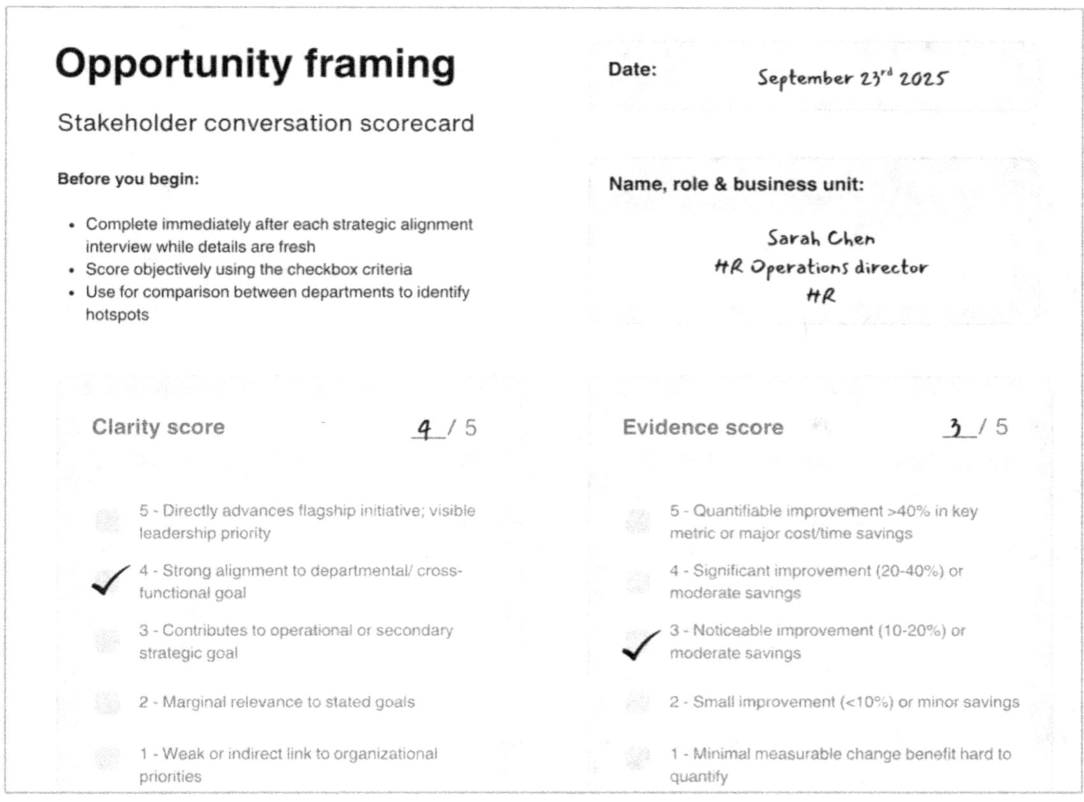

Figure 1-6. Stakeholder conversation scoring template

This scoring approach transforms subjective conversation impressions into objective data you can compare across departments, revealing which areas are truly ready for agent development versus those that need more foundational work.

Download the stakeholder conversation scorecard template from

```
https://github.com/Apress/Value-By-Design-with-Microsoft-
Copilot-Studio
```

Figure 1-7 below shows what this could look like in practice when added to a dashboard or similar for comparison. Three departments have been scored and documented, revealing Customer support and HR onboarding as clear hotspots, while Finance shows mixed results that might require further investigation.

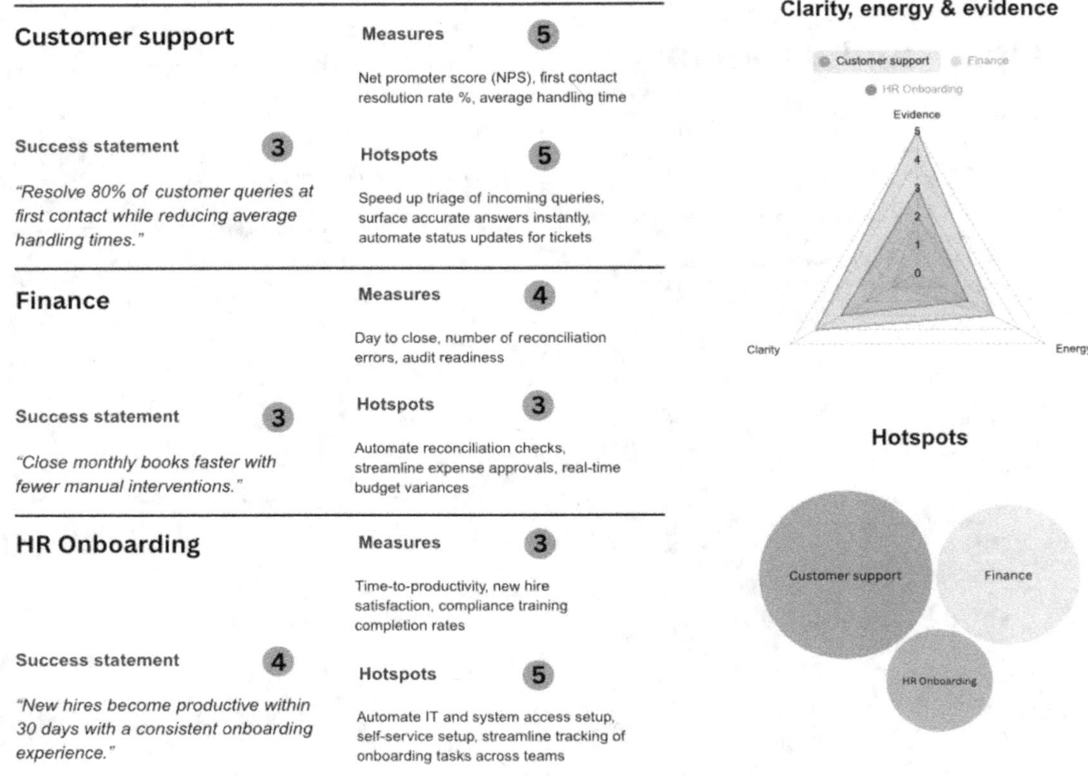

Figure 1-7. *Dashboard mockup – hotspot portfolio*

Quick recap: strategic alignment foundations

- Strategic alignment ensures agents contribute to organizational direction, not just solve interesting problems.

- Use the three-filter approach: Accountability, proximity, and influence to find the right stakeholders.

- Score conversations on clarity, evidence, and energy to identify the strongest foundations for agent development.

Strategic alignment gives you direction, but direction alone is not enough. Most departments can articulate goals; far fewer can pinpoint where work is breaking down in ways that meaningfully constrain those goals.

Once you have clarity on what success looks like, the next step is to find the places where agents can move the needle most reliably: the friction points, bottlenecks, and recurring failure patterns that quietly drain time, quality, or momentum.

Chapter 2 focuses on hotspot identification. It shows you how to translate strategic context into a focused set of high-potential hotspots, and how to separate "interesting ideas" from opportunities with the strongest evidence of impact.

CHAPTER 2

Hotspot Identification

By now, you've completed the **strategic alignment stage**: you've identified the objectives that matter, held structured conversations with stakeholders, and scored each department on **clarity, evidence and energy**. You also recorded the results in a consistent artifact, giving you a comparable set of outputs across the business.

This creates a new challenge: **you have data, but you need direction**.

The scoring framework gives you numerical data for each department.

But identifying where to focus your agent development efforts requires looking at patterns across your entire portfolio of conversations.

When you step back and look across these results, patterns start to emerge. Some business units, teams, or areas within your organization consistently show higher alignment – they are clearer on success, have stronger evidence of measurable impact, and display more energy for change. Others appear cooler, where objectives are vague, signals are weak, or appetite is low.

These differences reveal what we call **value hotspots**: the places in your organization where AI agents are most likely to make a measurable, lasting impact.

The shift from alignment to hotspots isn't a new assessment; it's the intelligent aggregation of the work you've already done.

Understanding hotspots changes how you think about opportunity:

- **Clarity** becomes **strategic importance**: Is the function directly tied to goals leadership cares about?

- **Evidence** becomes a **measurable impact**: Are there tangible metrics that would move if this area improved?

- **Energy** becomes **readiness for change**: Are people motivated and prepared to adopt a solution?

When all three conditions are strong, you've found a promising hotspot: a part of the business where multiple opportunities are waiting to be explored, not just one.

© Steve Jeffery 2026

S. Jeffery, *Value by Design with Microsoft Copilot Studio*, https://doi.org/10.1007/979-8-8688-2613-9_2

How to Identify Your Hotspots

To identify hotspots from your scoring data, look for departments that score consistently high across all three dimensions (clarity, evidence, energy), not just those with the highest single scores. A department with perfect clarity (5) but weak energy (2) signals strategic alignment without organizational readiness. A hotspot needs strong performance across the board.

Use this simple process:

1. Calculate total scores for each department (clarity + evidence + energy)

2. Flag high performers – Departments scoring 12+ out of 15 total points.

3. Check for balance – Ensure no dimension scores below three.

4. Validate access – Confirm you can still reach the stakeholders who provided these insights.

Departments that meet all four criteria become your priority hotspots for agent development.

When you visualize the scores across departments, you begin to see where the "heat" is concentrated across the organization, as shown in Figure 2-1.

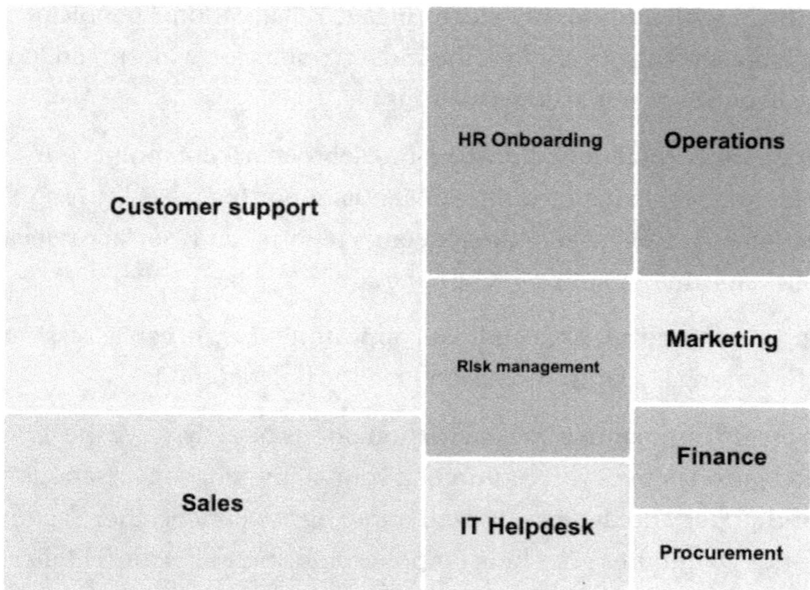

Figure 2-1. *Visualizing opportunity hotspots across departments*

Identifying hotspots gives you a portfolio view of where agents are most likely to deliver impact. However, **a hotspot is not a single idea** – it's a place in the business where multiple opportunities live. Inside Customer Support, for example, you might find opportunities ranging from faster triage of queries to automating status updates or surfacing policy answers.

From Hotspots to Specific Opportunities

Once you've identified your hotspots, the next step is diving deeper to uncover specific agent opportunities within them. Here, you systematically explore the friction points your stakeholders have already identified.

Return to your conversation template outputs for each hotspot department. The friction points you documented become your starting point for opportunity discovery.

Use these techniques:

- **Reference your stakeholder insights**: Review what each stakeholder type said was slowing them down. Process owners often identify the most actionable friction points.

- **Validate with additional voices**: Engage 2–3 additional people in each hotspot area to confirm the friction points are widespread, not isolated to your initial conversations.

- **Scope individual opportunities**: Break broad friction points into specific, testable opportunities. "Manual reporting takes too long" becomes "Automate compliance status reports" and "surface relevant policy information during case review."

Once you've captured a list of candidate opportunities, you can assess each one for its potential by scoring it against three factors in the hotspot model:

- **Strategic importance**: Which friction points directly serve the strategic objectives you captured in your alignment conversations? If the strategy holder emphasized reducing escalations, then "agent spends 20 minutes searching for policy information" scores higher than "printer frequently jams."

- **Measurable impact**: Which friction points offer quantifiable improvement in metrics the business already tracks? "Manual reporting takes 3 days" has clear measurement potential. "Communication could be better" is vague and hard to measure.

- **Readiness for change**: Which friction points can actually be addressed given current constraints? Consider change capacity (are teams already overwhelmed?), data readiness (is the information accessible and reliable?), and integration complexity. Problems requiring major system changes or competing with other initiatives score lower on readiness.

The prioritization process:

1. Score each friction point 0–5 on all three dimensions.

2. Calculate total scores (max 15 points).

3. Focus first on friction points scoring 12+.

4. Within high scorers, prioritize based on which dimension matters most to your organization (strategic importance may well trump everything).

This gives you objective criteria for choosing which 1–2 friction points to tackle first, rather than picking based on what seems easiest or most technically interesting.

To implement this scoring process systematically, use the friction point opportunity assessment template. This template walks you through converting each friction point into a specific agent opportunity, then applies the three-dimensional scoring framework to generate objective prioritization data.

Download the friction point opportunity assessment template from

```
https://github.com/Apress/Value-By-Design-with-Microsoft-
Copilot-Studio
```

Once you've scored individual friction points within your hotspot departments, visualize the results to guide prioritization decisions. Plotting each opportunity on a radar chart (for example) using your three-dimension scoring (strategic importance, measurable impact, readiness for change) makes it easy to compare options and identify the strongest candidates.

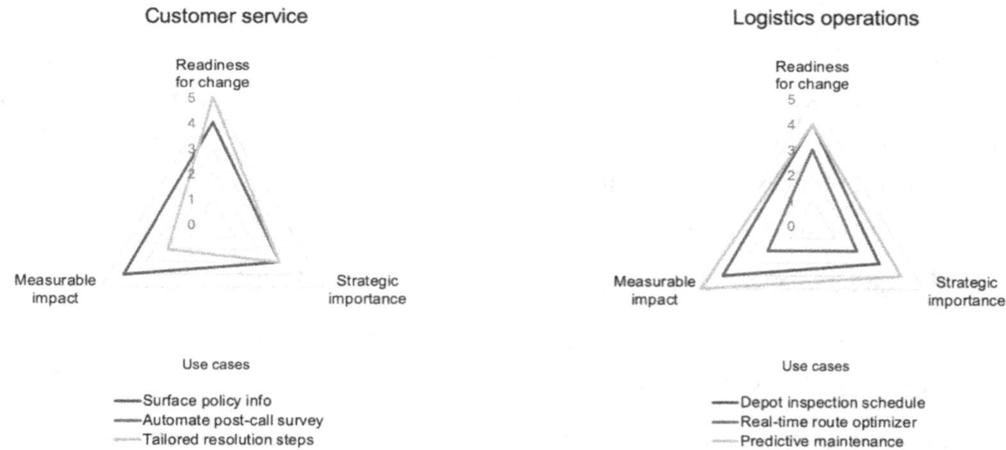

Figure 2-2. *Comparing candidate use cases within value hotspots*

The radar charts above show the profile of each friction point across your three scoring dimensions. Look for opportunities that

- **Score consistently high across all dimensions**: These are your immediate priorities. Strong strategic importance, clear measurable impact, and high readiness create ideal conditions for agent success.

- **Show balanced profiles**: An opportunity scoring 4-4-4 often delivers better results that one scoring 5-3-2, even with the same total score. Balanced opportunities avoid the risk of strategic relevance without measurable outcomes, or high impact without organizational readiness.

- **Reveal trade-offs**: Compare the customer service and logistics examples above. Customer service opportunities show higher readiness but lower strategic importance. Logistics opportunities align strongly with strategy but require more organizational change. These profiles help you choose approaches that match your organizations' current capacity and strategic priorities.

Building Your Opportunity Portfolio

Your friction points scores guide portfolio construction, but individual scores aren't everything. Use the 2x2 matrix below to balance your selection across the different types of opportunities. The goal here isn't to pick the highest scorers, it's to create a portfolio that delivers both immediate value and strategic progress.

Plot each opportunity based on

- Strategic alignment (how directly it serves leadership priorities)

- Implementation effort (based on your readiness for change scores and technical complexity)

The matrix helps you visualize which opportunities deliver immediate impact, which build long-term strategic advantage, and where trade-offs are required.

Figure 2-3 shows how to balance opportunities across strategic impact and ease of delivery when constructing your opportunity portfolio.

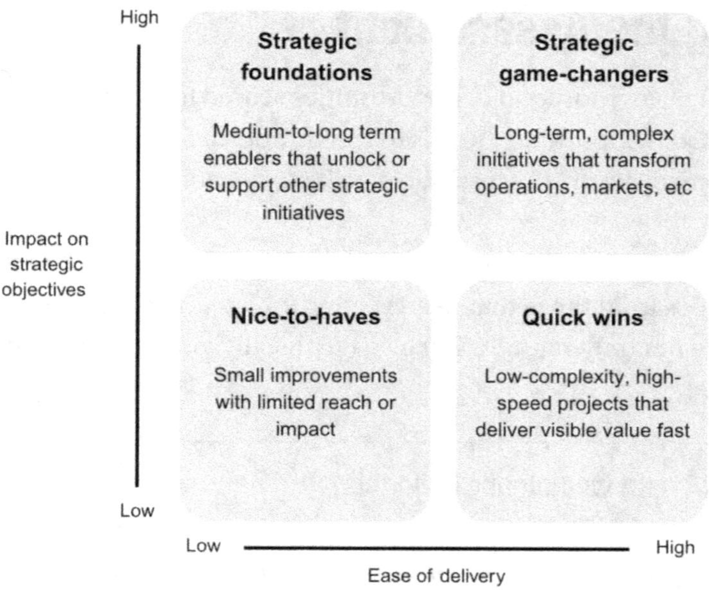

Figure 2-3. *Value classification grid*

Aim for a portfolio that includes

- **2–3 quick wins** (high strategic value, lower effort) to prove concept and build momentum.

- **1–2 strategic investments** (high strategic value, higher effort) to deliver transformational impact.

- **Avoid the other quadrants** unless they serve specific portfolio needs (proving capability, learning, etc.).

Avoid these portfolio potholes:

- All quick wins (no strategic impact)

- All strategic investments (no early momentum)

- Picking highest scores only (ignoring organizational readiness)

- More than five concurrent opportunities (diluted focus)

Deepening the Assessment

At this stage, you have a portfolio of opportunities scored for value. The next step is to apply reality. Each opportunity needs to run through a feasibility and governance lens: Is the data ready, is the process stable, will people adopt it, and can it be delivered responsibly?

These filters won't shrink your pipeline to nothing – but they will separate "ready now" opportunities from those that need staging for later. The result is a shortlist of use cases that are not only valuable but also technically, operationally, and ethically deliverable.

Reality check   can we actually build this?

Before moving your prioritized opportunities into development, run them through a simple feasibility filter. This phase is about asking practical questions that reveal obvious blockers early.

Most agent projects that struggle do so because teams skip this reality check. They discover fundamental barriers only after investing time in development. A focused feasibility review takes a few hours but can save weeks of wasted effort.

The comprehensive agent feasibility assessment template structures this review across four critical dimensions: technical readiness, adoption readiness, risk tolerance, and cost feasibility. Use this template to systematically evaluate each high-scoring opportunity before committing development resources.

Download the feasibility assessment templates from

```
https://github.com/Apress/Value-By-Design-with-Microsoft-
Copilot-Studio
```

The Four-Question Feasibility Filter

For each prioritized opportunity, work through these four areas with the people who understand the current reality:

- Technical readiness

- Adoption readiness

- Risk tolerance

- Cost assessment

Technical Readiness: Do We Have What We Need to Build This?

The core question: Can you access the data and systems this agent needs through Power Platform's connector ecosystem and Copilot Studio's capabilities?

Key checks:

- **Data access**: Which data sources does your agent need? Copilot Studio excels with Microsoft content (SharePoint, OneDrive, Dataverse) but also connects to enterprise systems through Power Platforms 1000+ connector library.

- **Copilot Studio capabilities alignment**: Does your opportunity match platform strengths? Copilot Studio handles natural language conversations, knowledge retrieval from approved sources, workflow orchestration, and integration with Power Automate exceptionally well.

- **Process stability**: Is the underlying workflow predictable enough to automate? Are there too many exceptions or judgment calls?

Who to ask? Power Platform administrators, data owners, process experts

Red flags: Critical data is locked away, processes change frequently based on undocumented factors, or integration requires major system changes.

Adoption Readiness: Will People Actually Use This?

The core questions: Does this agent fit naturally into how people work, or does it require unrealistic behavior changes?

Key checks:

- **Workflow integration**: Does the agent enhance existing workflows, or force people to work differently?

- **Change capacity**: Are users already dealing with other major changes? Do they have bandwidth for something new?

- **Trust factors**: Will people trust the agent's recommendations? Are there concerns about job displacement?

Who to ask? Representative end users, team leaders, change coordinators

Red flags: Users are resistant to change, the agent requires significant workflow modifications, or there are unresolved concerns about automation replacing jobs.

Risk Tolerance: Are We Comfortable with What Could Go Wrong?

The core question: If this agent makes mistakes or fails, can we handle the consequences?

Key checks:

- **Failure impact**: What's the worst thing that happens if the agent provides incorrect information or stops working?

- **Oversight mechanisms**: Can we monitor agent performance and intervene when needed?

- **Compliance basics**: Does this align with existing data policies and security requirements?

Who to ask? Business owners, compliance teams, security leads

Red flags: Agent failures could cause significant business disruption, no clear oversight process exists, or compliance requirements aren't understood.

Cost Feasibility: Can We Afford to Build and Run This?

The core question: What's the realistic total cost of ownership for this agent, and does the expected value justify the investment?

Cost assessment requires understanding both up-front development costs and ongoing operational expenses. Agent costs vary significantly by type and complexity, making it essential to align your cost expectations with the scope of what you're building.

Cost categories to assess:

- **Licensing and capacity**: Power Platform,[1] Copilot Studio, Microsoft 365, third-party systems all require licenses

- **Development effort**: Internal team time, external consulting, testing, and iteration cycles

- **Ongoing operations**: Content updates, monitoring, maintenance, user support, and training

Development complexity framework:

Different types of agents have predictable cost profiles. While we'll explore agent types in detail in the next section, you can use this complexity assessment for initial cost estimation (you will need to update cost ranges and currency based on your organization):

- **Simple agents (information lookup, basic guidance)**: $5–15K annually

- **Moderate agents (workflow assistance, recommendations)**: $15–35K annually

- **Complex agents (multi-system coordination, autonomous actions)**: $35–75K annually

Development effort sizing:

- S (small): 2–4 weeks, single system integration, standard capabilities

- M (medium): 1–3 months, multiple systems, custom workflows

- L (large): 3–6 months, complex integration, advanced features

- XL (extra-large): 6–12 months, enterprise-scale, extensive customization

---

[1] https://learn.microsoft.com/en-us/power-platform/admin/pricing-billing-skus

Key cost assessment questions:

- What development effort size applies based on complexity? (S/M/L/XL)

- How many systems beyond standard Power Platform connections are required?

- Will this need dedicated support resources or specialized skills?

Note   The specific agent type (retriever, assistant, orchestrator, etc.) will help refine these cost estimates. We'll cover the six agent types and their detailed cost implications in the following section.

Who to ask: Finance teams, Power Platform administrators, procurement leads.

Red flags: Total cost exceeds expected value by more than 3:1, requires ongoing specialized skills not available internally, or ongoing costs consume more than 30% of expected annual benefits.

Making Feasibility Decisions

Document your findings using this simple framework:

Opportunity	Technical	Adoption	Risk	Cost	Decision
Invoice query deflection	Green	Green	Amber	Moderate agent, M effort	Proceed with enhanced monitoring
Contract analysis support	Red	Green	Red	Complex agent, L effort	Defer until data access resolved
Expense approval routing	Amber	Green	Green	Moderate agent, S effort	Proceed with custom connector

Decision logic

All green: Proceed with confidence

One amber: Proceed with specific mitigation (noted in decision column).

Any red: Address blocking issues before development, or choose a different opportunity.

Mental exercise: Applying feasibility filters

Think about an agent opportunity in your organization (real or hypothetical). Work through the three-question filter:

1. **Technical readiness**: What data would this agent need? Which systems would it connect to? Are there any obvious technical barriers?

2. **Adoption readiness**: Who would use this agent daily? How does it fit into their current workflow? What might make them resist?

3. **Risk tolerance**: If this agent made a mistake, what would be the business impact? Who would need to be involved in oversight?

Based on your answers, would you proceed, address specific issues first, or choose a different opportunity?

This exercise helps you internalize the feasibility thinking before applying it to real opportunities.

Beyond Feasibility: Responsible Deployment

Once an opportunity passes feasibility review, consider what level of safeguarding it needs.

By safeguarding, we mean the practical controls, oversight, and constraints required to ensure the agent behaves appropriately, remains trustworthy, and can be safely adopted in its intended context.

Simple safeguarding assessment:

Low-risk agents (information retrieval, general guidance):

- Basic content filtering and usage monitoring

- Clear disclaimers about limitations and scope

- Simple user feedback mechanism

Medium-risk agents (recommendations, process routing):

- Human review for edge cases or high-value decisions

- Audit trails for agent decisions

- Regular performance evaluation against known scenarios

High-risk agents (autonomous decisions, sensitive data):

- Multi-layer validation of agent outputs

- Explainable decision-making capabilities

- Continuous monitoring with immediate intervention capabilities

The goal is **proportionate safeguarding**. Over-engineering controls for low-risk agents creates unnecessary friction. Under-protecting high-risk agents creates unacceptable exposure.

With feasibility confirmed, you have one final assessment: determining which agent type best fits your opportunity. Different agent patterns deliver value in fundamentally different ways and require different development approaches. A simple information lookup requires different capabilities, governance, and success metrics than a complex process orchestrator. Getting this match right early prevents costly problems and ensures realistic planning from the start.

Quick recap: From hotspots to opportunities:

- Hotspots are business areas where agents are most likely to succeed (high clarity + evidence + energy).

- Break friction points into specific, scoreable opportunities.

- Build portfolios with 2–3 quick wins and 1–2 strategic investments, avoiding more than 5 concurrent opportunities.

The next challenge is defining exactly what success looks like; not just for the agent's functionality but for the people and processes it will impact.

Stage two shifts focus from selecting opportunities to defining success. Here we move from "this agent should help with expense approvals" to "this agent will reduce approval time from 3 days to 4 hours while maintaining 100% policy compliance, delivering value to employees through faster reimbursement and to finance through improved cash flow visibility."

This stage establishes three critical foundations that shape everything that follows:

- **Value clarity:** Who experiences value, what kind of value matters most to them, and how those different perspectives connect to measurable outcomes.

- **Success definition:** Specific, testable criteria that determine whether the agent is achieving its intended impact across different stakeholder groups and time horizons.

- **Behavioral alignment:** Understanding what must change in people's daily work for value to be realized, and ensuring the agent design supports rather than fights those changes.

Stage two ensures that every design choice – from conversation flow to integration points – serves the outcomes that matter most to the people who will determine the agent's ultimate success or failure.

Value Foundations

Picture two teams launching customer service agents on the same day. Both agents can answer policy questions, route tickets, and surface knowledge articles. Both teams report a successful deployment, and user adoption looks great.

Six months later, one agent is being expanded across multiple departments. The other has no further investment, quietly running in the background.

What made the difference?

The successful team knew exactly **who** would benefit, how they'd measure improvement, and what behaviors needed to change for value to emerge. They could articulate why a 30% reduction in average resolution time mattered to frontline agents, how improved first-call resolution rates would affect customer satisfaction scores, and why executives should care about the compliance audit trail the agent generated.

The second team had built something technically sound that people used, but they couldn't explain why it mattered beyond "it saves time."

Value clarity is what separates successful agents from expensive experiments.

The Challenge of Defining Success

Completing stage one gives you a portfolio of opportunities.

You know what to build.

However, knowing what to build is different from knowing how to build it for maximum impact.

I've seen many teams jump straight from opportunity identification to solution design. They move from "expense approval takes too long" directly to "build an agent that speeds up approvals." This leap skips the most critical design question: What does success actually look like?

Without this foundation, it is difficult to demonstrate lasting value. It might satisfy immediate users but fail to build the broader stakeholder support needed for scaling and continued investment.

Stage two bridges this gap. Here, we move from "this agent should help with expense approvals" to "this agent will reduce approval time from three days to four hours while maintaining 100% policy compliance, delivering value to employees through faster reimbursement and to finance through improved cash flow visibility."

Figure S1-1 makes this shift explicit, contrasting vague notions of success with clearly defined outcomes across different audiences.

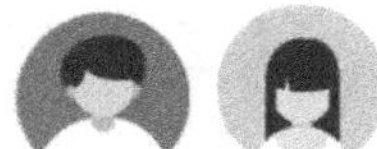

Figure S1-1. *Defining success for multiple audiences*

This specificity transforms everything that follows. Every design choice, from conversation flows to integration points, serves clearly defined outcomes rather than vague aspirations.

You will deliver this clarity through three connected steps that transform vague aspirations into measurable business cases. Figure S1-2 sets out the three connected steps that make up the value foundations stage.

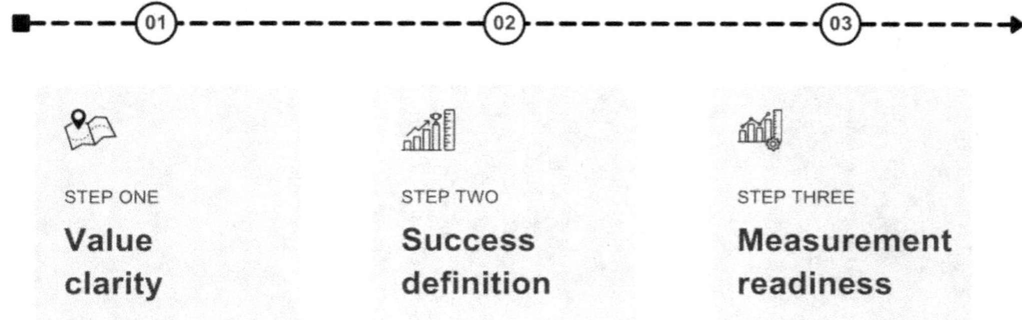

Figure S2-2. *The steps of value foundations*

Stage two establishes three critical foundations that shape everything that follows:

- **Value clarity**: Who experiences value, what kind of value matters most to them, and how those different perspectives connect to measurable outcomes

- **Success definition**: Specific, testable criteria that determine whether the agent is achieving its intended impact across different stakeholder groups and time horizons

- **Measurement readiness**: The mechanisms, metrics, and communication strategies needed to track progress and tell the value story as it unfolds

The difference between agents that thrive and those that struggle often comes down to how clearly value was defined before building began. When you start with precise outcomes, technical decisions become easier because they're anchored to purpose. Conversely, when you start with vague aspirations, every choice becomes subjective, and value becomes accidental.

The first foundation – value clarity – requires understanding that value is never experienced uniformly across an organization or agent opportunity. The same agent that transforms daily work for one group might barely register as useful for another. The same efficiency gain might be measured as time saved by users, cost reduction by managers, and risk mitigation by executives.

This is the reality we need to design for.

CHAPTER 3

Value Clarity

Remember the two customer service teams from our opening example? Both built technically sound agents that people used. Only one could explain why their agent mattered beyond "it saves time."

The difference wasn't technical capability; it was **value clarity**.

The successful team understood that their agent delivered different benefits to different people. More importantly, they could map exactly when each group would experience those benefits and what trade-offs they'd need to accept. When budget reviews came around, they could explain not just what their agent did but why each outcome mattered to specific stakeholders.

Value clarity begins with recognizing a fundamental truth: perceived benefit depends entirely on where you stand.

The Value Benefit Lens

To support more intentional conversations about value, we use the **value benefit lens** – a simple model that helps categorize the different types of value agents can deliver. It breaks value into three layers:

Value layer	Description
Operational	Efficiency gains such as time saved, error reduction, or reduced manual effort
Strategic	Business improvements such as better decision-making, insight, compliance, or scalability
Transformational	Behavioral or structural shifts, such as enabling new ways of working, empowering new roles, or changing how services are delivered

S. Jeffery, *Value by Design with Microsoft Copilot Studio*, https://doi.org/10.1007/979-8-8688-2613-9_3

These layers are not mutually exclusive. A single agent may deliver operational savings in the short term, while contributing to strategic or transformational outcomes over time. What matters is that the intended value is understood and made explicit at the outset.

The Reality: Everyone Experiences Value Differently

The same agent functionality creates completely different experiences depending on where you sit in the organization. Figure 3-1 makes this difference visible, showing how the same agent outcome is experienced differently across organizational roles.

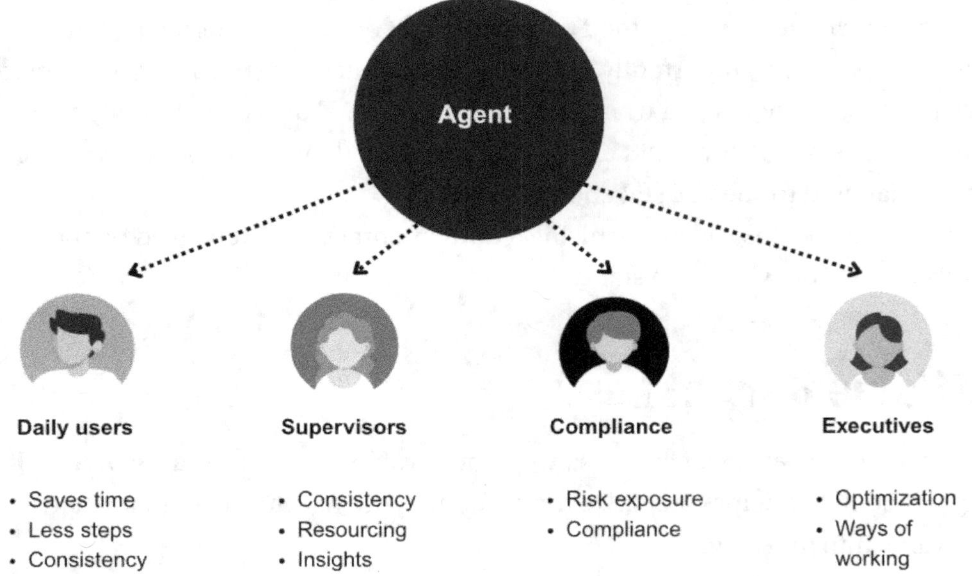

Figure 3-1. *How different groups of users experience value*

The same agent outcome can simultaneously be

- A time saver for daily users

- A quality improver for supervisors

- A risk reducer for compliance teams

- A cost optimizer for executives

These are **different lenses** on the same solution, not competing definitions of value.

Understanding these perspectives early allows you to design agents that create meaningful impact across organizational levels rather than optimizing for a single viewpoint.

Let's explore how the same functionality of an agent can deliver different types of value to different stakeholders, and why designing for multiple perspectives strengthens, rather than dilutes your solution.

Value Progression Over Time

In a logistics operation for a large organization, a small health and safety (H&S) team was responsible for overseeing compliance across more than 90 depots. With just nine people on the team, they relied on a paper-based system to plan and record inspections. While well-intentioned, the process introduced inconsistencies: some depots were inspected multiple times in short succession, while others were inadvertently missed. Scheduling was reactive. Oversight was fragmented. And despite everyone's best efforts, it was difficult to track patterns or improve proactively.

A member of the team developed an agent that digitized and standardized inspections. The new system introduced a consistent structure for how inspections were performed, how follow-ups were tracked, and how visits were scheduled. This immediately reduced duplication, increased coverage, and improved visibility across the estate. Let's look at how value was realized:

Operational value (immediate impact)

- H&S auditors saved time and reduced admin by working from a single, consistent digital process.

- Depot managers gained clarity on upcoming audits and post-inspection actions.

- Compliance teams could easily access records and monitor site coverage.

Strategic value (emerging insights)

As the system matured, the team began to recognize the value of the data they were collecting. Patterns emerged, certain sites reported repeat incidents, while others had recurring gaps in training or signage. The team used these insights to run proactive safety campaigns targeting the most relevant depots, leading to a measurable reduction in common incidents.

- Compliance leads began using data to prioritize interventions based on real risk.

- Drivers and site staff saw tangible improvements in signage, training, and depot design.

- Executives received evidence-backed reporting that linked investment in safety to reduced incident rates.

In time, the solution helped reframe how safety was viewed. Not just as compliance obligation but as an area of operational excellence. The organization shifted from reactive auditing to proactive risk management, and the platform became a template for similar improvements in other areas of frontline operations.

Transformational value (long-term impact)

- H&S culture evolved from inspection-led to insight-led.

- Data became a strategic asset for continuous improvement.

- The platform became a model for grassroots innovation at scale.

This is a story of how **value can emerge in stages**, and how that value differs depending on where you sit. For auditors, it was about saving time. For depot managers, it was visibility. For compliance teams, it was coverage. For leadership, it was evidence of progress on a critical risk area.

Crucially, by building with a clear purpose, and evolving the solution as its value became clearer, the team delivered operational, strategic, and transformational outcomes with a single system.

Figure 3-2 provides a simplified view of how operational, strategic, and transformational value tend to emerge and compound over time.

This kind of value progression is rarely linear. It unfolds through intentional iteration – where each version builds capability and unlocks new outcomes.

- **Operational value appears early**: In the first release, the agent often focuses on immediate, measurable efficiency gains – reducing manual work, speeding up routine steps, or improving data entry accuracy. These benefits tend to level off once the easiest gains have been captured.

- **Strategic value builds more gradually**: As the agent matures, integrates with more systems, or is trusted to support more critical processes, its contribution to decision-making, insight, and scalability increases, typically over the medium-term.

- **Transformational value is usually the most disruptive**: It often arrives as a step-change when a new capability, integration, or shift in behavior enables entirely new ways of working. This may be months or even years after the initial deployment.

Importantly, the overall value of the solution is the combination of these layers. An agent delivering well in all three can have a sustained and compounding impact; one that starts with immediate operational improvements and grows into a driver of strategic and even organizational change.

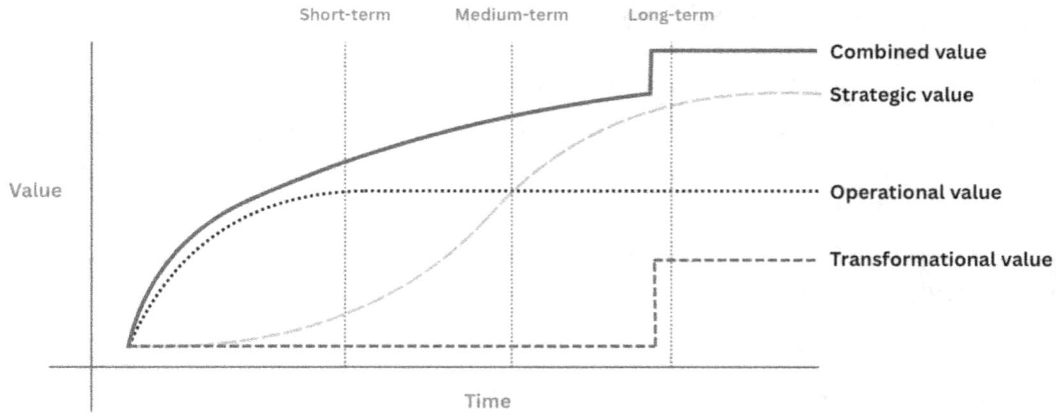

Figure 3-2. *Value over time: operational, strategic, transformational*

Understanding value in its different forms – operational, strategic, and transformational – gives us a language for describing the benefits an agent can bring. Seeing how those layers combine over time makes it clear that value is not static, and that it can evolve in ways that may not be obvious at the outset. Figure 3-3 brings these dimensions together, showing how different stakeholders experience value at different points in time – and how those layers combine to deliver sustained impact.

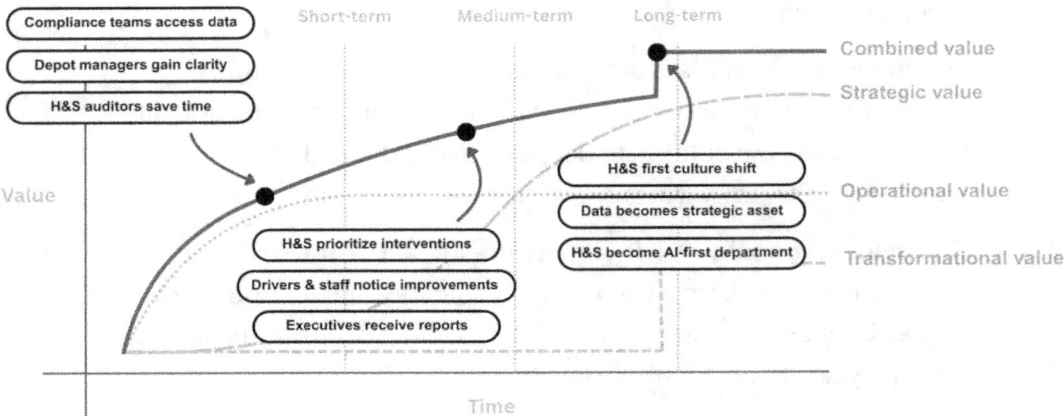

Figure 3-3. *Stakeholder value mapped over time*

The Multi-stakeholder Reality

Teams often begin agent development by asking "what should it do?". We need to shift this mindset to a more fundamental question: **"who should it help, and how?"**.

Consider this scenario: an organization builds an intelligent document processing agent. The IT team celebrates its technical sophistication; it can parse multiple file types, extract key information, and route documents automatically. Usage metrics look strong, but six months later, different stakeholders have vastly different perspectives on its value:

- **Finance team**: "It's faster than manual processing, but the categorization is inconsistent."

- **Compliance teams**: "We can finally audit document flows, but we need better approval trails."

- **Operations team**: "It handles routine stuff well but struggles with exceptions that matter most."

- **Leadership**: "The efficiency gains are unclear; how does this impact our quarterly targets?"

Each group experienced the same agent differently because they brought different priorities, workflows, and success criteria to the interaction. The technical capabilities remained constant, but the perceived value varied dramatically based on perspective.

This illustrates why stakeholder value mapping is essential before design begins. It ensures you're building for real needs rather than assumptions about what people want. However, understanding stakeholder perspectives is only the foundation. The critical next step is converting diverse viewpoints into concrete design guidance that can actually shape what you build.

The tools that follow are designed to do exactly that; helping teams translate stakeholder needs, constraints, and priorities into clear agent behaviors, boundaries, and success criteria.

Tool 1: The Stakeholder Value Map

When we talk about value, we are really talking about *perceived benefit* – and perception depends on where you stand. Capturing the perspectives of stakeholders early helps ensure the design serves multiple audiences, not just the most vocal one.

The stakeholder value map draws on well-established traditions of **stakeholder analysis**,[1] **value mapping**[2] in business model design, and **impact mapping**[3] in product management. What's unique here is the synthesis: combining these practices specifically for agent development to make the different ways stakeholders perceive and measure visible before design begins.

Traditional stakeholder analysis excels at identifying who has power and interest but often stops short of understanding what they value.

Value mapping captures what outcomes matter but can miss implementation realities and behavioral requirements.

Impact mapping connects goals to capabilities but sometimes oversimplifies stakeholder complexity.

---

[1] Freeman, R.E (1984): Strategic Management: A Stakeholder Approach

[2] Osterwalder & Pigneur (2010): Business Model Generation: A Handbook for Visionaries

[3] Adzic (2012): Impact mapping: Making a Big Impact with Software Products and Projects

The agent-specific synthesis addresses these limitations by ensuring you identify the right people, understand what matters to them, and connect agent capabilities to stakeholder outcomes through realistic behavioral change.

The four-category framework

Drawing from Freeman's stakeholder theory (1984), we begin by systematically identifying who will be affected by the agent's deployment and outcomes. Traditional stakeholder analysis uses power-interest matrices to map influence relationships. For agents, we adapt this to focus on **value dependency** and **adoption influence.** Figure 3-4 introduces a practical way to think about who matters for an agent opportunity, grouping stakeholders by how they experience value and influence adoption.

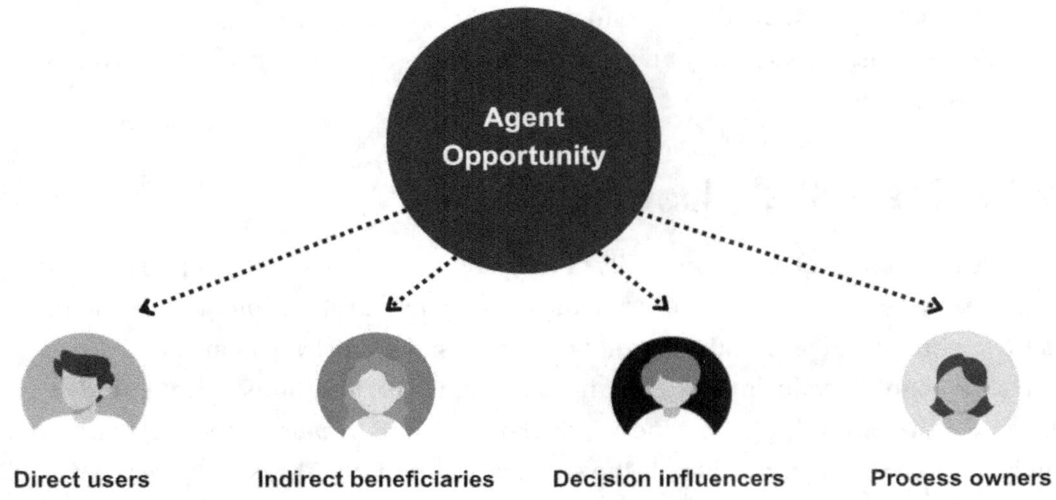

Figure 3-4. *Stakeholder mapping for an agent opportunity*

Direct users – People who interact with the agent as part of their daily work. Their adoption directly determines whether the agent succeeds operationally.

Indirect beneficiaries – People who feel the agent's impact through improved processes, better data quality, or enhanced services, even without direct interaction.

Decision influencers – People who can champion, fund, or constrain the agent's development and expansion. Their support determines resource allocation and strategic positioning.

Finally, **process owners** – People responsible for the workflows and outcomes the agent affects. Their buy-in determines whether the agent integrates smoothly or creates organizational friction.

The 5-minute stakeholder discovery assessment

Spend 5 minutes identifying who actually matters for your agent's success. Answer these questions for your specific use case.

Quick discovery questions:

1. **Who will use this agent daily?** Write down specific job titles, not departments. "Customer service representatives," not "customer service team." These are your direct users.

2. **Which stakeholder category should they be assigned?**

3. **Who can cancel this project?** Identify anyone with veto power. Budget holders, compliance officers, or influential skeptics.

4. **Who has to change how they work?** Think beyond direct users. Who trains people? Who updates procedures? Who handles exceptions?

5. **Who will be blamed if this goes wrong?** These people need the strongest risk mitigation story.

The template output should capture specific individuals and their relationships to your agent opportunity. Figure 3-5 below shows how this assessment would look for an HT onboarding agent project.

Stakeholder discovery

Five-minute stakeholder discovery assessment

Assessor: *S Jeffery*   Date: *07/06/2025*

Opportunity: *HR onboarding agent*

Direct users

Who will use this agent daily?

Name/ title: *Sarah Chen, HR Ops Director*

Department: *HR*

Stakeholder group: ☐ Direct user ☐ Indirect beneficiary ☑ Decision influencer ☐ Process owner

Name/ title: *Brian Jones, HR Administrator*

Department: *HR*

Stakeholder group: ☑ Direct user ☐ Indirect beneficiary ☐ Decision influencer ☐ Process owner

Name/ title:

Department:

Stakeholder group: ☐ Direct user ☐ Indirect beneficiary ☐ Decision influencer ☐ Process owner

Decision makers

Who can cancel this project?

Name/ title: *Sarah Chen, HR Ops Director*

Veto reason:

☑ Budget authority

☑ Strategic misalignment

☑ Compliance concerns

Name/ title:

Veto reason:

☐ Budget authority

☐ Strategic misalignment

☐ Compliance concerns

Workflow changes

Who has to change how they work?

Accountability

Who has accountability for this project?

Figure 3-5. *Stakeholder discovery template*

Download the stakeholder discovery template

```
https://github.com/Apress/Value-By-Design-with-Microsoft-
Copilot-Studio
```

Stakeholder value discovery

Once you've identified and categorized specific people, you need to understand what value means to each of them. You can gather these insights through direct interviews or automated surveys. Both approaches use the same core questions but scale differently.

Option one: direct interviews (high touch)

Use this approach when you have a small number of stakeholders, or need deep, qualitative insights.

Current state questions

1. "Walk me through how you handle [process] today"

2. "What part of that process frustrates you most?"

3. "What would happen if that frustrating part went away?"

4. "How do you currently measure whether [process] is working well?"

   Further questions: The aim of current state questions is to be able to articulate the scale of the challenges being faced. The following questions help identify how large the current pain points are:

5. "Let's get specific about the numbers. Roughly, how many [queries/cases/requests/] do you handle per [day/week/month]?"

   If they don't know, follow up with estimations: "Would it be closer to 10, 50, 100 per week?"

6. "On average, how long does [specific task] currently take?"

   If they don't know, challenge with "Is it minutes, hours, or days typically?"

7. "What percentage of the time does this process work smoothly, versus causing problems?"

   If they don't know, suggest: "Is it working well most of the time (70%+) or causing frequent issues (less than 50%)

Why these questions matter: Current state questions establish baseline reality and reveal pain points that may not be obvious to outsiders. They prevent you from solving problems that don't exist while uncovering friction points that stakeholders experience daily. The measurement question is particularly important, it identifies metrics the organization already tracks, making it easier to demonstrate agent value later. Here's how to score their responses:

- 5 = Critical daily pain with clear business impact and existing measurement

- 4 = Significant frustration with business consequences and some measurement

- 3 = Moderate issues with workarounds and basic measurement

- 2 = Minor inconveniences with limited measurement

- 1 = No significant current problems

Value questions

1. "What would make this agent genuinely valuable to you in your role?"

2. "When would you expect to start seeing that value – immediately, after a few weeks, or months, or longer term?"

3. "How could we track whether you're getting that value, and who else would need to see that evidence?"

4. "What would need to be true for you to trust this agent's outputs or recommendations?"

   Further questions: The following enhanced questions are designed to identify the benefits expected or required from the agent use case:

5. If this agent could improve [metric we discussed], what would be a meaningful improvement?

   If they can't answer: "Would reducing from [current baseline] to [estimated target] make a real difference to you?"

6. "How does this connect with your department's objectives or what leadership measures?"

   Or, to steer the conversation, try "Which of your quarterly goals or KPIs would this help with?"

7. "What would 'good enough' look like versus 'exceptional' performance?"

   Or: "At what point would you say this agent has earned its keep?"

Why these questions matter: Value questions help stakeholders articulate benefits in their own terms while establishing realistic timelines for when those benefits should appear. The timing question prevents unrealistic expectations and helps sequence agent capabilities appropriately. The tracking question identifies measurable signals and key stakeholders who need visibility into results. Trust requirement's surface adoption barriers that must be addressed in design. Together, these questions ensure you understand not just what value means but when and how it can be demonstrated. You can score them as follows:

- 5 = Specific, measurable benefits with immediate timeline and clear tracking

- 4 = Clear benefits with short-term timeline and good measurement plan

- 3 = General benefits with medium-term timeline and basic measurement

- 2 = Vague benefits with unclear timeline and weak measurement

- 1 = No clear benefits articulated

Trade-off questions

1. "What would you be willing to give up to get [benefit they mentioned]?"

2. "What's the worst thing that could happen if this agent made a mistake?"

3. "Who would you need to convince to support this?"

Why these questions matter: Trade-off questions reveal what stakeholders value most by forcing prioritization decisions. They surface constraints and concerns that could derail adoption if not addressed. The influence question identifies additional stakeholders you may need to consider and helps you understand the political dynamics around agent deployment. Here, use the following for scoring:

- 5 = willing to accept trade-offs, manageable risk tolerance, has influence to drive adoption

- 4 = Accepts reasonable trade-offs, understands risks, can help with adoption

- 3 = Limited trade-off acceptance, moderate risk concerns, neutral influence

- 2 = Reluctant to change, focused on risks, may resist

- 1 = Unwilling to change, sees mostly risks, will likely oppose

These conversations serve **three critical purposes** that determine whether your agent succeeds or becomes another failed experiment:

1. **Surface roadblocks before you build**: Every question is designed to reveal potential adoption barriers, technical constraints, or organizational resistance. It's far cheaper to discover that stakeholders won't trust AI recommendations or that key data isn't accessible during interviews than after months of development.

2. **Establish realistic value timelines**: By understanding when different stakeholders expect to see benefits, you can sequence your agent's capabilities appropriately and set realistic expectations. This prevents the disappointment that kills projects when early results don't match inflated expectations.

3. **Maximize production readiness**: These insights help you design an agent that people will actually use, that delivers measurable value, and that has sufficient organizational support to survive budget reviews and leadership changes. Every answer brings you closer to an agent that makes it from proof of concept to production.

After completing these surveys, your output should look as in Figure 3-6.

Role	Name	Stakeholder category	Has veto power?	Must change behavior	Bears risk?	Value	Current state	Trade-off
Customer service rep	Steve J	Direct user		✓		4	3	4
CS Team lead	Phil R	Indirect beneficiaries		✓		4	4	5
IT security	Vasavi B	Decision influencers	✓		✓	3	2	3
VP Customer experience	Manuela T	Decision influencers	✓		✓	5	3	5
CS Manager	Greg H	Process owner		✓	✓	4	4	4

Figure 3-6. *Stakeholder map*

Option two: automated surveys (scalable)

Use this approach when you have many stakeholders or want to gather baseline data efficiently.

Survey implementation

Deploy the same core questions through your organization's survey platform (Microsoft Forms, SurveyMonkey, etc.). Add these elements for better data quality:

Survey design tips:

- Keep it under 10 questions to ensure completion.

- Use a mix of multiple choice and open text fields.

- Include stakeholder category as a filter question.

- Send personalized invitations mentioning the specific agent opportunity.

Sample survey structure:

1. Stakeholder category (dropdown: direct user, indirect beneficiary, decision influencer, process owner)

2. Current process frustration (rating scale + open text)

3. Value priorities (rank order of options)

4. Success measures (open text)

5. Trust requirements (multiple choice + other)

6. Acceptable trade-offs (open text)

7. Risk concerns (open text)

Let's look at an example: **HR onboarding agent**.

Consider an organization developing an agent to streamline employee onboarding. Using the four-category framework, you have identified the following stakeholder groups, as shown in Figure 3-7 below.

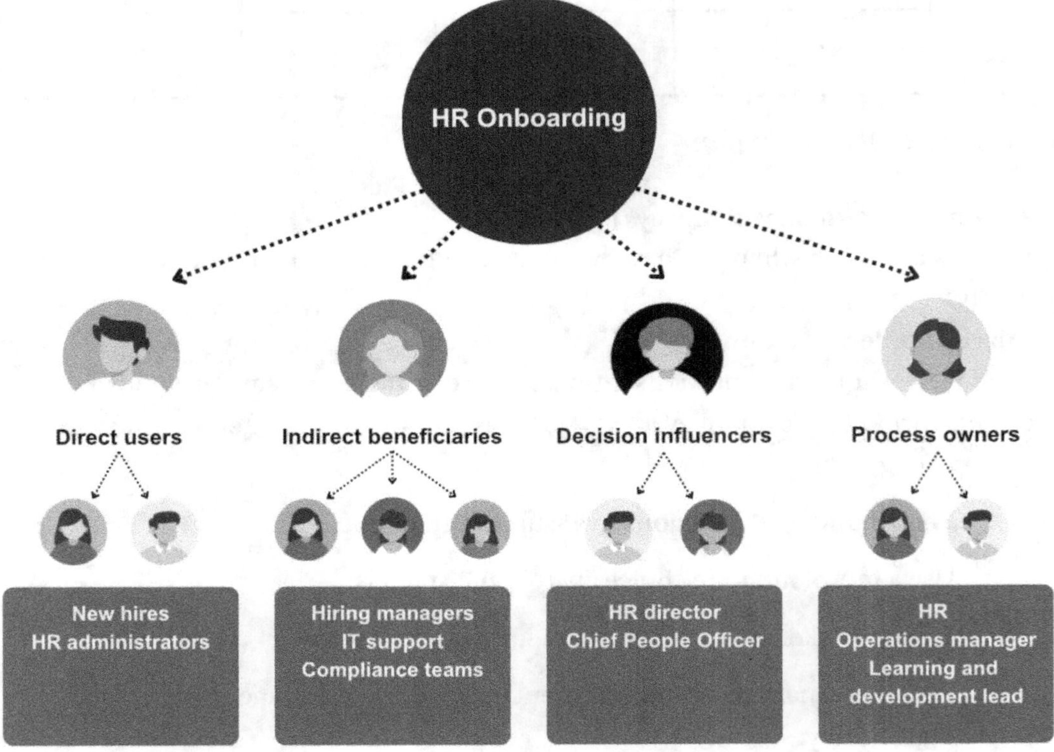

Figure 3-7. *Example stakeholder groups for an HR onboarding agent*

Prioritization scoring:

Analysis: As per Figure 3-8 above, four stakeholder groups emerge as high priority to detailed value mapping: new hires, HR administrators, HR director, and Learning and Development.

Role	Stakeholder category	Has veto power?	Must change behavior	Bears risk?	Value	Current state	Trade-off
New hires	Direct user				4	3	4
HR administrators	Direct user		✓		4	4	5
Hiring managers	Indirect beneficiaries				3	2	3
IT support	Indirect beneficiaries				5	3	5
Compliance teams	Indirect beneficiaries				4	4	4
HR director	Decision influencer	✓		✓	4	5	5
CPO	Decision influencer	✓		✓	5	4	4
HR Ops manager	Process owner			✓	3	3	4
L&D lead	Process owner			✓	4	3	4

Figure 3-8. *Example prioritization table*

Expanding the details

By now, you have a good view on stakeholders and their relative priorities based on interview scores. The value discovery process has given you rich insights into what each stakeholder wants, when they expect to see results, how they would measure success, and what concerns them most.

The critical part here is to document these insights in a structured way that transforms subjective interview responses into objective design guidance. This documentation serves multiple purposes: it creates a shared reference point for design decisions, establishes accountability for delivering specific stakeholder value, and provides the foundation for measuring agent success.

The stakeholder map below captures the essential elements from your interviews in a format that can guide subsequent design choices.

HR onboarding agent – stakeholder value map, as shown in Figure 3-9 below

Stakeholder	Value they want	Timeline	How to measure	Key concerns
New hires	Fast answers without bothering people	Immediate	Time to answer, satisfaction surveys	Getting wrong information
HR administrators	Stop answering repeat questions so I can focus on complex cases	First month	# Deflected queries, hours saved per week	Agent giving incorrect policy information
Hiring managers	New team members productive faster with less hand-holding	2 - 6 weeks	Time to productivity, reduced buddying time with basic questions	Making onboarding feel impersonal
IT support	Reduce setup tickets from new hires who don't understand the process	1 - 3 months	IT support ticket volume from new hires	If the agent bypasses security controls
HR director	Consistent onboarding with complete audit trail	3 - 6 months	Policy adherence rates, audit readiness, consistency metrics	Creating more work for managers, not improving compliance

Figure 3-9. *Example stakeholder map table*

Tool 2: Success Definition Framework

Understanding trade-offs in the HR onboarding agent

It's rare for every stakeholder to experience the same level or type of benefit from a change. In fact, improving value for one group can sometimes reduce it for another. These trade-offs are not signs of failure – they're an inevitable part of designing systems that serve multiple audiences. What matters is spotting these tensions early, understanding their impact, and deciding how to address them.

The HR onboarding scenario illustrates three common trade-off patterns (Figure 3-10):

Figure 3-10. *Trade off – speed vs. security*

Trade off one: Speed vs. security

Design resolution: Implement layered access, where general information (office locations, basic policies, team contacts) is immediately available, while sensitive information (salary details, performance systems, confidential policies) requires verification via Single Sign-On. Behind the scenes, the agent would check if the user is in a secure environment (e.g., corporate network, or approved IP range, if sensitivity label permissions match document classification, whether the request complies with Data Loss Prevention [DLP] and Microsoft Information Protection [MIP] policies). All of the interactions are audited, adding layers of security, while at the same time delivering success metrics for both sides.

- **New hire satisfaction**: Questions answered quickly

- **IT security compliance**: Verification for sensitive information access, zero security protocol bypasses

Trade-off two: Automation vs. human touch

Figure 3-11. *Trade-off: automation vs. human touch*

Design resolution: Automate routine informational queries while preserving and enhancing human touchpoints for relationship-building. The agent handles "where is the cafeteria?" but escalates "how do I succeed in this role?" to the hiring manager with context about what the new hire has already learned.

Success for both sides:

- **HR efficiency**: Reduction in routine queries handled automatically

- **Manager connection**: New hire satisfaction scores for "feeling supported by manager" maintain or improve

Trade-off three: Consistency vs. flexibility

Figure 3-12. *Trade-off: consistency vs. flexibility*

Design resolution: Create a standardized core experience for company-wide policies and procedures, with configurable modules for department-specific content that local managers can customize within approved guidelines. This achieves success for both sides by measuring compliance with core onboarding requirements across all locations, while allowing department-specific completion rates to either match or exceed company-wide averages.

Each trade-off resolution becomes a design principle that guides specific feature decisions.

In practice, teams should be able to explain how they arrived at these resolutions; what options were considered, which stakeholder outcomes were prioritized, and which constraints were non-negotiable. This doesn't require exhaustive documentation, but it does mean making the trad-offs explicit before any veto is exercised.

Next, validate your trade-off resolutions against stakeholder interview scores.

Primary stakeholders (have veto and/or responsibility) must be satisfied. If your resolution doesn't address the core concerns of HR directors, HR administrators, and IT support, reconsider the approach.

Secondary stakeholders should benefit where possible. New hires and hiring managers get value, but not at the expense of primary stakeholder needs.

Design principles are non-negotiable: Security requirements from IT cannot be compromised, even if it slows down the experience for new hires.

Mental exercise: the trade-off test

Imagine: you're designing a customer service agent for a financial services company. After stakeholder interviews, you've discovered conflicting needs that can't all be satisfied simultaneously. Work through this scenario:

The situation

Your agent handles account queries, transaction disputes, and policy questions. Three high-priority stakeholders have emerged with conflicting requirements, as shown in Figure 3-13.

Stakeholder	Value they want	Timeline	Key concerns
Customer service reps	Handle complex queries so I can focus on relationship building and sales opportunities	Immediate	What is customers get frustrated with wrong answers and take it out on me?
Compliance officer	Every financial advice interaction must have complete audit trails and escalation to licensed representatives	First month	What if the agent gives financial advice without proper oversight and we get fined?
Operations director	Reduce call center costs by 30% while maintaining customer satisfaction scores about 4.2/5	2 - 6 weeks	What if this creates more work for managers or doesn't deliver the cost savings we primised the board?

Figure 3-13. *Example of conflicting stakeholder priorities and timelines*

The constraint

Your company has committed to a six-month deployment timeline to demonstrate AI value to the board. Due to competing priorities, you can only get two weeks of dedicated time from one key stakeholder group during the critical solution shaping phase, as shown in Figure 3-14.

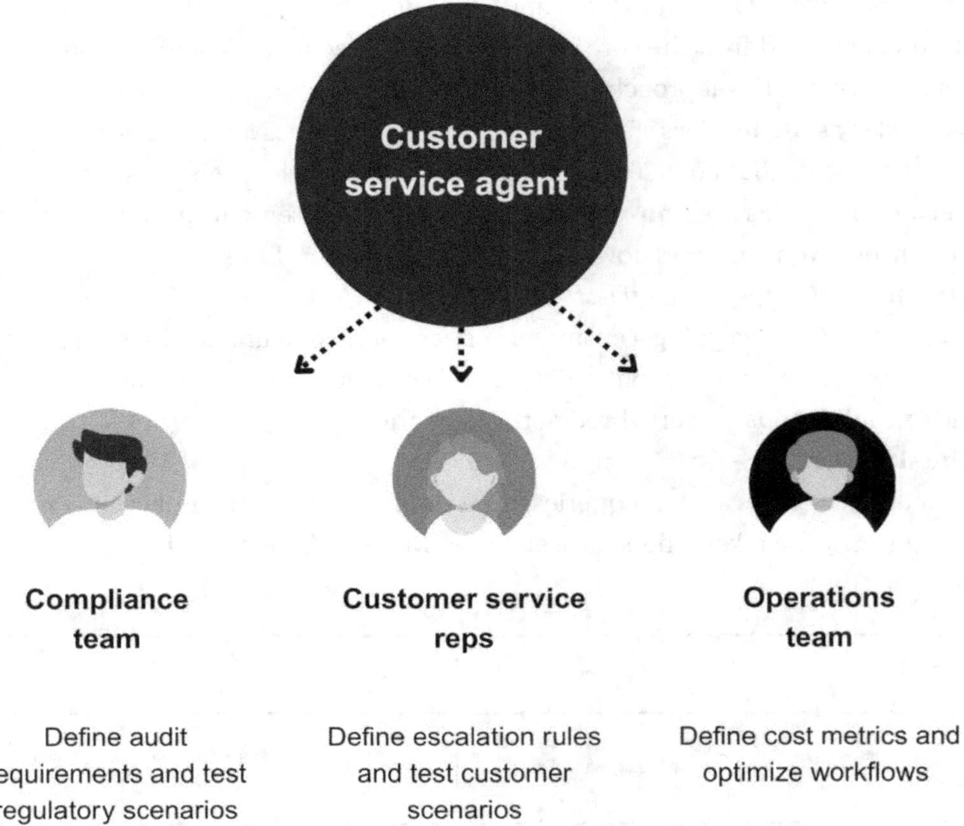

Figure 3-14. *Prioritizing stakeholder engagement under delivery constraints*

Whichever group you don't prioritize for intensive collaboration will only be able to provide feedback during standard review cycles, potentially missing critical requirements that could require significant rework later.

Trade-off scenarios

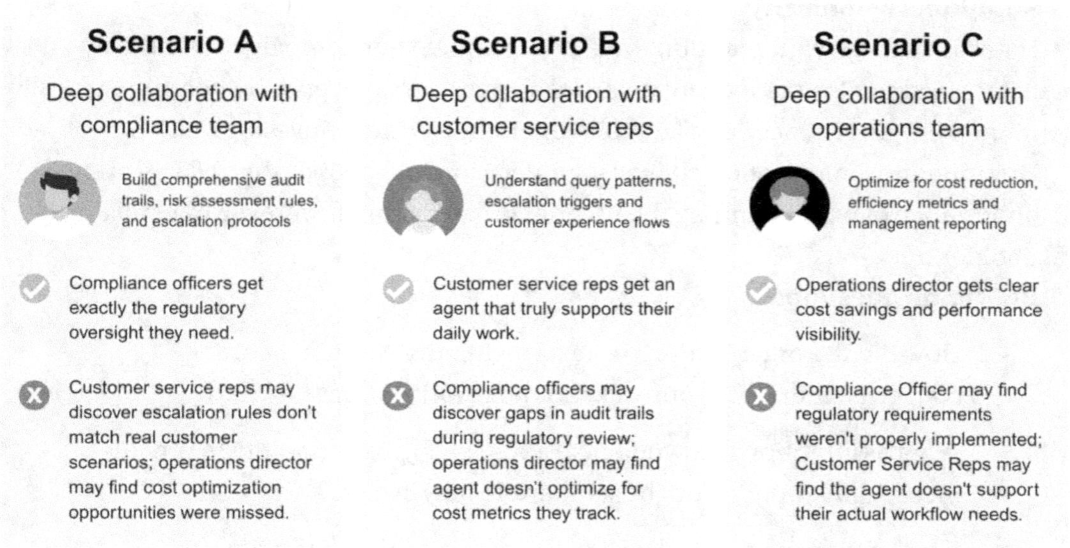

Figure 3-15. *Alternative collaboration trade-offs across stakeholder groups*

Your challenge

Choose one scenario and justify your decision by addressing these questions:

1. **Stakeholder priority analysis**: Based on interview scores (Compliance officer: 14, Customer service reps: 13, Operations director: 12), whose needs should take precedence and why?

2. **Risk assessment**: What's the worse-case scenario for each stakeholder if you don't prioritize their intensive collaboration? Which risk is the company least able to accept?

3. **Mitigation strategy**: How would you measure whether your collaboration choice was correct six-months after deployment? Which metrics would tell you if you chose the wrong group to prioritize?

4. **Stakeholder communication**: How would you explain to the non-prioritized stakeholders why their group wasn't selected for intensive collaboration, while maintaining their engagement and support?

Additional complexity

Halfway through your planning, you discover that your company was cited by regulators last year for inadequate financial advice oversight, and the board specifically mentioned "AI governance" as a key concern in the quarterly investor call.

How does this information change your decision? What does this tell you about the importance of understanding the broader organizational context when making stakeholder trade-offs?

Reflection questions

- How did the organization context (regulatory citation, board concerns) influence your stakeholder prioritization?

- What assumptions did you make about each group's ability to provide meaningful input through "standard review cycles"?

- If you had to make this decision in a real-world project with incomplete information, what additional data would you seek out?

This exercise wasn't about "correct" answers, but your reasoning process should demonstrate understanding of stakeholder priorities, organizational risk management, and practical project constraints that exist in real-world agent development.

In Chapter 3, we've established the foundation that separates successful agents from expensive experiments: value clarity. You now understand that value is never experienced uniformly across an organization. The same agent functionality creates completely different experiences depending on where stakeholders sit – frontline workers care more about daily efficiencies, managers focus on process improvements, and executives measure strategic impact.

We've introduced the value benefit lens, which categorizes agent value into three layers: operational (immediate, efficiency gains), strategic (medium-term business improvements), and transformational (long-term behavioral shifts). These layers typically emerge sequentially, with operational benefits appearing first and transformational impact developing over months or years.

Most importantly, you've built a systematic approach to stakeholder value discovery. Through structured interviews covering current state pain points, value expectations, and trade-off willingness, you've moved beyond assumptions about what people want, to evidence-based understanding of what they actually need. The stakeholder value map you've created captures who experiences value, what that value means in their own words, when they expect to see results, and what concerns them most.

You've also learned that trade-offs are inevitable when serving multiple stakeholders. Rather than trying to satisfy everyone equally (which usually satisfies no one), you've established principled approaches to resolving tensions between competing needs. These design principles become guardrails that prevent scope drift and ensure consistent decision-making throughout agent development.

Looking Ahead: From Value Clarity to Success Definition

Value clarity tells you what different stakeholders want from your agent. The next critical step is **translating those insights** into specific, measurable success criteria that guide design decisions and prove impact. In Chapter 4, we'll use tools to convert stakeholder desires into concrete agent outcomes, establish multi-level success criteria that work across organizational levels, and create measurement mechanisms that demonstrate your agent delivers the value it promised.

Success Definition

Introduction: The Measurement Gap

In Chapter 3, you discovered what value means to different stakeholders through structured interviews and analysis. You now understand who experiences value, when they expect to see it, and what concerns them most. Your stakeholder value map captures these insights in a structured format that shows different perspectives on what the agent should achieve.

But there's a critical gap between "understanding value" and "defining success." A stakeholder saying "I want faster access to policy information" provides direction but falls short of establishing what "faster" means in measurable terms, or how you'll know when you've achieved it. This transition from insights to outcomes reduces the chances of building an agent that isn't delivering value.

The Challenge Many Teams Face

Teams often jump directly to building the agent. They hear "we need faster onboarding" and immediately start designing features: a conversational experience, knowledge base integration, automated task routing, etc. These are reasonable technical responses, but they skip the crucial step of defining what success actually looks like in concrete, measurable terms.

Without this definition, several problems emerge:

Ambiguous goals become moving targets. When you haven't specified what "faster onboarding" means quantitatively, stakeholders can shift expectations after seeing results. What seemed like a success gets reframed as insufficient because someone expected more without ever articulating that expectation up front.

S. Jeffery, *Value by Design with Microsoft Copilot Studio*, https://doi.org/10.1007/979-8-8688-2613-9_4

Design decisions lack clear criteria. Without specific outcomes, every feature debate becomes subjective. Should the agent handle complex exceptions or focus on common scenarios? Should it prioritize speed or completeness? These trade-offs can't be evaluated rationally without knowing what specific outcomes you're optimizing for.

Measurement becomes an afterthought. Teams realize too late that they never defined how to measure success, leading to the measurement gap problem described earlier. You've built something, people use it, but you can't prove it delivers the value stakeholders expected because you never specified what that value was.

This chapter bridges this gap by teaching you how to convert stakeholder insights into specific, measurable success criteria. This approach ensures your success criteria are concrete enough to guide design decisions and prove business impact.

The outcome conversion process provides a systematic method for transforming the qualitative insights captured in your stakeholder value map into quantitative success specifications that can guide agent design and validate achievement.

The Role of Success Definition in Your Value by Design Journey

Before diving into the mechanics of outcome conversion, understand where this work fits in your broader journey.

From chapter one and two (opportunity framing): You identified strategic hotspots where agents could deliver meaningful impact and selected specific opportunities based on friction points that mattered to organizational goals.

From chapter three (value clarity): You mapped stakeholders, conducted interviews to understand their needs, and captured their perspectives on what value means to them in their own words.

In chapter four (success definition – where we are now): You transform those stakeholder perspectives into specific, measurable outcomes that everyone agrees represent success. This creates the design specification your agent must satisfy.

Coming in chapter five (measurement readiness): You'll build the infrastructure to track whether those outcomes are being achieved, establishing baselines and implementing monitoring systems.

Eventually, in later chapters: You'll design and build the agent with clear success criteria guiding every decision, then measure actual results against the outcomes defined here.

Success definition is the bridge between qualitative understanding (what stakeholders want) and quantitative measurement (proof that you delivered it). Without this bridge, you can't build with confidence or prove with evidence.

The Journey Ahead

Your stakeholder value map contains rich insights from interviews; statements about what people want, when they expect to see results, and what concerns them most. These insights are valuable, but they're expressed in the natural language people use when describing their needs and frustrations.

Look back at your stakeholder value map from Chapter 3. You likely have entries that sound like this:

- "We need faster access to information."

- "The process should be more consistent."

- "Employees shouldn't have to wait days for answers."

- "We want better visibility into what's happening."

These statements are genuine expressions of stakeholder needs. They reflect real pain points and legitimate desires for improvement. But notice what they don't tell you. We already covered this in the introduction: how fast is faster? What does consistent mean? How long is too long? What kind of visibility?

The outcome conversion process solves this problem. It provides a systematic method for taking the qualitative insights from your stakeholder map and transforming them into specific, measurable outcome statements that everyone agrees represent success.

Think of it as a translation process.

You take the natural language stakeholders use to describe their needs; "faster," "more consistent," "better vision," and translate it into clear, measurable outcome statements that can guide design and be tracked over time.

This ensures the human element is understood clearly enough to build something that actually delivers what people need.

The Outcome Conversion Process: An Overview

Before we dive into the detailed process, understand the basic transformation you'll be making. You'll take each entry from your stakeholder value map and convert it through a structured formula that answers five critical questions.

1. What will change?

2. From what current state?

3. To what target state?

4. By when?

5. How will we know?

Let's see what this means in practice. Your stakeholder value map will likely have entries like

- "Fast answers without bothering people"

- "Better visibility into processes"

- "Consistent experience across locations"

- "Reduce manual effort"

These statements describe desired outcomes but are not specific enough to design or measure against.

Before we dive into the details, there's an important foundation to establish. When stakeholders describe what they want, they're often describing different types of improvements without realizing it. "Faster answers" is about efficiency; doing things quicker. "Consistent experience" is about effectiveness; doing things reliably. "Better visibility" is about empowerment; enabling better decisions.

Before you can convert stakeholder insights into measurable outcomes, you need a shared vocabulary for describing what type of value you're trying to deliver. This vocabulary helps you have more precise conversations with stakeholders and ensures your converted outcomes capture what they actually care about.

This is where value benefits come in.

Understanding Value Benefits

Value benefits are the positive, measurable outcomes resulting from agent behavior. They provide a common language for describing different types of improvements, helping you translate vague desires into specific categories of change.

Value benefits generally fall into five categories, as shown in Figure 4-1 below.

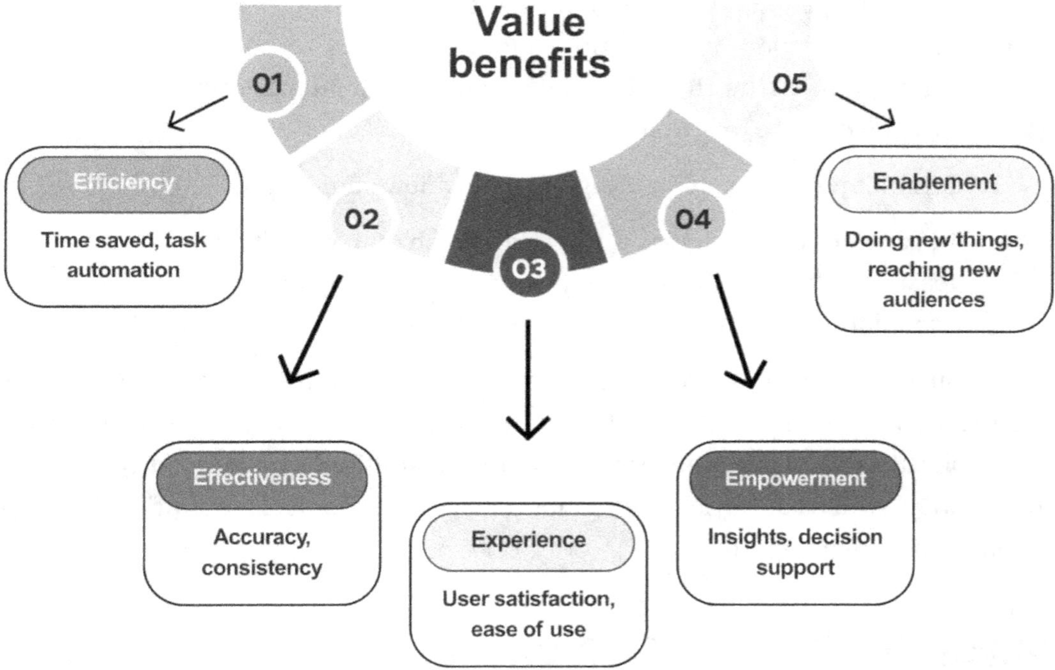

Figure 4-1. *Five categories of value benefits*

1. **Efficiency:** Time saved, task automation

    Making existing processes faster and requiring less human effort. Efficiency improvements reduce the cost or time required to complete current tasks without changing what gets accomplished.

2. **Effectiveness:** Accuracy, consistency

   Making existing processes more reliable and producing better quality outcomes. Effectiveness improvements ensure work is done correctly and consistently across people, locations, and time.

3. **Experience:** User satisfaction, ease of use

   Making interactions more pleasant, intuitive, and less frustrating. Experience improvements focus on how people feel about their work rather than just how quickly or accurately they complete it.

4. **Empowerment:** Insights, decision support

   Providing people with better information, analysis, or recommendations to make more informed choices. Empowerment improvements give people capabilities they didn't have before, like real-time data or predictive insights.

5. **Enablement:** Doing new things, reaching new audiences

   Making possible activities, services, or reach that weren't feasible before. Enablement improvements open up entirely new capabilities rather than improving existing ones.

Every successful agent delivers value benefits across multiple categories. A customer service agent might deliver efficiency (faster query resolution), effectiveness (consistent policy application), and experience (reduced user frustration) simultaneously. Understanding which categories matter most to your stakeholders helps prioritize where to focus measurement efforts.

Convert Stakeholder Insights into Specific Outcomes

For each stakeholder, extract three elements from their interview responses:

1. What they want (from value questions)

2. Current pain points (from current state questions)

3. Success measurements (from value and current state questions)

Then apply this conversion formula, as shown in Figure 4-2 below.

[Verb] + [current baseline] + [target level] + [time frame] + [measurement method]

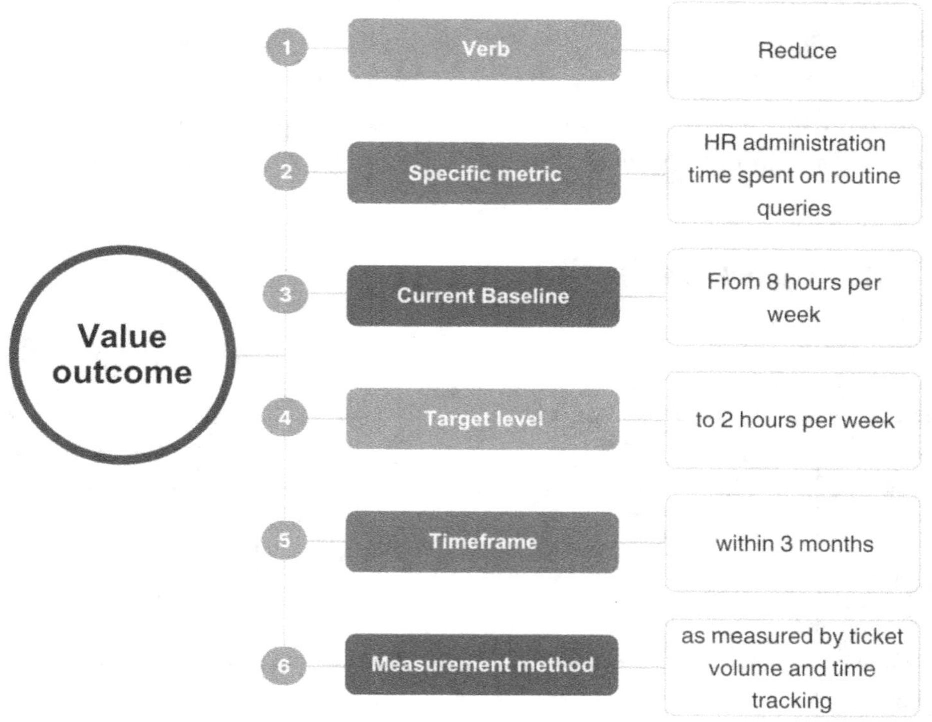

Figure 4-2. *Stakeholder insight-to-outcome conversion formula*

Example:

Once you've applied the conversion formula to transform stakeholder insights into specific outcomes, you need to document these systematically to create your success specification. This documentation becomes the foundation for all design decisions and measurement planning.

Introducing the Stakeholder Outcome Template

The stakeholder outcome template brings together everything you've learned through your alignment and discovery process. It translates qualitative insights into measurable outcomes, ensuring every stakeholder's value need is visible, tracked, and linked to success measures.

This table becomes your source of truth for value definition, showing not just what each stakeholder wants to achieve but how progress will be observed over time. By documenting original insights, converted outcomes, and associated value categories, you create a living specification of what "working" means for your agent.

The template below in Figure 4-3 provides a structured format to record these details consistently. Each row representing a stakeholder's perspective, captured from early interviews and alignment sessions, and refined into tangible, measurable goals.

Stakeholder definition

Stakeholder outcome template

Assessor: S Jeffery   Date: 07/06/2025

Opportunity: HR onboarding agent

Stakeholder	Original insight	Converted outcome	Value category	Current baseline	Target	Timeline	Measurement method
New hire	"Get answers fast without bothering people"	Increase onboarding satisfaction scores from 3.2/5 to 4.5/5 within two months	Experience	3.2/5	4.5	2 months	Post-onboarding survey

Figure 4-3. Example: Stakeholder outcomes

Guidelines

Consistency in language: Use active verbs that clearly indicate the direction of change: "increase," "reduce," "improve," and "achieve." Avoid passive language like "there will be better" or "users should experience."

Specific timelines: Every outcome must have a realistic timeline that aligns with stakeholder expectations captured in interviews. Depending on the outcome, this might be expressed in hours or days (for operational improvements), weeks or months (for adoption or behavioral change), or phased milestones rather than a single date for more strategic outcomes. Avoid vague time frames like *"in the fullness of time."*

Measurable baselines: Document current performance levels using actual data where possible, or stakeholder estimates when data doesn't exist. This baseline becomes your starting point for measuring improvement.

Clear ownership: Each outcome should connect to a stakeholder who can verify whether it's been achieved and who cares about the result.

Value category mapping: Assign each outcome to one of the five value benefit categories to ensure comprehensive coverage.

Your stakeholder outcome table should show value distribution across both value category and timelines. If all outcomes fall into a single category (like efficiency) and similar timelines, consider whether you're missing opportunities to deliver broader value.

Mapping Stakeholder Outcomes to the Value Lens

Each outcome captured in your stakeholder outcome template represents a discrete contribution to value. When viewed together, these outcomes form a timeline that shows how value builds operationally, strategically and eventually, transformationally.

This mapping is the practical expression of your value lens. It connects the individual improvements experienced by stakeholders to the broader organizational outcomes they enable. Rather than viewing these value layers as isolated stages, the diagram below shows how each outcome contributes to a cumulative pattern of value growth over time.

Integrate this visual (shown in Figure 4-4) into your communication materials and dashboards. Use it to prioritize measurement focus, starting with operational metrics, then layering in strategic indicators as adoption grows.

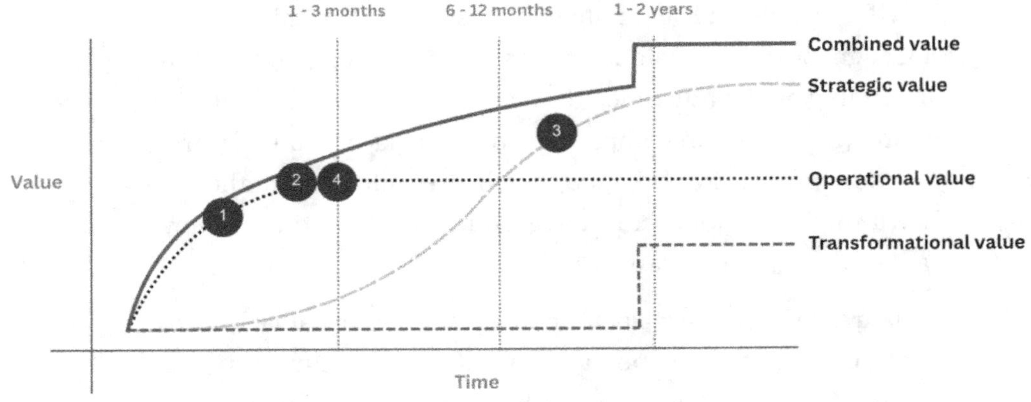

	Value category	Stakeholder	Value outcome
1	**Experience**	New hire	Increased onboarding satisfaction score
2	**Efficiency**	HR administrator	Reduced routine query time
3	Effectiveness	HR director	Increase compliance with onboarding policies
4	Efficiency	IT support	Reduction in setup tickets

Figure 4-4. Stakeholder outcomes mapped to the value lens

Stakeholder Outcomes Template As Design Specification

This completed table becomes your agent's design specification. Every feature decision can be tested against these outcomes: "Does this capability help achieve the value outcomes we've committed to delivering?"

The table also provides objective criteria for trade-off decisions. When features conflict or resources are limited, prioritize capabilities that serve multiple stakeholder outcomes or address the highest-priority stakeholders based on the scoring from Chapter 3.

However, individual stakeholder outcomes don't exist in isolation. They need to be structured into a measurement framework that works across organizational levels and provides the right information to the right people at the right time.

Bridging Success Definition and Measurement: Microsoft Copilot Studio Evaluations

You've now defined what success looks like across operational, strategic, and transformational value layers. You have stakeholder outcomes documented with baselines, targets, timelines, and measurement methods. Your success architecture shows how individual outcomes build toward broader organizational impact. There is still a lingering question: "How will you actually prove this is working?"

Microsoft Copilot Studio's evaluation capabilities are specifically designed to address this question. Rather than treating "measurement" as something you figure out after deployment, evaluations become integral to how you validate, track, and continuously improve the success outcomes you've just defined.

What Are Copilot Studio Evaluations?

Evaluations are systematic assessments of agent performance that operate across three phases of the agent lifecycle, directly supporting the success outcomes in your stakeholder table:

- **Pre-deployment evaluation** validates your agent works correctly before users encounter it. You create test scenarios covering expected questions, edge cases, and potential failures. The agent evaluation feature runs these tests automatically, simulating hundreds of conversations simultaneously, and provides clear pass/fail indicators showing where your agent succeeds and where it needs refinement.

- **Production monitoring** tracks real-world performance continuously after launch. The enhanced analytics dashboard automatically captures

  - **Conversation outcomes**: Which sessions were resolved successfully? Which escalated to humans? Which were abandoned?

  - **Answer quality**: AI-powered analysis evaluates whether responses are complete, relevant, and grounded in reliable sources.

  - **Knowledge source effectiveness**: Which content sources successfully answer questions versus those causing problems?

- **User satisfaction**: Thumbs up/down reactions and CSAT surveys reveal how users feel about their experience.

Most valuable of all, the system generates daily insights by clustering unanswered queries into themes and providing actionable recommendations. Instead of manually reviewing hundreds of conversations to find patterns, the AI identifies the top five improvement opportunities for you each day.

- **Business value measurement** connects agent usage to financial impact. Through Viva Insights integration, the platform calculates

  - **Agent assisted hours**: Time saved based on resolved sessions and knowledge source usage

  - **Agent assisted value**: Monetary impact using your organization's actual labor costs

  - **Business impact correlation**: How agent usage correlates with specific business KPIs you upload

However, evaluations are only part of the measurement story. When an executive asks "did we achieve the x% reduction" (or some other value benefit), you'll need multiple sources. Using our HR onboarding example

- **Copilot Studio evaluations provide conversation-level data**: Resolution rates, user satisfaction, answer quality

- **The HRIS system provides the business outcome**: Actual onboarding completion timestamps

- **Support ticket system provides the operational context**: Volume and nature of escalations

- **Custom tracking provides the connecting tissue**: Conversation outcome parameters that link agent interactions to business processes

Evaluations don't replace the measurement infrastructure (we'll discuss this in great detail in later chapters), they complement it. The power comes from correlation: combining agent usage data from Copilot Studio with business outcomes from your operational systems to demonstrate causal relationships between agents' interactions and business improvements.

CHAPTER 5

Measurement Readiness

The Measurement Gap Problem

Let's revisit a scenario we used earlier: the *HR onboarding agent*. The HR director thought everything was perfectly planned. The team had completed thorough stakeholder interviews for their employee onboarding agent. They'd validated success outcomes. The stakeholder outcome table looked impressive: "reduce onboarding task completion time from five days to 48 hours within three months, as measured by HRIS analytics tracking task timestamps."

Six months after deployment, the HR director faced an uncomfortable reality during the quarterly business review. The agent was technically successful, new hires loved it, HR administrators reported fewer routine questions, and everyone could see that onboarding was smoother. When the CFO asked for ROI calculation on the onboarding transformation initiative, the confidence evaporated.

The measurement infrastructure that everyone assumed would be straightforward revealed itself as a complex web of integration challenges, data quality issues, and attribution problems. The "HRIS analytics tracking" that seemed so clear during planning turned out to require custom reporting that hadn't been budgeted. HRIS tracked when tasks were assigned and marked complete, but not the actual time spent on each task. Multiple factors were influencing onboarding efficiency simultaneously: new manager training, revised policies, updated system access procedures, making it impossible to isolate the agent's specific contribution. External factors like hiring volume fluctuations, remote work policies, and department-specific conditions made it difficult to prove the agent deserved credit for the improvements everyone could see happening.

This story illustrates the **measurement gap problem** – the disconnect between clearly defined value benefits and the practical reality of proving those outcomes have been achieved.

S. Jeffery, *Value by Design with Microsoft Copilot Studio*, https://doi.org/10.1007/979-8-8688-2613-9_5

The Hidden Complexity of Agent Measurement

Traditional business applications generate value through indirect mechanisms. A CRM system doesn't directly improve sales performance; it provides tools that enable better sales processes. Measuring CRM success focuses on adoption metrics: how many people use it, how completely they enter data, whether it integrates with other systems.

Agents work differently.

They don't just provide tools; they actively participate in business processes. They make decisions, take actions, and influence outcomes directly. This creates both opportunity and complexity for measurement.

The opportunity is quite compelling: **agents can be measured on business outcomes**, not just technical metrics. A customer service agent can be evaluated on resolution rates and satisfaction scores, not just uptime and response speed. This direct connection to business value is what makes agents potentially transformational.

The complexity emerges because business outcomes are influenced by multiple factors beyond agent performance. When customer satisfaction improves after deploying a service agent (e.g., an advisor or assistant), how much credit belongs to the agent versus concurrent training programs, process changes, or other organizational or environmental conditions? When warehouse efficiency increases, is it the agent, new staff, improved processes, or seasonal factors?

This measurement attribution challenge becomes more acute because agents often work alongside human collaborators rather than replacing them entirely. A financial planning agent might provide recommendations that humans review, modify, and implement. Measuring the agent's contribution requires disentangling its influence from human expertise, judgment, and relationship-building.

Why Measurement Planning Fails

Many measurement failures aren't technical; they're conceptual. Teams develop measurement approaches that look comprehensive during planning but break down when confronted with operational reality.

The Assumption Trap

Planning discussions about measurement often proceed with implicit assumptions that prove wrong:

> **Assumption:** *"We'll compare onboarding performance before and after agent deployment to measure impact."*
>
> **Reality:** Multiple initiatives launched simultaneously, new manager training programs, updated IT provisioning processes, revised policy documentation. Isolating agent impact requires more sophisticated analysis than simple before/after comparison.

Many measurement plans assume that because data exists in organizational systems, it's accessible and reliable for agent measurement. This assumption frequently proves false; here are a few reasons why:

- **Data exists but isn't available:** Information lives in systems that don't integrate easily, require specialized access, or have restrictions that prevent real-time measurement.

- **Data exists but isn't reliable:** Systems capture data inconsistently, contain gaps or errors, or reflect business rules that have changes over time without retroactive data cleaning.

- **Data exists but isn't granular:** Aggregate reporting provides general trends but lacks the specificity needed to measure agent impact. Monthly department-wide metrics can't reveal daily individual agent contributions.

- **Data exists but isn't timely:** Measurement requires recent data to support rapid iteration and improvement, but some systems batch process or delay reporting.

Figure 5-1 summarizes the most common ways measurement plans break down in practice, even when data technically exists. These gaps explain why many teams struggle to prove agent impact despite having access to organizational systems:

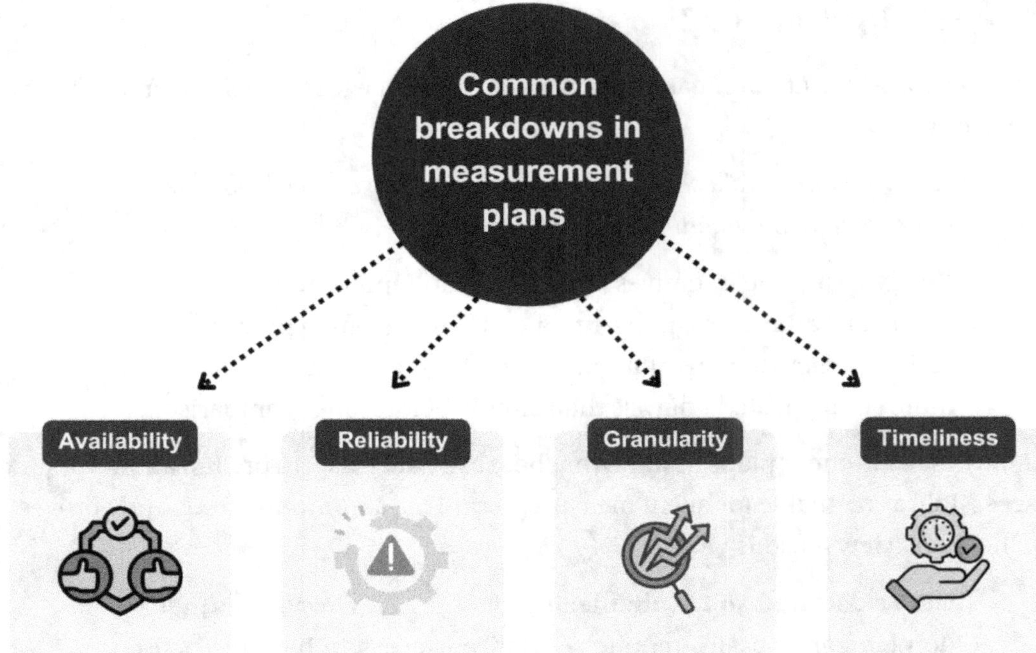

Figure 5-1. *Why existing data often fails agent measurement*

The Stakeholder Measurement Mismatch

During planning, stakeholders often agree to measurement approaches that seem reasonable in theory but prove problematic in practice.

The proxy problem: Stakeholders accept proxy measurements during planning but lose confidence when actual results rely on indirect indicators. A reduction in support tickets seems like a good measure of agent effectiveness until stakeholders realize that users might be getting help but through different channels that aren't tracked.

The baseline problem: Establishing accurate baselines requires historical data that may not exist, may not be comparable to post-agent conditions, or may reflect exceptional rather than typical performance.

The frequency problem: Stakeholders want regular progress updates but don't consider the practical challenges of measuring business outcomes on short cycles. Some improvements only become visible over months, not weeks.

Quick recap: why measurement plans collapse

- Data assumed to exist often lacks the fields you need.

- Access, privacy, and integration take longer than teams expect.

- Outcomes are multi-casual, so attribution is partial.

- Proxies can work, but only if stakeholders accept them up front.

- Baselines are a design activity, not an afterthought.

The Cascade Effect of Measurement Problems

When teams can't demonstrate agent value through reliable metrics, stakeholder confidence erodes gradually. Initial enthusiasm based on anecdotal evidence gives way to skepticism as business reviews demand quantitative justification.

The erosion typically follows a predictable pattern. Figure 5-2 shows how measurement readiness shapes stakeholder confidence over time, illustrating the divergent paths teams experience when value can, or cannot, be demonstrated consistently.

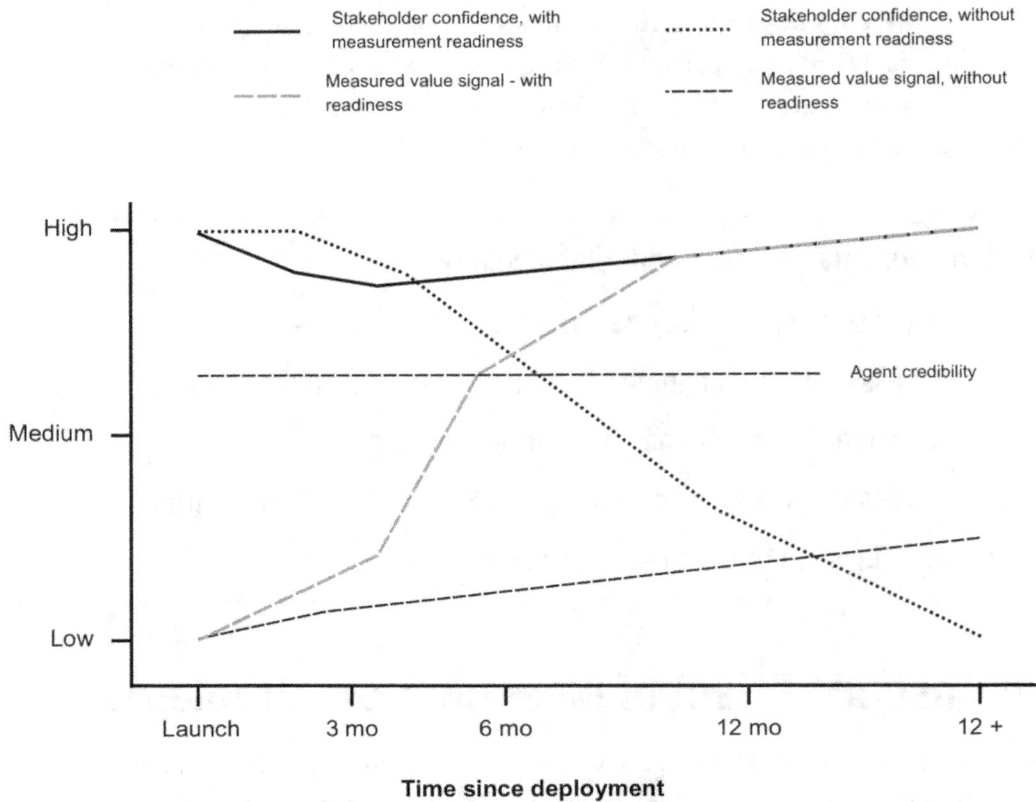

Figure 5-2. *Measurement readiness determines whether confidence grows or erodes*

Months 1–3: Stakeholders focus on adoption metrics and user feedback, both generally positive for well-designed agents.

Months 4–6: Business impact questions emerge. Stakeholders begin asking for ROI calculations and business metric improvements.

Months 7-12: Without clear business impact measurement, support wavers. Competing priorities emerge, and agent investment faces scrutiny.

Beyond 12 months: Agents that can't demonstrate measurable business value struggle to maintain organizational support, regardless of user satisfaction or technical performance.

When credible value signals emerge before scrutiny peaks, agents sustain support. When they don't, confidence declines, even when the agent is working.

The Path Forward

The measurement gap problem is real, but not insurmountable. Organizations that succeed at agent measurement build **practical systems** that provide sufficient evidence to maintain stakeholder confidence and support improvement decisions.

The solution isn't eliminating measurement challenges but designing around them. This requires accepting that attribution will often be partial, that proxies sometimes substitute for direct measurement, and that measurement infrastructure needs to evolve alongside agent capabilities.

Most importantly, it requires recognizing that measurement readiness; having practical systems to track progress toward validated outcomes is as critical to agent success as technical performance or user adoption.

The following sections provide frameworks and practical approaches for building measurement systems that bridge the gap between success definition and value proof, enabling organizations to demonstrate agent impact with confidence while avoiding the complexity traps that derail measurement efforts.

Key Components of Measurement Readiness

The measurement gap problem reveals why good intentions and clear success definitions aren't enough. Bridging the gap requires systematic infrastructure assessment that maps the practical realities of measurement before your agent launches. This isn't about building perfect analytics systems; in fact, it's about **establishing the minimum viable measurement infrastructure** that can capture the signals proving your agent delivers promised value.

Measurement readiness consists of three interconnected components that transform your validated success outcomes into trackable, reportable metrics. Each component addresses a specific aspect of the measurement challenge while building toward a comprehensive measurement capability.

Measurement Infrastructure Assessment

Your stakeholder outcome table defines what you need to measure. Infrastructure assessment determines whether you can actually measure it. This assessment reveals the practical constraints, opportunities, and investments required to track your agent's impact reliably.

The infrastructure assessment works systematically through three layers:

- Data source mapping (where measurement data lives)

- Baseline establishment (creating reliable starting points)

- The technical implementation (building measurement capabilities)

Each layer builds on the previous one, creating a foundation that supports evidence-based value communication.

Reality check: Are your metrics measurable?

- Can you name the exact fields needed to calculate each metric?

- Have you personally checked sample records in the source system?

- Do you have permission to extract the data on a recurring basis?

- Would you trust the data enough to show it to a CFO?

Data Source Mapping

Data source mapping identifies where each success metric currently lives, how accessible it is, and what integration work is required to make it useful for agent measurement. This is critical to avoid the common failure of assuming where data exists only to discover significant barriers after deployment.

Work through these questions for each metric in your stakeholder outcome table. Do the work yourself, don't delegate this or accept assurances that "the data exists."

Question 1: What Specific Data Points Do I Need?

Take your metric and list over piece of data required to calculate it, like in this example:
"Reduce onboarding time from 5 days to 2 days"
You need:

- When the employee started

- When each onboarding task was assigned

- When each task was completed

- What counts as being "complete"

Write it down. If you can't list the specific data points, your metric isn't clear enough yet.

Question 2: Does This Data Actually Exist, and Where?

For each data point, open the system and pull 10 or so recent records.
Check if

- The fields exist

- They have values (e.g., they are not blank)

- The value makes sense

- The value is standardized (think date, we always get derailed by differing date formats!)

Three outcomes:

- **Found it:** Data exists and looks right > document the system, field name, and data type/format.

- **Found something else:** Data exists but doesn't match what you need > write down what is different.

- **Nothing there:** Data doesn't exist > stop looking and note this.

Don't spend hours searching. If you can't find it in 15–30 minutes, it probably doesn't exist in usable form.

Question 3: Can I Access This Data?

For each system with data, you need to check if you have access. Try to extract a sample. If it works, you're done with this system.

If you don't have access, find the system owner (IT admin, DBA, data steward), ask them what you need to do to access this data, and how long it will take.

Flag anything requiring

- Privacy review

- Security assessment

- Executive approval

- Cross-department coordination

Why? These take weeks, not days. Start the process now!

Question 4: Is the Data Reliable Enough?

Pull 20–30 records. Look for problems:

Missing data: Count how many records have blank fields – over 20% missing? That's a problem.

Wrong data: Pick five records and verify them against reality (ask someone who knows). If more than one is wrong, investigate why.

Changed definitions: Ask the data owner if the field has meant the same thing for the past six months. If no, your baseline period may be comparing apples to oranges.

Rate each source:

- Good enough to use

- Usable with known limitations

- Not reliable enough

If it's not reliable enough, you need either better data, or a different metric.

Question 5: How Hard Is It to Get This Data Regularly?

You need to measure this data every day/week/month after the agent launches. Ask yourself:

Can I automate it? If there's an API and you know how to use it (or can learn, or have a developer that can help), rate this "easy."

Does someone need to export it? If it requires a person to remember to download data and send it to you, rate this "Manual" and identify who the person or team is.

Does it need building? If you'd need to create new connections, write code, or combine multiple systems, rate this "Complex."

For anything marked "Manual," ask yourself if that person will actually do this every day/week/month for the next year. If you're not confident, find a different approach. Document what you found, using the data source mapping template.

Download the data source mapping template:

https://github.com/Apress/Value-By-Design-with-Microsoft-Copilot-Studio

---

Measurement readiness

Data source mapping

Assessor: S Jeffery Date: 07/06/2025

Opportunity: HR onboarding agent

Success metric	Primary data source	Data owner	Quality assessment	Integration complexity	Measurement readiness score
Onboarding completion time	HRIS workflows	HR analytics	Moderate - captures system events, not the actual work	High - requires custom reporting, cross-system correlation	6/10
New hire satisfaction	Quarterly engagement survey	HR operations	High - established methodology	Low - existing survey infrastructure	8/10
HR admin time savings	Currently unmeasured	No owner	Poor - no baseline exists	High - requires new measurement system	3/10

Figure 5-3. *Data source mapping worksheet*

Complete this for every metric. When you're done, you'll have one of three situations for each:

- **Ready**: Data exists, you can access it, quality is acceptable, extraction is doable – proceed with baseline.

- **Needs setup**: Data exists, but you need to configure access or build extraction – start that work now, expect 1–3 weeks (maybe longer, depending on setup requirements).

- **Blocked**: Data doesn't exist, can't get access, or quality is unusable – change the metric, you can't measure it.

What This Investigation Tells You

Count your metrics:

- How many are ready?

- How many need setup?

- How many are blocked?

If more than half are blocked, you have a measurement problem that needs solving before worrying about baselines. Go and talk with stakeholders about either changing metrics or investigating in measurement infrastructure.

If most are ready, you can proceed. The "needs setup" items become parallel workstreams while you establish baselines for ready metrics.

You might find this investigation reveals that your most important metric has no data. That's painful to discover, but better now than after agent deployment when stakeholders are expecting to see "did it work?" and you have no answer.

Take the time to do this properly. Two or three days of investigation saves months of scrambling to prove value with data that doesn't exist.

Baseline Establishment

The baseline you establish today becomes the evidence you'll use to prove value tomorrow.

Invest the time to get it right.

Reliable measurement requires understanding current performance before your agent launches.

Baseline establishment creates the reference points that prove improvement and enable attribution. This does, however, present several challenges that teams must address systematically.

Typically baseline establishment follows one of two paths, each with distinct implications for your agent development timeline:

> **Scenario 1:** Historical data exists (measure before building).
> When reliable historical data exists in accessible systems, baseline measurement becomes a pre-development activity. This is the ideal scenario, you can analyze patterns, establish benchmarks, and validate measurement approaches before investigating in agent development.

Scenario 2: No baseline exists (build measurement first). When historical data is absent, unreliable, or inaccessible, you face a critical decision: delay agent development to establish baselines or proceed with parallel measurement infrastructure development. Parallel measurement rarely works. Without baselines, you cannot prove your agent caused observable improvements. Any number of factors – seasonal variations, process changes, staff experience, etc. could explain the changes you see.

Making the Baseline Measurement Investment Decision

When baseline establishment requires delaying agent development, stakeholders need clear criteria for deciding whether to proceed.

Proceed with baseline measurement when

- Strategic value is high (high being subjective is hard to suggest, but, for example, $500K annually), and value attribution is required.

- Regulatory or compliance reporting requires evidence.

- Multiple initiatives could claim credit for improvement.

- Agent success determines future AI investment decisions.

Consider parallel development (accepting measurement risks) when

- Operational value is obvious and immediate.

- Organization accepts qualitative evidence initially.

- No competing initiatives could claim attribution.

- Speed to market outweighs measurement precision.

Never skip baseline establishment when

- Board-level reporting requires ROI calculations.

- Investment exceeds $100K in development costs.

- Success metrics appear in executive KPIs.

- Failure would damage AI adoption credibility.

The Baseline Challenge Matrix

Not all outcomes are equally easy to baseline. Different types of value introduce different measurement challenges, and each requires a deliberate approach before an agent is deployed.

Metric type	Baseline challenge	Establishment approach
Efficiency (time, effort, throughput)	Historical data may not reflect current conditions	Capture 4-8 weeks of pre-agent performance under current conditions
Effectiveness (accuracy, consistency, compliance)	Existing measurement may be informal or inconsistent	Implement formal measurement 4-6 weeks before agent launch
Experience (satisfaction, ease of use)	Previous surveys may not include relevant questions	Conduct baseline survey with agent-specific questions
Business impact (cost, revenue, strategic KPIs)	Multiple factors influence these metrics beyond agent scope	Establish correlation methodology between agent metrics and business outcomes

Figure 5-4. *Baseline establishment challenges across value metrics*

Scenario One: Data Exists, Baseline Establishment Process

Phase 1: Historical Analysis

Historical analysis establishes whether existing data can serve as your baseline, and if so, what that baseline actually tells you about current performance. The aim of baseline measurement is establishing a defensible reference point that the agent stakeholders accept as representing "before agent" reality.

Conducting historical analysis

Step 1: Define the baseline period

Identifying which historical time frame provides the most representative baseline data requires systematic investigation, not gut feel or convenience. The wrong period can invalidate your entire measurement approach – making improvements look smaller than they are or creating false positives that don't reflect agent impact.

Decision criteria:

- **Recency**: More recent data better reflects current conditions.

- **Stability**: Period should have consistent processes, systems, and staffing.

- **Completeness**: Data musts be available and reliable for the entire period.

- **Comparability**: Conditions must be similar enough to post-agent state.

Establishing a baseline is not a mechanical step; it's an analytical decision that directly shapes how agent impact will be interpreted (shown in Figure 5-5). The time frame you choose determines what patterns are visible, what noise is amplified, and whether improvements appear meaningful or misleading.

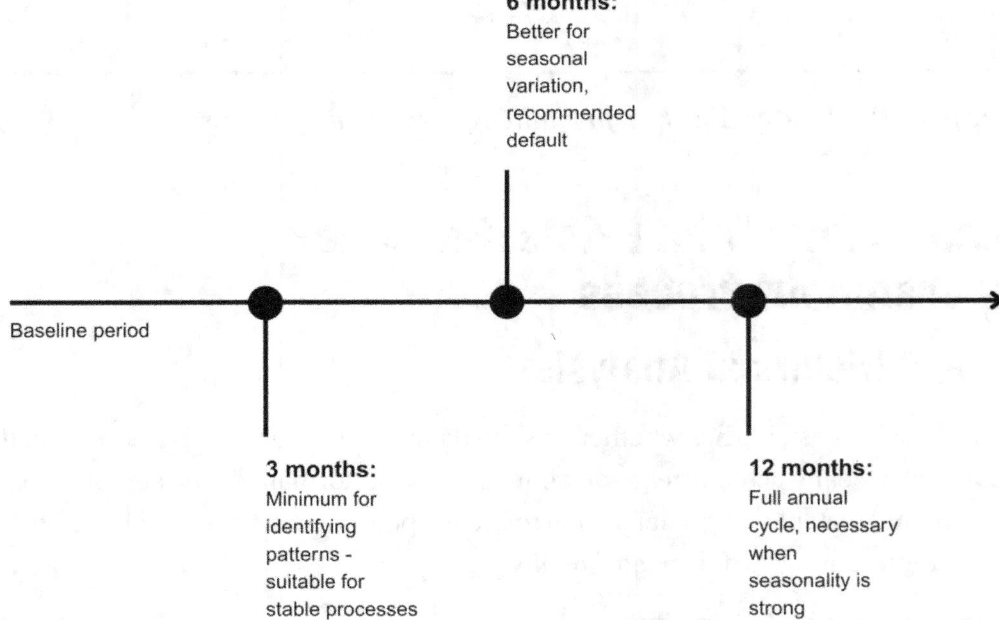

Figure 5-5. Baseline period selection for agent measurement

Shorter baselines favor speed but risk distortion; longer baselines improve confidence but delay insight. The right choice depends on process stability and decision stakes.

Phase a: Assemble the investigation team

Baseline period selection isn't a solo decision. You need input from people who understand process history, data systems, and organizational context.

Required perspectives:

- **Process owners**: Know when procedures changed, when problems occurred, when things were "normal."

- **Data stewards**: Understand data quality issues, system migrations, reporting changes.

- **Business stakeholders**: Remember organizational events that affected operations.

- **IT/Systems team**: Know when systems were upgraded, integrated, or replaced.

Phase b: Map the organizational timeline

Before looking at data, create a timeline of events that could affect baseline validity.

Timeline mapping considerations

System changes:

- Were major systems implemented, upgraded, or replaced?

- Did data collection methods change?

- Did integrations between systems start/stop?

Process changes:

- Did procedures significantly change?

- Were new policies introduced?

- Did staffing models change?

Organizational changes:

- Were there restructures, mergers, or acquisitions?

- Did leadership changes occur?

- Did strategic priorities shift?

External factors:

- Did market conditions change dramatically?

- Did regulatory changes take effect?

- Did unusual events occur (pandemic, economic shifts)?

The organizational context that determines whether a period is suitable: process changes, staffing shifts, system migrations, external events – live in the minds of people across different functions (your investigation team).

The baseline period assessment workshop brings these perspectives together systematically. By gathering an investigation team (process owners, data stewards, business stakeholders, and IT representatives) for a focused 90-minute session, you create a timeline that reveals which periods provide reliable baselines and which are compromised by confounding factors.

Workshop approach for timeline mapping

Schedule a 90-minute session with your investigation team with the objective of building the timeline collaboratively.

Structure:

First 20 minutes – system changes review

Data stewards present known system changes chronologically. The IT team adds integration changes and data structure modifications. Document each change with the data and impact on data comparability.

Focus question: "When did we change how we collect or store this data?"

Next 20 minutes – process changes review

Process owners describe when procedures changed. Look for policy updates, workflow modifications, or staffing model changes. Note whether changes were sudden or gradual.

Focus question: "When did we change how we do the work this agent will affect?"

Next 20 minutes – organizational context review

Business stakeholders provide strategic context. Identify restructures, leadership transitions, and priority shifts. Note external events that influenced operations.

Focus question: "When did something happen that changed how our business operates?"

Final 30 minutes – timeline synthesis

Consolidate all events into a single timeline view. Mark periods with stable conditions in green. Flag unsuitable periods in read. Mark periods requiring careful consideration in yellow.

The output is a visual timeline showing 12–18 months of history.

HR Onboarding example (Figure 5-6)

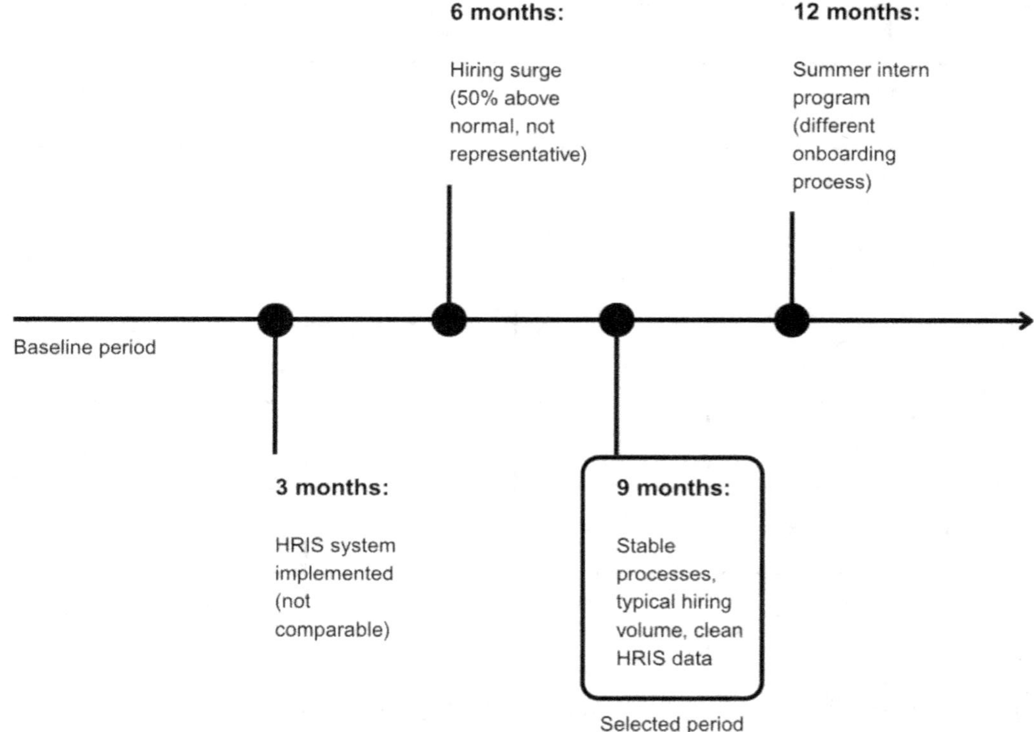

Figure 5-6. *Example of baseline period selection using historical context*

The HR team reviews potential baseline periods.

Is this level of investigation needed?

Many teams might skip this investigation and simply grab "the last 6 months of data" without questioning whether it's appropriate. This creates three problems:

1. The baseline gets challenged later.

2. You miss confounding factors.

3. You waste time on unusable data.

Baseline length is not a fixed rule; it depends on volume, variability, and how stable the underlying process is.

The table below in Figure 5-7 provides practical guidance for selecting an appropriate baseline period on common operating scenarios, balancing statistical confidence with relevance to current conditions.

Scenario	Minimum period	Recommended period	Rationale
High volume, stable processes (100+ observations/month)	1 month	2-3 months	Large sample size enables statistical confidence quickly
Medium-volume process (20-50 observations/month)	2-3 months	3-6 months	Needs sufficient sample for confidence intervals
Low-volume process (<20 observations/month)	3-6 months	6-12 months	Must capture full seasonal cycle
High seasonal variation	12 months	12 months	Must capture full seasonal cycle
Moderate seasonal variation	3-6 months	6 months	Enough periods may not be comparable to future
Rapidly changing environment	1-2 months	2-3 months	Longer periods may not be comparable to future
Stable, mature processes	3-6 months	6 months	Standard baseline for most scenarios

Figure 5-7. *Baseline period selection guidance by operating scenario*

Selecting a baseline is ultimately a trade-off decision rather than a purely technical one (Figure 5-8).

Longer periods provide

- ✓ Larger sample sizes
- ✓ Better statistical confidence
- ✓ Capture seasonal variations
- ✗ Risk of including process changes
- ✗ Less recent/relevant data
- ✗ More time to establish baseline

Longer periods provide

- ✓ More recent/relevant data
- ✓ Less risk of process changes
- ✓ Faster to establish baseline
- ✗ Smaller sample size
- ✗ Wider confidence intervals
- ✗ May miss seasonal patterns

Figure 5-8. Trade-offs in baseline period length selection

Phase 2: Validate Data Quality

Data existing in a system is not the same as data being reliable. Fields might be populated but contain errors. Definitions might have shifted subtly without documentation. Data entry practices might vary across teams or locations. These quality issues can invalidate your entire baseline if discovered after you've built measurement frameworks around flawed data.

The data quality validation process

Pull a representative sample from your selected baseline period. For the HR example, 75 onboarding events were pulled. A sample of 15 to 20 records (around 25%) provides sufficient coverage for quality assessment. Don't cherry pick the sample, use random selection or systematic sampling (e.g., every fourth record) to ensure representativeness.

For each sampled record, validate completeness, accuracy, and consistency. If data quality assessment reveals problems, you have three options.

- When issues are minor (like a low [<15%] missing data), proceed with documented limitations.

- When issues are moderate, you might expand your baseline period to include more data points that compensate for quality gaps.

- When issues are severe, you cannot use this period of data as a reliable baseline.

You should return to your timeline from the workshop and identify an alternative period or acknowledge that scenario 2 (no baseline exists) better describes your situation.

Phase 3: Calculate and Document Baseline Metrics

With data quality validated, calculate the baseline metrics that will serve as your comparison points after agent deployment. These calculations should directly connect to the success outcomes you defined in Chapter 4.

Return to your stakeholder outcome table. Each outcome specifies a measurement method. Your baseline calculations must use those exact measurement methods so post-deployment comparisons are valid.

The calculation process

For each metric, calculate three statistical measures: mean (average), median (middle), and standard deviation (variability). The mean gives you the typical performance. The median protects against outliers skewing results. Standard deviation tells you how consistent current performance is, high variability suggests unpredictable processes where improvement is hard to prove. Let's look at an example.

The sample:

The HR team selected a 25% sample from their baseline period, 20 cases randomly selected from their 75 total onboarding events. Here are the actual onboarding completion times in days for those 20 cases.

CaseId	TimeToComplete	CaseId	TimeToComplete
1	4.5	2	3.8
3	6.1	4	5.5
5	4.0	6	8.3
7	3.2	8	5.2
9	4.7	10	3.9
11	5.0	12	4.8
13	4.2	14	3.5
15	5.8	16	4.8
17	6.5	18	4.1
19	11.5	20	5.3

Figure 5-9. *Baseline sample illustrating variation in onboarding completion time*

Looking at the numbers, you can see they vary quite a bit. Some new hires completed training in under four days, while others took more than a week. One case took 11.5 days. Understanding this variation is important, it tells you whether your current process is consistent or unpredictable.

Calculating the mean (average):

Add all 20 together, and divide by 20:

```
Total: 4.5 + 3.8 + 6.1 + 5.5 + 4.0 + 8.3 + 3.2 + 5.2 + 4.7
+            3.9 + 5.0 + 7.2 + 4.2 + 3.5 + 5.8 + 4.8 + 6.5 + 4.1 +
11.5 + 5.3 =

101.2 days

Mean: 101.2 / 20 = 5.06 days
```

The mean tells you that on average, onboarding takes about five days. This becomes your primary comparison point. If post-deployment average drops to 2.5 days, you've achieved roughly 50% improvement.

Calculating the median (middle value):

The median represents the middle point of your data. Half of your cases finish faster than this number, half finish slower. To find it, first sort all your completion times from shortest to longest:

```
3.2, 3.5, 3.8, 3.9, 4.0, 4.1, 4.2, 4.5, 4.7, 4.8, 5.0, 5.2, 5.3, 5.5, 5.8,
6.1, 6.5, 7.2, 8.3, 11.5
```

Now you need to find the middle value. Since we have 20 records (an even number), there's no single middle value – instead, there are two middle values sitting right in the center.

Looking at our sorted list, count to the tenth and eleventh positions. The tenth value is 4.8 days; the eleventh value is 5.0 days. To find the median, take the average of the two middle numbers:

```
Median: (4.8 + 5.0) / 2 = 9.8 / 2 = 4.9 days
```

The median tells you the typical experience. Half of new hires completed onboarding in less than 4.9 days, half took longer.

Notice the median (4.9 days) is slightly lower than the mean (5.1 days). This tells you something important: a few unusually long onboardings (like that 11.5 days record) are pulling the average up, but they don't represent the typical experience. The median gives you a better sense of what "normal" looks like because it isn't affected by those extreme cases.

Understanding the range

The shortest onboarding took 3.2 days. The longest took 11.5 days. That's a range of 8.3 days, a huge variation for a process that should be fairly standardized. Looking at the sorted list, most cases cluster between 3.5 and 6.5 days. The 11.5 day outlier stands out dramatically. Investigate what happened.

What this tells you about your baseline:

Your baseline isn't a single number. Your baseline is a picture of current performance that includes typical cases and outliers. When documenting your baseline, you would write

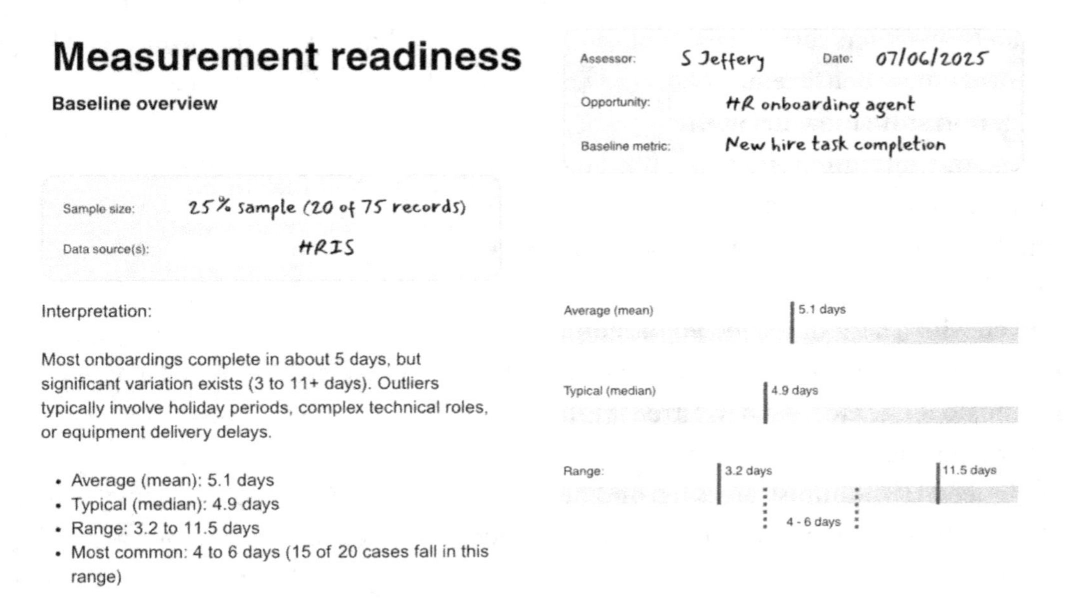

Figure 5-10. *Baseline performance profile for an HR onboarding process*

Practical guidance for your baseline:

When calculating your own baseline metrics, follow this simple process:

First, pull your sample. Take at least 25% of your baseline period data, ensuring random or systematic selection rather than cherry-picking cases that look normal.

Second, sort the data from the lowest to highest. This visual arrangement helps you spot patterns, identify outliers, and understand the range of current performance.

Third, calculate the middle value (median). Count halfway through your sorted list. That number represents typical performance better than the average when outliers exist.

Fourth, calculate the average (mean). Add everything up and divide by the number of cases. This gives you the single number most stakeholders will ask about.

Fifth, describe the range and variation in plain language. Don't just report "5.1 days average"; explain that most cases fall between 4 and 6 days, with occasional outliers extending to 11+ days due to identifiable causes.

Finally, investigate outliers before finalizing your baseline. That 11.5 day onboarding wasn't a data error, or a process failure. Why did it take so long?

Understanding why outliers exist helps you interpret post-deployment results accurately. If outliers disappear after agent deployment, that suggests the agent is making the process more consistent, which is valuable beyond just reducing average time.

Current state measurement

Baseline measurement tells you what performance looked like during a past period that represents normal operations. Current state measurement captures performance immediately before your agent deploys. Both are necessary for reliable baseline establishment.

Even with a carefully selected baseline, conditions change between when your baseline period ends and when your agent deploys. This gap creates a risk that the baseline no longer represents current reality.

Looking back to our HR example, staff turnover might affect performance. If experienced HR administrators left and new staff joined, onboarding times might have shifted. Process refinements might improve outcomes independently of the agent. The team might have made small adjustments to their onboarding checklist or streamlined certain approval steps. Seasonal factors might create variations. External events might create temporary disruptions: year-end freezes, holiday schedules, or budget cycle pressures could all influence onboarding performance.

Current state measurement validates that your historical baseline still reflects reality. It provides the most recent reference point for immediate comparison, giving you the confidence that changes observed after deployment represent agent impact rather than underlying trends. It also creates the measurement rhythm your team will continue post-deployment. Rather than scrambling to establish new tracking approaches after the agent launches, you've already practiced the measurement protocol during current state capture.

Begin current state measurement four to six weeks before planned agent deployment. This timing provides sufficient data collection duration without excessive delay that might introduce new confounding factors. For high-volume processes generating more than 100 events per week, four weeks capture adequate samples to validate baseline stability.

Current state measurement protocol

Use identical measurement methods you plan for post-agent tracking. This consistency enables direct comparison across baseline, current state, and post-deployment periods. If Copilot Studio analytics, or Azure Application Insights will measure resolution rates after deployment, establish a proxy measurement now that captures similar signals.

Track manual resolution of queries that the agent will eventually handle. Document time spent, outcomes achieved, and challenges encountered.

Document the measurement process and any challenges encountered. Note when data collection was difficult, when staff forgot to log information, when systems didn't capture what you expected. These practical challenges inform post-deployment measurement design. If manual time logging proved unreliable during current state measurement, don't depend on it post-deployment; instead, find automated alternatives or accept that metric won't be trackable.

Comparing current state to historical baseline

Once current state data is collected, compare it to your historical baseline metrics. Look for three patterns:

Consistency indicates your historical baseline remains valid. If current state performance matches historical patterns within expected statistical variation, proceed with confidence that your baseline represents current reality. Calculate whether differences fall within your documented standard deviation; if they do, the baseline remains valid.

Improvement suggests something changed between baseline period and current state. Investigate what drove the improvement so you don't mistakenly attribute it to your agent later. Process changes, system updates, staff training, or external factors could explain improved performance. Documenting these changes to post-deployment measurement can account for them, your agent cannot claim credit for improvements that preceded its existence.

Decline requires understanding whether deterioration represents temporary conditions or new normal. If temporary (staff on leave, system issues), wait for resolution before deploying. Starting from an artificially degraded baseline makes even most agent performance look impressive, creating false confidence. If decline represents new normal (process complexity increased, resource constraints), update your baseline to reflect current reality rather than using outdated historical data.

Phase 3: Baseline validation and stakeholder sign-off

You've now conducted historical analysis to select a baseline period, validated data quality from that period, calculated baseline metrics with appropriate statistical measures, and confirmed through current state measurement that the baseline still represents current reality. Before agent development proceeds to deployment, secure stakeholder validation and formal sign-off on the baseline methodology and metrics.

Sign-off creates shared accountability for measurement methodology. When stakeholders formally approve the baseline, they commit to accepting post-deployment comparisons based on it. This prevents retrospective challenges where stakeholders question measurement approaches after seeing results they find surprising or disappointing.

Sign-off ensures everyone understands limitations and assumptions built into the baseline. No baseline is perfect. Data quality issues exist, measurement methods have constraints, practical realities force trade-offs. Making these limitations explicitly and getting stakeholder agreement creates shared understanding of what baseline can and cannot tell you about agent impact. The final point to cover is that sign-off creates the documented approval trail needed for governance and audit requirements. If regulatory compliance requires demonstrating agent impact, or if investment decisions require ROI calculations, the signed baseline record provides evidence that measurement followed rigorous, approved process with stakeholder oversight.

Documenting sign-off

Create a formal sign-off record capturing stakeholder agreement on baseline validity and success criteria. Include

- Baseline summary (period, sample size, key metrics)

- Data quality assessment and documented limitations

- Current state validation results

- Stakeholder questions raised and resolutions

- Success threshold agreement (what improvement level constitutes success)

- Measurement approach post-deployment

- Timeline for results review

Secure documented approval from all key stakeholders. This documented agreement becomes your contract with stakeholders. When you report results after deployment, you measure against thresholds they approved, using methodology they validated, accounting for limitations they accepted. The sign-off protects your team from retrospective objections while holding everyone accountable to the measurement framework they agreed represented fair evaluation of agent impact

Scenario Two: When No Baseline Exists

Not every agent opportunity has the luxury of historical data. Sometimes data was never collected. Sometimes systems changed too fundamentally for historical records to be comparable. Sometimes the process itself is new, making historical baselines impossible.

When you discover during data source mapping that reliable baseline data doesn't exist, you face a critical decision: delay agent development to establish measurement infrastructure first or proceed with agent deployment accepting measurement limitations.

The Reality of Proceeding Without Baselines

Building and deploying an agent without established baselines creates a fundamental attribution problem. You cannot prove your agent caused observable improvement. Without knowing what performance looked like before the agent, and changes you observe after deployment could be explained by numerous factors: seasonal variations, learning curves as people adapt to any new system, concurrent process improvements, staff experience growth, organizational changes, or external market conditions.

Stakeholders may observe improvements and credit them to your agent based on intuition rather than evidence. This feels like success initially but creates fragility. Imagine when budget reviews require ROI justification, or when competing initiatives claim credit for the same improvements, your lack of baseline data leaves you unable to defend the agent's contribution.

When to Proceed Without Baselines

Despite these risks, some situations justify proceeding with agent deployment before establishing comprehensive baselines.

- **Operational value is immediate and obvious:** When agent benefits are self-evident and undeniable, elaborate baseline measurement adds bureaucratic overhead without changing deployment decisions. An agent that answers questions instantly when the alternative is multi-day email chains creates obvious value regardless of precise time savings calculations.

- **Organizational culture accepts qualitative evidence initially**: Some organizations operate with lower measurement formality, making decisions based on directional evidence and stakeholder feedback rather than requiring quantitative proof for every initiative. If your organization culture accepts "this seems to be helping" as sufficient justification for modest investments, baseline establishment may be unnecessary overhead.

- **No competing initiatives could claim attribution**: When your agent operates in isolation without other concurrent improvements to the same process, attribution becomes less ambiguous. Changes observed after agent deployment are more likely to be agent-driven when nothing else changed simultaneously.

- **Speed to market outweighs measurement precision**: Strategic timing sometimes matters more that measurement rigor. Demonstrating AI capability to key stakeholders, responding to competitive pressure, or capturing limited-time opportunities may justify accepting measurement limitations to accelerate deployment.

This being said, there are times when you should **never skip baseline establishment**. Some situations demand baseline rigor, regardless of pressures.

- **Board-level reporting requires ROI calculations**: Executive leadership and board members expect quantitative justification for significant investments. Without baselines, you cannot provide credible ROI figures.

- **Investment exceeds significant threshold:** Define your organization's threshold for requiring baseline measurement. For many organizations, investment exceeding $100K in development or licensing costs warrants formal baseline establishment.

- **Success metrics appear in executive KPIs:** When your agent's intended outcomes connect to metrics executives are accountable for delivering, they need baseline evidence showing the agent contributed to improvements rather than claiming credit for achievements their existing teams drove.

- **Failure would damage AI adoption credibility:** If this agent serves as proof point for broader AI adoption, measurement rigor protects the larger program. A failed agent undermines confidence in future AI initiatives. Inability to prove a successful agent's value creates similar skepticism.

Alternative Measurement Strategies When Baselines Don't Exist

If you proceed with agent development despite lacking baseline data, implement these alternative approaches to capture what evidence you can

- **Comparative measurement:** If multiple locations, teams, or processes exist where the agent could deploy, stage rollout to create comparison groups. Deploy to location A while location B continues current process. Measure both locations simultaneously. Performance differences between locations provide evidence of agent impact, even without historical baselines. This approach introduces complexity – locations must be sufficiently similar for comparison validity, and staged rollout extends overall deployment timeline.

- **Capability-based measurement:** Instead of measuring business outcomes the agent influences, measure the agent's direct capabilities. Track queries handled, tasks completed, recommendations provided. Document time saved per interaction based on estimated manual effort. These metrics don't prove business impact but demonstrate agent activity and usage. They provide defensible evidence of value when baseline business metrics don't exist.

- **Qualitative evidence collection:** Gather structured stakeholder feedback, user testimonials, and case studies documenting specific instances where the agent delivered value. While not statistically rigorous, qualitative evidence can be compelling when well-documented. Create templates for collecting evidence systematically rather than relying on ad hoc examples.

- **Rapid baseline establishment post-deployment:** Deploy the agent to a subset of users while maintaining current process for others. Measure both approaches simultaneously for four to eight weeks. This creates a quasi-baseline using concurrent measurement rather than historical comparison.

Communicating Measurement Limitations

If you proceed without baseline establishment, be explicit about measurement limitations in all stakeholder communications. Include standard language in status reports and presentations. This level of transparency protects both your credibility and that of the agent. Stakeholders who understand measurement limitations from the start won't feel misled when ROI calculations prove impossible later. They made informed decisions about acceptable evidence levels rather than discovering constraints retrospectively.

From Measurement Readiness to Value Delivery

You've now completed the foundational work that separates agents that prove their value from those that struggle to justify continued investment. The measurement infrastructure you've established, whether through comprehensive historical baselines, current state validation, or carefully chosen alternative approaches, provides the evidence framework that will demonstrate whether your agent delivers on its promise.

The journey through measurement readiness has taken you from identifying what needs to be measured, through assessing whether measurement is feasible, to establishing the baselines that will prove impact. You've documented your measurement approach, secured stakeholder agreement on success thresholds, and created the infrastructure to track progress from day one of deployment.

What You've Accomplished

You've assessed your measurement infrastructure systematically, identifying where data exists, evaluating its quality and accessibility, and documenting what can and cannot be measured with current systems. You've established reliable baselines using historical analysis, current state validation, and stakeholder sign-off, or you've made explicit, documented decisions about proceeding with alternative measurement approaches when baselines weren't feasible.

You've created measurement protocols that will continue beyond deployment, ensuring consistent tracking that enables fair comparison between baseline performance and agent-enabled outcomes. You've secured stakeholder agreement on what constitutes success, preventing retrospective debates about whether results meet expectations.

Most importantly, you've built shared accountability. Stakeholders who approved your measurement methodology, accepted documented limitations, and agreed on success thresholds cannot later claim measurement was inadequate or that standards were unclear. They committed to the framework that will evaluate agent impact.

The Measurement Mindset

Measurement readiness is not only having the right data and systems in place. It is also about establishing a discipline that will guide how you think about value throughout the agent's life cycle. The baselines you've established become reference points for every design decision. The success thresholds you've defined become criteria for prioritizing capabilities and resolving trade-offs.

This measurement discipline prevents the drift that undermines many agent projects, the gradual shift from solving important problems to building interesting features, from delivering stakeholder value to exploring technical possibilities, from proving business impact to generating activity metrics.

With measurement foundations established, you're ready to move into solution design. The next stage of value by design focuses on translating your validated success outcomes and measurement framework into specific agent capabilities. You'll determine which agent type best fits your opportunity, design interaction patterns that serve your stakeholders' need, and architect solutions that can be measured against the baselines you've established.

The hard work of measurement readiness creates the foundation for confident design, credible reporting, and sustained stakeholder support. You've built that foundation. Now it's time to design the agent that will deliver on it.

Solution Shaping

You know what success looks like. You've defined it, measured it, and secured stakeholder agreement on it. The outcomes are clear. The baselines are established. The measurement infrastructure is ready.

Now comes the moment that separates theoretical value from real impact: translating what you want to achieve into what you're going to build.

This is where many agent projects stumble. Teams jump straight into Copilot Studio, building what's technically possible rather than what's strategically necessary. They create agents that work but don't deliver the value stakeholders expected.

The gap here is **design discipline**.

An agent can answer questions flawlessly yet fail to reduce support burden. It can complete workflows perfectly yet fail to reduce support burden. It can complete workflows perfectly yet fail to improve user satisfaction. It can integrate with every system yet fail to move the metrics that matter. Technical success without value delivery is just expensive automation.

But there's another gap that's equally important: **the gap between automation and augmentation**.

The most successful agents amplify what people do best. They handle the routine so humans can focus on the complex. They provide information so people can make better decisions. They coordinate logistics so teams can concentrate on outcomes. They remove tedium while preserving meaning.

This is important because agents don't deliver value in isolation. They deliver value through people.

If an HR agent answers routine questions, HR staff can spend more time on the challenging cases that require empathy and judgement. If your finance agent handles standard approvals, finance managers can focus on strategic planning and risk analysis. If your customer service agent resolves common issues, human agents can build relationships and solve novel problems.

Yes, roles evolve. Some tasks shift entirely to automation and should. Fully automated invoice processing, standard compliance checks, routine data transfers – these are processes where human involvement adds cost without adding value. However, even here, the design question matters: Are you automating to free people for higher-value work, or simply eliminating roles without considering what's lost? The distinction is both ethical and practical. Organizations that design automation with empathy for job impact create smoother transitions, stronger adoption, and better long-term outcomes than those that treat headcount reduction as the primary goal.

The Frontier Firm Evolution: From Copilot to Autonomous Function

We're witnessing a fundamental shift in how organizations deploy AI – a progression toward what many call "frontier firms."[1] This evolution happens in stages, each representing a different relationship between humans and agents.

Stage one: Copilot (AI assisting individuals)

Individual agents help people do their work better. An HR professional has a copilot that helps draft policies, answer questions, or analyze data. The human remains fully in control, with AI as a capable assistant that amplifies individual productivity.

Stage two: AI managers (employees managing teams of agents)

Individuals orchestrate multiple specialized agents working together. That same HR professional now manages a team of agents: one handles routine inquiries, another processes leave requests, another generates compliance reports. The human's role shifts from doing tasks to directing agent teams, focusing on strategy, exceptions, and judgement calls that agents can't handle.

Stage three: Autonomous functions (fully automated workflows)

---

[1] https://www.microsoft.com/en-us/worklab/work-trend-index/2025-the-year-the-frontier-firm-is-born

Entire business functions operate with minimal human intervention. Agent teams coordinate among themselves, handling end-to-end processes with human oversight at strategic decision points rather than operational ones. The HR function might have agents managing most transactional work, with humans focused on organizational design, culture, and complex employee relations.

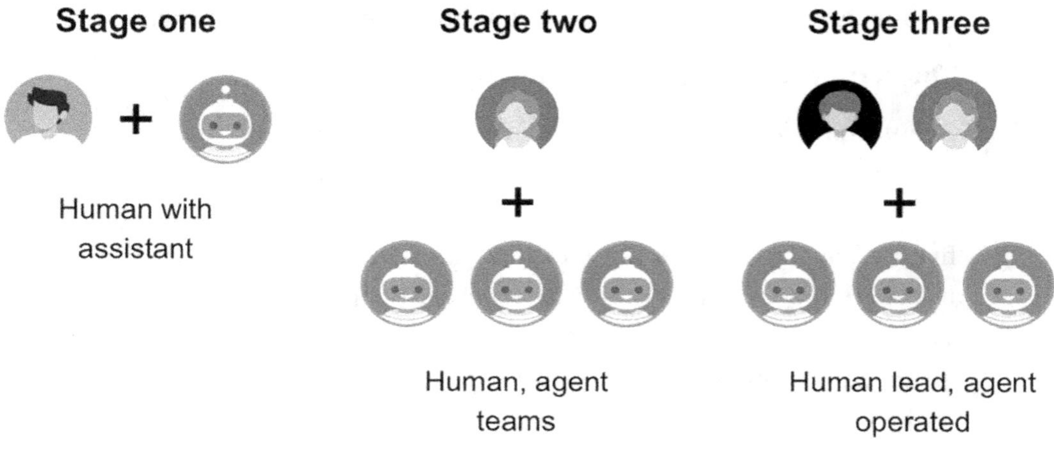

Many organizations I speak to are in stage one, building individual Copilots. Many are experimenting with stage two, letting people work with and manage small agent teams. Very few have reached stage three, and those that have focus on well-bounded, low-risk functions where full automation creates clear value without unacceptable consequences.

The design focus here is on which stage serves our current value outcome while building foundations for future evolution. Trying to jump directly to stage three autonomous functions usually fails, not because the technology can't handle it, but because organizations lack the trust, governance, and change readiness required. Starting at stage one and designing for evolution succeeds because it builds capability, confidence, and organizational learning progressively.

Three critical decisions shape every successful agent:

First: What kind of agent are you really building?

Not all agents serve the same purpose. A retriever that surfaces information requires fundamentally different capabilities than an orchestrator that coordinates workflows. Understanding the distinction helps you design agents that complement human work rather than compete with it.

Second: How should people interact with it?

The spectrum from open conversation to structured workflow isn't just a technical choice. It determines how much agency and judgement remain with the people using your agent. The right architecture balances efficiency with human context and control.

Third: How you design for humans, not just processes?

Agents that optimize for process efficiency without considering human experience can create friction, resistance, and diminished value. Human-centered design means building agents that fit naturally into how people work, that earn trust through transparency, and that respect the expertise people bring. This question evolves across stages of frontier firm but never disappears. In stage one, it means building agents that enhance individual capability. In stage two, it means designing for humans as orchestrators who direct agent teams. In stage three, it means ensuring autonomous functions remain aligned to human values and organizational purpose even when humans aren't in every loop. Human-centered design means building agents that fit naturally into how people work today while enabling trust through transparency, security, and maintaining meaningful human agency at every stage.

This stage gives you the frameworks, patterns, and principles to make these decisions well. You'll learn how to **select the right agent type** by mapping your value profile to capability requirements; how to choose **interaction architecture** that respects both efficiency and appropriate human involvement; and how to design for trust, adoption, and sustained usage across different frontier firm stages.

CHAPTER 6

Agent Type Selection

You've completed the foundational work that many teams skip. You know which stakeholders need value, what that value looks like in measurable terms, and how you'll prove the agent delivered it.

Your stakeholder outcome table defines success.

Your baselines establish the starting point.

Your measurement infrastructure is ready to track progress.

Now comes a critical question that shapes everything that follows: **what kind of agent are you actually building?**

This isn't a technical question about which Copilot Studio features to use. It's a strategic question about the role the agent will play in delivering your defined outcomes. The answer determines your development approach, governance requirements, risk profile, and ultimately, your ability to deliver the value stakeholders expect.

The Six Agent Types

Not all agents are created equal.

While they may share common capabilities: natural language processing, integration with business systems, and the ability to act, they serve fundamentally different roles in how work gets done. Understanding these differences is essential because each agent type has distinct development requirements, risk profiles, and value patterns.

The six agent types below represent the most common patterns I see in successful enterprise deployments. Each fills a specific niche in the spectrum, from simple information retrieval to autonomous process execution (Figure 6-1).

© Steve Jeffery 2026

S. Jeffery, *Value by Design with Microsoft Copilot Studio*, https://doi.org/10.1007/979-8-8688-2613-9_6

Retriever

Finds and delivers relevant information to support a person's task or decision.

HR agent that surfaces benefits information or company policies instantly from approved sources.

Collaborator

Works with people or systems to get things done.

In marketing, an agent that collects inputs from multiple stakeholders and compiles a unified campaign brief.

Orchestrator

Coordinates a series of steps across systems or teams.

In operations, and agent that manages onboarding activities across departments, updating multiple systems as tasks are completed.

Assistant

Helps a person complete a task or make a decision.

In IT support, an agent that guides users through submitting a helpdesk ticket with all required details.

Advisor

Gives insights, guidance, or recommendations.

In sales, an agent that suggests next-best actions based on customer data and deal history.

Performer

Takes direct action and completes tasks autonomously.

In finance, an agent that updates a record when predefined conditions are met, such as posting journal entries.

Figure 6-1. *A practical classification of agent types used in enterprise deployments*

Why Are Agent Types Relevant?

Agent type determines everything from development timeline to operational risk. Development effort varies dramatically across types – a retriever agent might take days to build with simple data lookup and formatting, while an orchestrator might require weeks or months of complex integration and error handling. Each agent presents **fundamentally different engineering challenges**.

Risk and governance profiles differ just as dramatically. When a retriever makes a mistake, users see incorrect information displayed: annoying, but most times recoverable. When a performer makes a mistake, it takes autonomous actions that might be difficult or expensive to undo. The risk difference should shape both your governance approach and your portfolio strategy.

Value metrics align naturally to agent types, which matter for measuring value and securing continued investment. Retrievers succeed through query deflection rates and response accuracy. Advisors prove their worth through recommendation uptake and measurable decision quality improvements. Orchestrators demonstrate value via process completion rates and error reduction.

Architecture patterns are also type-specific, affecting both development approach and long-term operational costs. Retrievers need robust search capabilities and content management systems. Orchestrators require workflow engines and sophisticated transaction handling. Advisors depend on analytics platforms and model management infrastructure. Understanding these architectural needs early prevents expensive redesigns later.

The Value of Agent Type Matching and Assessment

Agent type assessment reveals an important design principle: while any agent can deliver multiple types of value, different agent types have natural strengths that influence where value typically **emerges first**.

Retrievers and assistants excel at immediate operational improvements: faster information access, guided task completion, reduced manual effort. These benefits appear quickly and are easy to measure, making them ideal starting points for demonstrating agent value.

Advisors and orchestrators can deliver operational benefits but are particularly powerful for strategic value: improved decision-making, process standardization, compliance automate. Their ability to coordinate across systems or provide insights makes them natural fits for business-level objectives.

Collaborators and performers span both operational and strategic value, but have unique potential for transformational impact; enabling entirely new ways of working, reaching new audiences, or automating what was previously impossible.

This doesn't mean a retriever agent can't contribute to strategic goals or that a performer can't save time on daily tasks. Rather, it suggests that understanding your agent type's natural strengths helps you sequence value delivery effectively; starting with what the agent does best, then expanding as adoption grows and organizational readiness increases.

Agent Types and Organizational Maturity

The progression from retrievers to performers mirrors a broader organizational journey toward the concept of frontier firms: organizations where AI agents evolve from helpful assistants to trusted business partners to autonomous operators.

Agent types don't just differ in what they do; they differ in what an organization must be ready to support. As agents take on more coordinated and autonomous roles, the organizational capabilities required to deploy them safely and effectively increase accordingly.

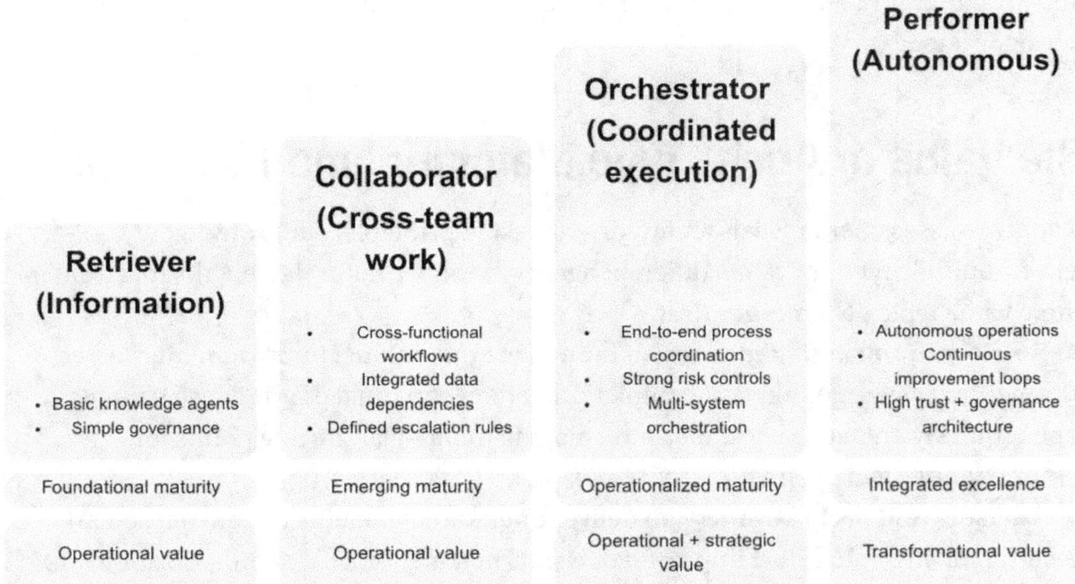

Figure 6-2. *Progression of agent types aligned to organizational maturity and value realization*

The frontier firm progression, as illustrated in Figure 6-2, is about building each capability layer deliberately. Organizations that jump straight into autonomous performers without establishing foundational infrastructure create risk exposure that undermines stakeholder confidence. Those that progress systematically through agent types build organizational muscle memory alongside technical capability.

This progression explains why your agent type choice matters beyond immediate use case requirements. Selecting a retriever when your organization has only basic governance isn't conservative; it's strategic. It lets you deliver value while building the infrastructure needed for more autonomous agents later

Agent Types and Governance Requirements

Each agent type carries distinct governance and oversight requirements, based on its autonomy level and potential impact. This is a powerful benefit of agent types – being able to plan governance, responsible AI, and risk mitigation before building your agent helps mitigate risks and ensure the agent has the correct level of governance oversight.

Retrievers and assistants need basic governance focusing on content safety and user feedback. Collaborators and advisors require standard governance with performance monitoring and approval workflows. Orchestrators and performers demand comprehensive governance, including model cards, isolated environments, and full audit capabilities.

When designing your governance strategy, start with a proportionate approach appropriate for your agent type, then enhance controls as complexity and organizational impact increase. This graduated approach ensures appropriate oversight without over-engineering simpler use cases or under-protecting high-risk autonomous agents.

Retriever	**Collaborator**	**Orchestrator**
Basic governance	Standard governance	Comprehensive governance
Usage analytics, user feedback mechanisms. Focus on data safety and response accuracy with minimal oversight.	*Environment separation, approval workflows, and performance monitoring. Requires business owner approval and audit trails.*	*Multi-environment deployment, sophisticated ALM pipelines, and process monitoring. Full change control and compliance reporting required.*
Assistant	**Advisor**	**Performer**
Basic governance	Standard governance	Comprehensive governance
Session logging, error handling; emphasis on guided interaction safety with standard Power Platform controls.	*Model performance tracking, decision audit trails, and human oversight workflows. Enhanced monitoring for recommendation quality and uptake rates.*	*Production isolation, comprehensive logging. Complete model cards, risk assessments and executive approval needed.*

Figure 6-3. *Governance requirements increase with agent autonomy*

Agent Type and Governance Implications

Real-world agents often serve multiple functions; a customer service agent might retrieve policy information for frontline staff, while also routing complex cases to specialists. This creates a governance, risk, and responsible AI challenge: which agent type's requirements apply?

In these cases, the most restrictive applicable governance model provides the answer. When an agent encompasses multiple types, apply the highest governance standards across all functions. If your agent serves as both a retriever (basic governance) and a collaborator (standard governance), govern it as a collaborator throughout.

This is an important point for value delivery.

- It prevents security gaps that could undermine stakeholder trust

- Simplifies compliance and audit requirements

- Ensures consistent user experience across all agent functions

- Reduces implementation complexity by avoiding multiple governance frameworks

This approach may seem conservative, but it protects your value objectives. An agent that fails governance requirements delivers no value regardless of its technical capabilities. The most restrictive model ensures your agent can deliver sustained value while meeting organizational risk standards.

Identifying the Right Agent Type for Your Opportunity

With this understanding of how agent types align with value patterns, you can systematically assess which pattern best fits each of your feasible opportunities. This assessment prevents misalignment between what you're building and how you're building it. For each feasible opportunity, work through these questions:

Primary function: What's the agent's main/primary job?

- Information finding: "Retriever"

- Task guidance: "Assistant"

- Process coordination: "Collaborator"

- Decision support: "Advisor"

- Workflow management: "Orchestrator"

- Autonomous execution: "Performer"

Autonomy level: How much oversight is needed?

- **High oversight**: Orchestrator, Performer

- **Medium oversight**: Collaborator, Advisor

- **Low oversight**: Assistant, Retriever

User-interaction pattern: How do people engage with this agent?

- **On-demand queries**: Retriever, Assistant

- **Structured workflows**: Assistant, Collaborator

- **Background processing**: Orchestrator, Performer

- **Advisory conversations**: Advisor

Decision authority: What level of decisions can this agent make?

- **Information display only**: Retriever

- **Process guidance**: Assistant

- **Routing and coordination**: Collaborator, Orchestrator

- **Recommendations with human approval**: Advisor

- **Autonomous actions within defined parameters**: Performer

These assessment questions are most useful when considered together rather than in isolation. The table below brings them into a single view, allowing you to compare agent types across function, autonomy, interaction pattern, and decision authority.

Use this as a practical decision aid: work row by row for a given opportunity, note where your answers cluster, and select the agent type that best matches the dominant pattern.

When answers span multiple columns, treat this as an early signal that your opportunity may require either scope refinement or more advanced governance.

Assessment dimension	Retriever	Assistant	Collaborator	Advisor	Orchestrator	Performer
Primary function	Information finding	Task guidance	Process coordination	Decision support	Workflow management	Autonomous execution
Autonomy level	Low	Low	Medium	Medium	High	High
User interaction pattern	On-demand queries	On-demand/ workflows	Structured workflows	Advisory dialog	Background processing	Background processing
Decision authority	Info only	Process guidance	Routing/ coordination	Recs with human approval	End-to-end workflow decisions	Autonomous actions within rules

Figure 6-4. *Assessing agent types by function, autonomy, and decision authority*

By working through these assessment questions, you've moved from a general opportunity to a specific agent type with clear functional requirements, risk profile, and architectural needs. This precision transforms how you approach the next stage of development.

The agent type assessment completes your opportunity foundation. You now have a strategically aligned opportunity that's technically feasible, organizationally ready, and matched to the right functional pattern.

Quick recap: Agent types and governance

- Six agent types serve different functions: retriever, assistant, collaborator, advisor, orchestrator, and performer.

- Agent type determines development effort, risk profile, and success metrics.

- For multi-functional agents, apply the most restrictive governance requirements across all functions.

From Outcomes to Agent Type: Practical Mapping

Let's make this concrete with the HR onboarding agent we've followed throughout the book. Your stakeholder outcome table contains these key outcomes:

- **New hires:** Reduce average time to find onboarding information from 45 minutes to 5 minutes.

- **HR administrators:** Decrease routine inquiry volume by 60% within three months.

- **HR director:** Achieve 100% compliance with mandatory training completion within first week.

- **IT security:** Maintain zero security protocol violations during onboarding.

Value Benefits Analysis

Looking at these outcomes through the value benefit lens:

- **Efficiency**: "45 minutes to 5 minutes" is pure efficiency gain – time saved through faster information access.

- **Effectiveness**: "100% compliance" requires consistent, reliable completion of required steps.

- **Experience**: Reducing routine inquiries suggests improving the HR administrator experience.

- **Empowerment**: New hires getting information when needed empowers self-service.

The dominant value pattern is efficiency and effectiveness with strong experience components. This profile suggests agent types that excel at information delivery and task guidance.

Autonomy and Risk Assessment

Review your stakeholder interviews:

- **IT security stakeholder scored high on risk concerns**: Any onboarding process touching system access requires careful oversight.

- New hire stakeholders valued getting answers quickly but also mentioned wanting to "understand why" for complex policy questions.

- HR director emphasized the need to track and verify compliance, not just assume it happened.

This risk profile suggests **moderate autonomy with human oversight at key decision points**, not full autonomous execution.

Interaction Pattern Requirements

Your stakeholders described their ideal interaction:

- **New hires**: "Ask a question and get an answer immediately, like asking a colleague."

- **HR administrators**: "Route standard questions automatically so I can focus on complex cases."

- **IT security**: "Ensure proper verification before any access provisioning."

These interaction preferences indicate a mix of **conversational inquiry (retriever)** for information needs and **structured guidance (assistant)** for process completion.

The agent type decision:

Bringing these strands together reveals why agent type selection is rarely a single, binary choice.

In the HR onboarding scenario, stakeholder outcomes, value benefits, risk constraints, and interaction preferences all point to a hybrid design. New hires need fast, conversational answers to common questions, while the organization also needs a guided, verifiable process that ensures mandatory steps are completed correctly and securely.

The illustration below shows how these inputs translate into a clear agent pattern: a primary assistant agent that guides onboarding tasks end-to-end, supported by retriever capabilities that surface policy and FAQ information on demand. This mapping, as shown in Figure 6-5, makes explicit how stakeholder needs drive both the dominant agent type and its supporting behaviors.

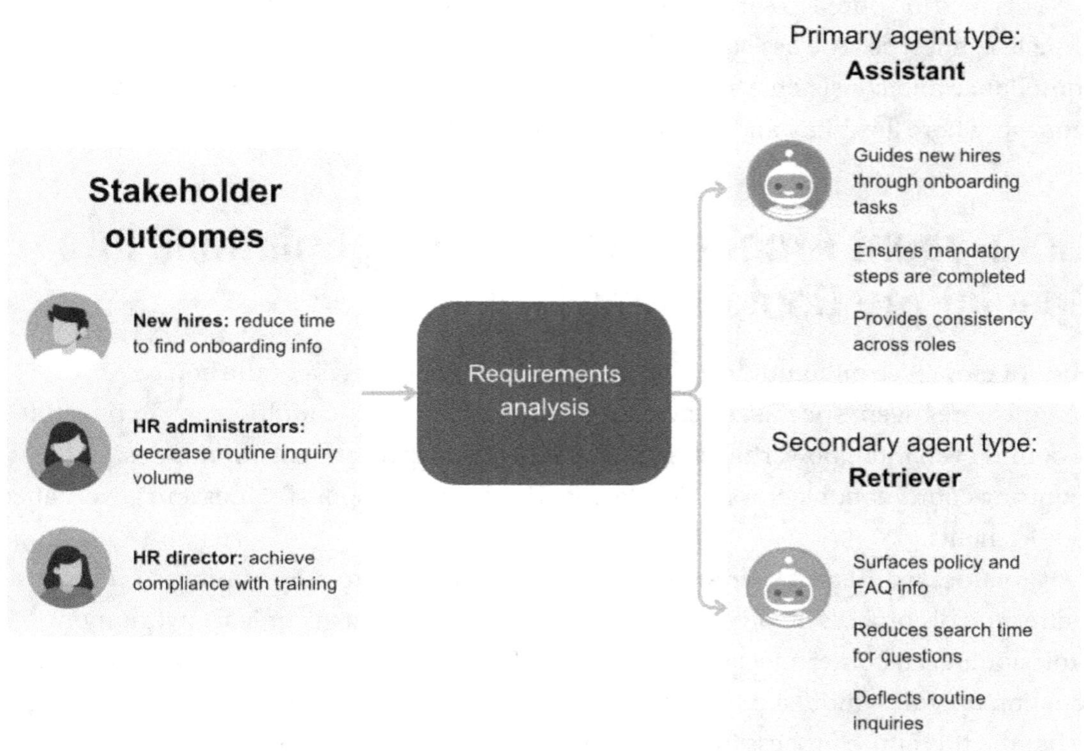

Figure 6-5. *Mapping stakeholder interaction needs to a hybrid agent design*

Primary type: Assistant

- Guides new hires through onboarding tasks with structured workflows

- Ensures mandatory steps are completed in the correct sequence

- Provides consistency while allowing flexibility for different roles and locations

Secondary type: Retriever

- Surfaces policy information, FAQs, and resources on-demand

- Reduces search time for specific questions

- Deflects routine inquiries from HR administrators

This hybrid approach serves your outcomes better than forcing everything into a single agent type. The assistant handles structured onboarding workflows where compliance and consistency matter. The retriever handles unstructured information requests where flexibility and quick access create value.

Multi-agent Architecture: Breaking Solutions into Specialized Components

The HR employee onboarding example we've followed throughout the book demonstrates agent specialization within a single department. Multi-agent architecture becomes even more powerful when processes span organizational boundaries, requiring coordination across departments with distinct responsibilities and governance requirements.

Consider a different scenario: Onboarding a new enterprise customer to your platform. This process involves legal compliance verification, technical environment provisioning, customer success planning, and financial system integration. Each function operates under a different ownership, timelines, and risk profiles. Attempting to handle this entire process in a single monolithic agent creates the coordination and governance challenges we've discussed. Instead, decomposing the solution into function-aligned specialized agents creates a more resilient, maintainable, and governable system.

The Modularity Principle

Rather than building one comprehensive "enterprise customer onboarding agent," we consider breaking the solution into specialized agents that align with departmental functions and natural process boundaries.

Compliance verification agent (advisor)

- **Purpose**: Reviews customer-submitted documentation against internal compliance requirements and regulatory obligations

- **Knowledge sources**: Compliance policy database, regulatory requirement catalogs, contract template library, historical compliance patterns

- **Integration points**: Document management system, contract repository, compliance tracking database

- **Interaction pattern**: Triggered by document submission; analyzes content against compliance rules; surfaces findings to legal team with risk assessment

- **Value delivered**: Reduces manual document review time, ensures consistent compliance checking exceptions, flags high-risk items for human attention

- **Governance**: Audit trail of all reviews, human verification required for any compliance exceptions, regular review of decision accuracy

Environment provisioning agent (performer)

- **Purpose**: Configures customer technical environment, including account creation, role assignment, service access, and security settings

- **Integration points**: Identify management system, cloud infrastructure APIs, access control systems, configuration management database

- **Interaction pattern**: Triggered by compliance clearance; executes provisioning workflow autonomously; reports completion status

- **Value delivered**: Eliminates manual provisioning steps, ensures configuration consistency, reduces time-to-activation from days to hours

- **Governance**: Pre-approved provisioning templates only, comprehensive logging of all actions, automated verification of security configurations, rollback capabilities for failures

Customer success planning agent (assistant)

- **Purpose**: Creates tailored onboarding journey based on customer profile, industry, and product selection

- **Knowledge sources**: Customer data platform, onboarding playbook repository, industry best practices, product usage analytics

- **Integration points**: CRM system, email, calendar scheduling system, customer portal

- **Interaction pattern**: Combines customer data with historical success patterns to generate personalized onboarding plan; guides customer success team through execution

- **Value delivered**: Ensures consistent high-quality onboarding experience, surfaces relevant best practices, automates routing communication scheduling

- **Governance**: Customer success manager approval of final plan, tracking of plan adherence, feedback collection on effectiveness

Financial integration agent (collaborator)

- **Purpose**: Establishes customer financial record, including billing configuration, payment method validation, and ERP system integration

- **Integration points**: ERP system, payment gateway, billing platform, accounts receivable system

- **Integration pattern**: Validates financial information, coordinates with finance team for exceptions, triggers billing setup workflow

- **Value delivered**: Reduces billing setup errors, ensures payment method validation before service activation, maintains data consistency across financial systems

- **Governance**: Finance team approval for non-standard billing terms, PCI compliance for payment data handling, audit trail of all financial record changes

Onboarding orchestration agent (orchestrator)

- **Purpose**: Coordinates the entire customer onboarding workflow across all functional agents, ensuring proper sequencing and handling exceptions

- **Integration points**: All specialized agents listed above, cloud flows, notifications, case management systems

- **Interaction pattern**: Monitors prerequisite completion for each stage, triggers appropriate agents when conditions are met, escalates exceptions to relevant teams

- **Value delivered**: Ensures nothing falls through the gaps between departments, maintains visibility into onboarding status, handles edge cases gracefully

- **Governance**: Exception escalation protocols, audit logging, SLA monitoring and alerting, regular review of orchestration patterns

Understanding When Multi-agent Architecture Makes Sense

The decision to build specialized agents versus a single comprehensive agent isn't always obvious. Many organizations default to building one agent per use case because it seems simpler. Sometimes that's correct. Often, it's not. The key is recognizing the patterns when decomposition creates more value than it costs.

When a Single Agent Is the Right Choice

Start with this reality: every additional agent introduces coordination complexity. If your solution genuinely serves a narrow, well-defined purpose with uniform governance requirements, a single agent may be optimal.

Consider a customer service agent that answers product questions. The entire purpose is information retrieval. All queries require the same governance approach: ensure accurate information, track common questions, measure response quality. All interactions follow the same pattern: someone asks, the agent answers.

The knowledge sources are related: product documentation, FAQs, support articles. There's no compelling reason to split this into multiple agents. The overhead of coordination would exceed any benefit from specialization. The same logic applies to a straightforward expense approval routing agent. It receives expense submissions, checks them against policy rules, and routes them to appropriate approvers. While this involves some decision-making (which expenses need which approvals), it's a linear workflow with consistent governance needs. A single assistant agent handles this effectively without requiring decomposition.

In both cases, the solution maps cleanly to a single agent type (retriever and assistant, respectively), serves stakeholders with aligned needs, operates without uniform governance requirements, and follows predictable interaction patterns. These characteristics suggest single-agent architecture makes sense.

When Multi-agent Architecture Becomes Necessary

The enterprise customer onboarding scenario demonstrates the opposite pattern. The process requires compliance verification, technical provisioning, success planning, and financial integration. These are fundamentally different functions managed by different departments with distinct governance requirements.

When compliance reviews customer documentation, the activity is analytical and advisory. The agent examines documents against rules, identifies potential issues, and recommends next steps to the legal team. The interaction is review-focused, the value comes from consistency and thoroughness, and the governance demands human oversight of risk assessments.

When IT provisions the customer environment, the activity is execution-oriented. The agent performs a series of technical actions: creating accounts, assigning permissions, configuring services. The interaction is automated, the value comes from speed and accuracy, and the governance requires comprehensive logging and verification but minimal human involvement for standard scenarios.

These functions have little in common beyond being part of the same overall process. Trying to handle both in a single agent creates problems. The analytical, recommendation-focused interaction needed for compliance review conflicts with the automated, action-oriented interaction need for provisioning. The human-in-the-loop governance appropriate for legal review doesn't fit the autonomous execution model that makes provisioning efficient. The prompt engineering that makes one interaction natural makes the other feel awkward.

More fundamentally, these capabilities have completely different ownership and life cycles. Legal owns compliance requirements and updates them as regulations change. IT owns provisioning logic and modifies it as infrastructure evolves. Finance owns billing configuration and adjusts it as pricing models change. Forcing all these functions into a single agent means coordinating every change across departments that operate on different timelines with different priorities.

This is the pattern that signals multi-agent architecture creates value.

When capabilities

- Are owned by different departments

- Require fundamentally different governance approaches

- Follow different interaction patterns and evolve based on distinct domain considerations

Functional Alignment

The enterprise customer onboarding scenario reveals another critical consideration: aligning agents with organizational functions creates natural ownership boundaries that support long-term maintainability. The compliance verification agent belongs to the legal department. They understand regulatory requirements, know which document characteristics signal risk, and can maintain the compliance rules as regulations evolve. Legal can enhance this agent's capabilities based on their domain expertise without coordinating with IT, customer success, or finance.

The functional alignment extends beyond just maintenance convenience. Each department can measure their agent's success using metrics they already track. Legal measures compliance review accuracy. IT measures provisioning and time-to-activation. Customer success measures plan effectiveness and customer engagement. Finance measures billing setup accuracy and payment method validation rates. The agents naturally align with existing departmental KPIs rather than requiring new cross-functional metrics.

If/when you find yourself asking "which department should maintain this capability?" and the answer spans multiple departments with different expertise, that's a signal for decomposition. Create specialized agents that align with functional ownership boundaries.

The Necessity of Orchestration

Multi-agent architecture for cross-functional processes introduces a new requirement that simpler scenarios don't need: explicit orchestration. Someone or something needs to coordinate the sequence, handle dependencies, and manage exceptions across the specialized agents.

In the enterprise customer onboarding scenario, compliance verification must complete before provisioning begins. You can't create customer accounts and configure access before legal confirms the customer meets compliance requirements. Provisioning must succeed before customer success activates the onboarding plan. You can't start scheduling welcome sessions and sending engagement emails if the customer doesn't have a working environment. Financial integration should happen in parallel with compliance verification to avoid delays, but billing can't activate until both provisioning succeeds and payment methods are validated.

These dependencies and sequencing rules don't naturally emerge from individual agents. The compliance agent doesn't know when provisioning should start, the provisioning agent doesn't track whether compliance review completed successfully. The customer success agent can't determine on its own whether it's safe to activate the onboarding plan.

In short, this is where the orchestration agent becomes essential. It maintains the overall process state, tracks which prerequisites are satisfied, triggers appropriate agents when conditions are met, and handles the inevitable exceptions. When compliance flags a high-risk item requiring legal review, the orchestration agent pauses provisioning and notifies the appropriate team. When provisioning fails due to infrastructure issues, it alerts IT and updates customer success that activation is delayed.

The orchestration agent doesn't do the work, it coordinates the agents that do.

This separation of concerns keeps specialized agents focused on their domain functions while ensuring the overall process executes correctly. It also creates a single place to implement process improvements. When you identify opportunities to parallelize steps or add new dependencies, you modify orchestration logic without touching the specialized agents.

Reusability Compounds Value

Beyond service, the immediate use case better, function-aligned agents often create broader organizational value through reusability across multiple scenarios.

The compliance verification agent doesn't just have to serve enterprise customer onboarding. It could also review contract amendments when customers upgrade services. It could validate documents for partnership agreements, or check regulatory compliance for new product launches.

Each scenario requires document review against compliance rules, and the specialized compliance agent could serve all of them with minimal modification.

Compare this to a monolithic onboarding agent that tightly couples compliance verification to the customer onboarding workflow. When legal needs compliance review for a partnership agreement, they can't use the onboarding agent because it's designed around the customer journey.

The same reusability logic applies across all the function-aligned agents. The provisioning agent serves customer onboarding today, but also handles environment setup for proof-of-concept trials, demo environments for sales, and sandbox environments for partner integrations tomorrow.

The most important thing here is to recognize that **functional capabilities will be needed across multiple scenarios**. Decomposing into specialized agents makes economic sense even if the immediate use case could technically work with fewer agents. You're **not** building for one workflow; you're building organizational capabilities that serve many scenarios.

Designing Agents for Reusability

The difference between single-use agents and reusable capabilities comes down to how you handle three design decisions: what you hardcode vs. configure, how you define inputs and outputs, and what you assume about context.

The most common reusability mistake is embedding workflow-specific logic into what should be a general capability. Consider the compliance verification agent. The core capability is comparing documents against rules sets and violations. This capability is useful across many scenarios. But if you hardcode assumptions about the customer onboarding workflow, checking for specific onboarding document types, routing findings to the customer onboarding team, updating the customer onboarding status tracker, you've created an agent that only works for customer onboarding.

Instead, design the agent around its essential capability and make workflow context configurable. The compliance verification agent should accept these as inputs: the document to review, which rule set to apply, what risk thresholds to use, and where to send findings. It shouldn't know or care whether the document is part of customer onboarding, partnership validation, or product compliance. The workflow orchestrator that calls the compliance agent provides that context.

Microsoft's document processing agent reference architecture[1] demonstrates this pattern effectively. The agent uses instructions that define its core capability, processing documents and extracting information without hardcoding assumptions about specific document types or workflows. Instead, it responds to status changes in a Dataverse table and calls appropriate actions based on those statuses.

Applying this same pattern to build a reusable compliance verification agent:

Use agent instructions that define capability, not workflow

The compliance verification agent's instructions should describe what it does, not which workflow it serves:

```
You are a compliance verification agent. You review documents against
specified rule sets and identify policy violations.

When asked to review a document with ID {documentId} using rule set
{ruleSetId}:


        -Call the extract compliance data action
        -Wait for the extraction to complete
        -Call the validate against rule sets action
        -Route findings based on the severity threshold provided

When the validation status changes to "Requires Review":
        -Call the escalate finding action with the specified
        routing target
```

These instructions work whether the document is a customer contract, partnership agreement, or product specification. The agent doesn't need to know; it just operates on the document and rule set it receives.

Store workflow context in Dataverse, not in the agent

The document processing reference architecture uses a state table in Dataverse to track document status and context. As documents move through processing stages, their status updates in the table, triggering the agent to take appropriate actions.

For the compliance verification agent, we would create a compliance review events table with columns:

---

[1] https://learn.microsoft.com/en-us/power-platform/architecture/
reference-architectures/document-processing-agent

- **DocumentId**: Which document is being reviewed

- **RuleSetId**: Which compliance rules apply (e.g., "customer contracts," "partnership agreements")

- **RiskThreshold**: Escalation sensitivity (e.g., "high," "medium," "low")

- **RoutingTarget**: Where findings should go (e.g., "customer ops," "legal team")

- **SourceWorkflow**: Which process triggered this review

- **Status**: Current stage (e.g., "New," "Extracted," "Validated," "Escalated")

- **ExtractedData**: Compliance findings in structured format

When customer onboarding needs compliance review, it creates a row with `RuleSetId = "customer-contracts"` and `RoutingTarget = "customer-ops"`. When partnership validation needs review, it creates a row with `RuleSetId = "partnership-agreements"` and `RoutingTarget = 'legal-team"`. The agent retrieves context from the table row, not from hardcoded assumptions.

Build agent flows that accept row IDs, not specific parameters

The document processing agent's actions receive a Data Processing Event ID as input. Each action retrieves the document and its context from Dataverse, processes it, updates the status, and lets the agent know what happened.

For the compliance verification agent, create flows following this pattern:

Extract Compliance Data flow:

```
Input: reviewEventId
1. Get row from compliance review events table using reviewEventId
2. Retrieve document using row.DocumentId
3. Review document using ReviewDocument prompt with rule set rown.RuleSetId
4. Store extracted findings in row.ExtractedData
5. Updates row-Status to "Extracted"
```

Validate against rules flow:

```
Input: reviewEventId
1. Get row from compliance review events table
2. Retrieve extracted data from row.ExtractedData
```

```
3. Apply validation rules based on row.RuleSetId and row.RiskThreshold
4. Update row.Status to "Validated" or "Requires Review" based on findings
```

Escalate finding flow:

```
Input: reviewEventId
1. Get row from compliance review events table
2. Retrieve findings from row.ExtractedData
3. Route to team specified in row.RoutingTarget
4. Include row.SourceWorkflow in notification for content
5. Update row.Status to "Escalated"
```

Each flow operates on whatever context exists in the table row. The core capability remains unchanged across scenarios, only the data in the compliance review events table differs.

Implementing Multi-agent Coordination

You've seen how the enterprise customer onboarding scenario required specialized agents coordinating across departments. How you implement that coordination depends on your workflow characteristics. Copilot Studio supports two distinct patterns, each suited to different scenarios.

Approach one: Dataverse state machine orchestration

This approach uses Dataverse tables to maintain process state and trigger agent tools based on status changes. It works well for long-running processes with multiple wait states, parallel execution paths, and requirements for comprehensive audit trails. Commonly, the orchestration agent monitors a master table and triggers agents based on status changes in this approach. The orchestration agent instructions might look like this:

```
You are an enterprise customer onboarding orchestration agent. You
coordinate the onboarding process across compliance, provisioning, customer
success, and finance teams.
Monitor the enterprise customer onboarding table for status changes:

When status = "initiated":
• Call create compliance review action with OnboardingId and CustomerId
• Update status to "Compliance Review"
```

- Set ComplianceReviewId from action response

```
When status = "Compliance approved":
```
- Check if FinancialRecordId exists
- If yes and financial validation complete, start ProvisioningAction
- If now, wait for Financial setup to complete
- Update status to "Provisioning"

The specialized agents update their own tables and their status in the master orchestration table. This creates a reliable coordination mechanism that persists across system restarts and handles long-running processes naturally. The orchestration agent doesn't need to stay continuously active; it responds to status changes whenever they occur.

Some steps can run concurrently. Compliance verification and financial setup don't depend on each other, so both run in parallel. The orchestration agent monitors both and only triggers provisioning when it sees that both prerequisites have completed.

Approach two: native agent-to-agent communication

Copilot Studio can transfer control to other agents within a conversation. This creates tighter coordination for user-driven workflows, the conversation flows naturally between specialized agents.

Instead of monitoring tables, the orchestration agent actively manages the conversation. When a user initiates customer onboarding, the orchestration agent collects basic information, then transfers the conversation to the compliance verification agent. The compliance agent interacts with the user, completes its review, then transfers control back to the orchestration agent with status details. The orchestration agent then determines next steps and potentially transfers to the provisioning agent.

The orchestration agent's instructions guide this conversation flow:

```
You are the enterprise customer onboarding coordinator. You guide users
through onboarding by connecting them with specialized agents.

When a user initiates new customer onboarding:
```
- Collect basic customer information: name, industry, product selection
- Transfer to compliance verification agent with customer details
- Wait for compliance agent to complete review

```
If approved, transfer to provisioning agent
```

If rejected, explain findings to user and offer next steps

When transferring to specialized agents:
- Provide all necessary context in transfer parameters
- Explain to user which team is now assisting them
- Remain available if user asks to speak with coordinator again

After each agent completes its work:
- Receive status and key details from specialized agent
- Update user on progress
- Determine next steps based on status received
- Transfer to next agent if prerequisites met

If any agent reports errors:
- Explain the issue to the user in plain language
- Offer options: wait for resolution, escalate to human, cancel onboarding
- Log error details for follow-up

The key difference from the state machine approach is that context passes through the conversation itself. When the orchestration agent transfers to the compliance agent, it includes customer details as transfer parameters. When the compliance agent transfers back, it includes review status and any findings. This creates a seamless conversational experience where users interact with different specialists without leaving the conversation.

Error handling happens conversationally too. If the compliance agent encounters an issue, it transfers back to orchestration with error details. The orchestration agent then explains the problem to the user in plain language and offers options: wait for resolution, escalate to a human specialist, or cancel the onboarding.

Quick recap:

- Good agents succeed because people succeed with them.

- Human-centered design is not optional; it is what unlocks adoption, trust, and real impact.

- Every design decision: interaction style, language, level of autonomy, transparency, shapes how people feel, behave, and ultimately deliver value.

- Process efficiency matters, but human experience determines whether that efficiency is realized.

Choosing Between Approaches

The decision comes down to your workflow characteristics. Use the Dataverse state machine when your process runs over hours or days, has multiple wait states where no one is actively engaged, or requires comprehensive audit trails showing every state transition. This approach handles long-running workflows reliably and allows multiple systems to query process status.

Use native agent-to-agent communication when your process completes within a single user session, user interaction guides the workflow progression, or hand-offs between specialists mirror how humans would naturally collaborate. This approach creates intuitive conversational experiences where users get real-time updates and explanations.

Figure 6-6 contrasts these two execution approaches and highlights the conditions under which each is the better fit.

Dataverse state-machine | **Native agent-to-agent**

Dataverse state-machine

- Process runs over hours or days with multiple wait states
- User is not continously engaged throughout the process
- Multiple systems need to query process status
- Audit trails must show every state transition with timestamps
- Process needs to survive system restarts or maintenance windows
- Manual intervention may be needed at various points

Native agent-to-agent

- Process completes within a single user session
- User interaction guides the workflow progression
- Context flows naturally through conversation
- Hand-offs between specialists mirror human organizational patterns
- User needs real-time updates and conversational explanations
- Errors should be explained conversationally rather than logged silently

Figure 6-6. Choosing between agent execution approaches based on workflow characteristics

Many complex workflows benefit from combining both approaches. The enterprise customer onboarding example works well as a hybrid: user conversations use agent transfers for the compliance discussion, while background processes like provisioning and financial integration use the state machine approach. This gives users a conversational interface where it matters, while handling complex background coordination reliably.

Conclusion

Agent type selection shapes everything that follows. The choice between retriever and orchestrator, single-agent and multi-agent architecture, state machine coordination, and native agent transfers are way more than technical decisions. As we've explored, they determine development timelines, governance requirements, risk profiles, and ultimately your ability to deliver the stakeholder value you defined in the earlier chapters.

The frameworks in this chapter give you systematic approaches to these decisions. When you evaluate an opportunity, you can now

- Map stakeholder outcomes to the six agent types based on primary function, autonomy requirements, interaction patterns, and decision authority.

- Assess whether single-agent architecture serves your needs or whether functional decomposition creates more maintainable, governable solutions.

- Choose coordination approaches that match your workflow characteristics, using Dataverse state machines for long-running processes and native agent transfers for conversational workflows.

- Design specialized agents for reusability across multiple scenarios, maximizing organizational value beyond the immediate use case.

Organizations that treat these decisions casually will often discover problems later in development. An orchestrator built when an assistant would suffice creates unnecessary complexity. A single monolithic agent serving cross-functional processes creates coordination nightmares when legal, IT, and finance teams all need to update different parts simultaneously. A native agent-to-agent implementation for a multi-day workflow loses context and frustrates users.

Getting agent type selection right early prevents these costly mistakes. More importantly, it establishes the foundation to agents that can evolve as organizational needs mature. The HR onboarding assistant you build today can grow into an orchestrator coordinating with specialized agents tomorrow, because you understood the architectural implications from the start.

Technical architecture alone doesn't determine agent success. You can build a perfectly orchestrated multi-agent system with flawless coordination that still fails because users don't trust it, don't understand how to interact with it, or find the experience frustrating rather than helpful.

The most valuable agents deliver value only when people actually want to use them. That requires different design thinking, moving from process logic and system architecture to conversation design, trust-building, and human-centered interaction patterns. It means understanding not just what your agent can do, but how people will experience working with it day after day.

Chapter 7 shifts focus from selecting the right agent architecture to designing agents that people embrace rather than avoid. We'll explore how conversation design, transparency, and user experience principles transform technically capable agents into solutions that stakeholders actively champion. Why? Because the best-architected agent in the world creates zero value if it sits unused.

Designing Agents People Want to Use

Imagine two organizations launch customer service agents at the same time. Both agents access similar knowledge bases, handle the same type of queries, and integrate with similar backend systems. Six months later, one agent handles 75% of customer inquiries with satisfaction scores matching human support. The other sits mostly unused, with customers actively seeking ways to bypass it and reach human agents instead.

The differences are not in technical capability. Both agents work. Both retrieve accurate information. Both complete transactions successfully when users persist through the conversation. The difference is that one agent feels like a helpful colleague who understands what you need, while the other feels like an obstacle course you must navigate to get basic help.

This gap between technical function and human adoption determines whether your agents deliver the value you've promised stakeholders. An orchestrator with flawless multi-agent coordination creates zero value if users find the experience frustrating. An assistant with perfect workflow logic sits idle if the experience feels robotic and unnatural.

Chapter 6 equipped you to select the right agent type and architecture. You can now access whether your opportunity needs a retriever or an orchestrator, whether single agent, or multi-agent architecture makes sense, and how to coordinate specialized agents across departmental boundaries. These decisions establish the technical foundation that makes value delivery possible.

© Steve Jeffery 2026

S. Jeffery, *Value by Design with Microsoft Copilot Studio*, https://doi.org/10.1007/979-8-8688-2613-9_7

But possible isn't the same as probable.

Technical foundation supports value delivery only when the agent actually understands what users need and responds appropriately. In Copilot Studio, this happens through generative orchestration; AI that interprets user requests semantically and selects the right capabilities to fulfill them. The job of building an agent isn't to script every possible conversation path. It's to design capabilities that the generative orchestrator can understand and use effectively.

This is fundamentally different from traditional bot design where you map utterances to intents to conversation flows. You're not building conversation trees. You're teaching an AI orchestrator how to interpret user needs, and which capabilities serve those needs. The orchestrator handles the conversation dynamically. You design the capabilities and describe them clearly enough so that the orchestrator knows when to use them.

The shift from "design conversation flows" to "design capabilities with clear descriptions" changes everything about how you approach agent development. It means

- **Writing descriptions that guide orchestration decisions**, not scripting dialog that handles every variation

- **Structuring knowledge sources for semantic understanding**, not organizing FAQ content by category

- **Defining capability boundaries explicitly**, not mapping every possible user utterance

- **Testing orchestration decisions**, not validating conversation paths

- **Refining based on how the AI interprets requests**, not fixing broken conversation branches

This chapter explores how to design agents that work with generative orchestration effectively. We're not abandoning human-centered thinking; understanding user needs remains foundational. However, we are applying that understanding differently. Instead of designing conversations, we're designing capabilities that an AI orchestrator can intelligently deploy based on semantic understanding of what users are trying to accomplish.

Poor capability design doesn't just frustrate users; it also undermines confidence in the entire AI strategy. When an agent consistently misunderstands requests and triggers wrong capabilities, users stop trusting not just that agent but possibly the organization's broader AI capabilities. When knowledge retrieval returns irrelevant information, users question whether agents can actually help with real work.

Conversely, agents designed for effective orchestration become proof points that AI can augment work effectively. Users become advocates. Stakeholders see evidence that agents deliver promised value. Leadership gains confidence to invest in more ambitious initiatives. The design choices you make in early agents shape organizational readiness for the autonomous capabilities you'll build later.

This matters because you're **not just designing individual agents. You're establishing patterns that will influence how your organization builds and deploys AI for years.** The HR onboarding assistant you design today creates user expectations for the finance advisory agent that you'll build next quarter. The orchestration patterns that work well get replicated. The failures get remembered and cited as evidence that "we tried AI and it didn't work here."

The design principles in this chapter apply across all agent types, but implementation varies significantly. A retriever answering questions requires different action descriptions than an orchestrator coordinating week-long processes. An advisory making recommendations needs different knowledge structure than a performer taking autonomous actions. We'll explore both the universal principles and the type-specific implementation patterns that make orchestration work effectively in practice.

We're building on the stakeholder understanding you developed in Chapter 3 but shifting focus from what value means to stakeholders to how agents will actually understand and serve their needs. The stakeholder analysis identified whose needs matter and what outcomes they expect. Now, we're designing capabilities and knowledge sources that generative orchestration can use to deliver those outcomes in ways that feel natural, trustworthy, and genuinely helpful.

The design work starts now, before you write your first action description, or upload a knowledge document. Because the most sophisticated generative AI can't compensate for poorly described capabilities or badly structured knowledge sources. When orchestration decisions seem random, users lose confidence. When knowledge retrieval returns irrelevant information, users stop asking. When capabilities don't align with how users naturally express needs, adoption fails regardless of technical sophistication.

Let's begin where all successful agent design begins: understanding the humans who will determine whether your agent succeeds or fails.

Understanding Your Users

Before you write a single action description, or structure any knowledge source, you need to understand the humans whose needs your agent will serve. Generative orchestration interprets user requests semantically, which means your agent can handle varied phrasings and unexpected requests. This is wonderfully flexible, but this flexibility only works if you've designed capabilities that align with how users naturally think about and describe their problems. An agent that understands "I need to enroll in benefits" but fails with "how do I sign up for insurance" has capability descriptions that don't account for how real users express the same need.

Who Will Actually Use This Agent?

Return to the stakeholder analysis from Chapter 3, but now focus on different design considerations.

Direct Users Versus Indirect Beneficiaries

Before we design capabilities or interaction patterns, we need to be clear about **who actually experiences value** from an agent and how that value flows through the organization.

In the HR onboarding example, the people who interact with the agent are not the only ones who benefit from it. A new hire asking questions or submitting requests receives immediate, visible value. However, those same interactions also create downstream effects: fewer interruptions for HR administrators, faster readiness for managers, and more consistent compliance for the organization.

Understanding this distinction between direct users and indirect beneficiaries is critical. Design decisions should be driven by the needs, language, and context of direct users because they determine whether the agent is adopted at all. Measurement and success criteria, however, must reflect the outcomes experienced by indirect beneficiaries because that is where organizational value is realized.

Figure 7-1 below shows how these two groups are connected, using the HR onboarding agent to make the flow of value explicit.

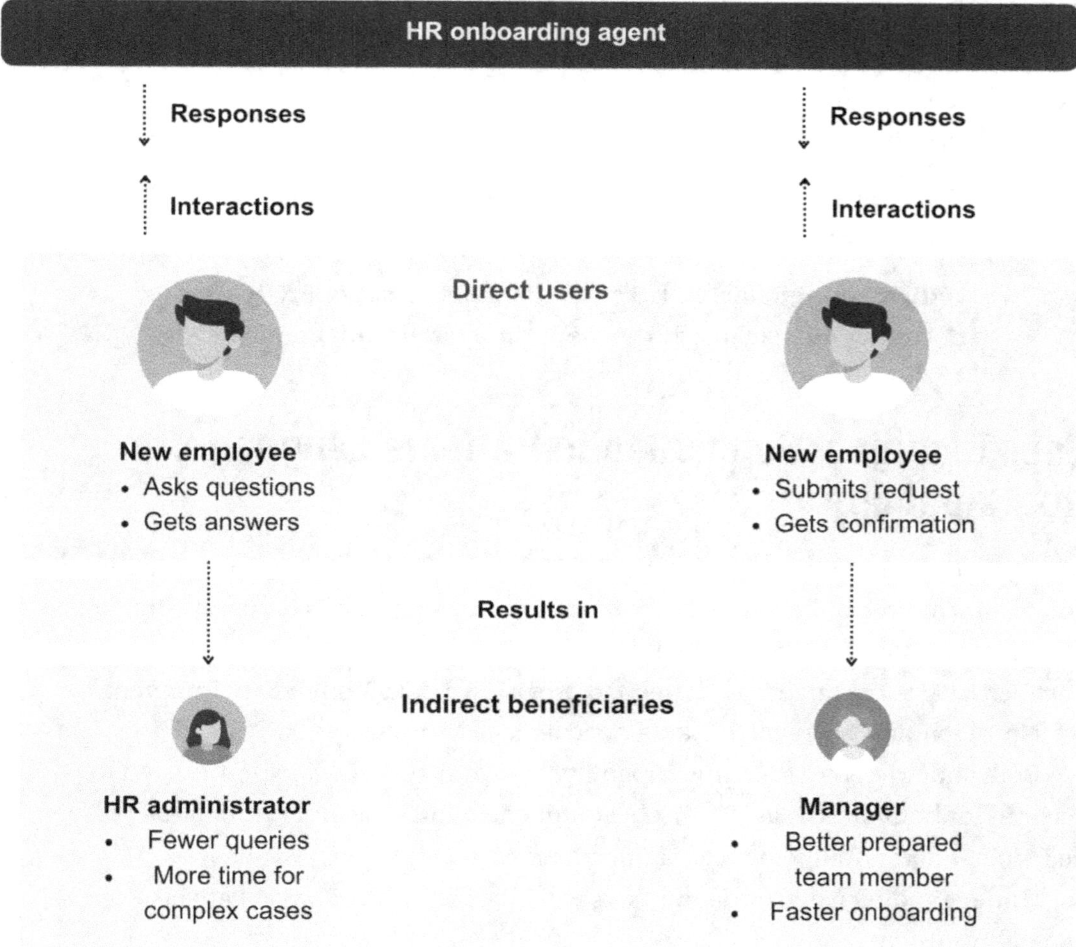

Figure 7-1. *Value flow between direct users and indirect beneficiaries*

Notice how value flows in two distinct pathways. On the left, a new employee asks questions and receives answers, immediate value for the direct user. However, this interaction creates downstream value for the HR administrator, who receives fewer interruptions and can focus on complex cases that truly require human expertise. On the right, a new employee submits a request and receives confirmation; again, immediate value. This generates downstream value for managers who receive better prepared team members through faster, more consistent onboarding.

This distinction shapes your design approach in fundamental ways. Designing for users determines orchestration decisions; you need to understand their language, their context, and their goals to build capabilities the agent can deploy effectively. Designing for indirect beneficiaries determines what you measure; you track the business outcomes they care about to prove the agent delivers organizational value, not just individual convenience.

For the HR onboarding agent:

- **Direct users**: New employees asking questions, completing enrollment

- **Indirect beneficiaries**: HR administrators whose query volume decreases, managers who get better-prepared team members

User Technical Sophistication Affects Language, Not Capability

With generative orchestration, you don't need to dumb down or simplify capabilities for less technical users. The AI handles varied sophistication levels naturally. But you do need to understand the language users actually use.

Technical users might say: "I need to provision a development environment."

Non-technical users might say "I need a place to test things."

Both should trigger the same capability, but your action descriptions need to account for both phrasings. The orchestrator can handle the interpretation if you've described the capability to match both contexts.

Understanding when and how users will interact with your agent affects capability design:

- **Time pressure**: Emergency IT provisioning versus routine account creation requires different response patterns. High-pressure scenarios need faster orchestration, clearer confirmations, more proactive status updates.

- **Multitasking environment**: Users juggling multiple responsibilities may need agents that can pause and resume gracefully, maintain context across days, or send proactive updates rather than requiring constant checking.

- **Physical environment**: Users on mobile devices need concise responses. Users at desks can handle more detailed information.

- **Cognitive load**: Users overwhelmed with onboarding information need agents that don't add to the complexity. Design for clarity and simplicity when users are already dealing with cognitive overload.

User Motivation and Trust Baseline

Some users approach agents optimistically ("this will help me"), others skeptically ("let's see if this actually works"). You can't change baseline trust through design alone but you can avoid destroying it.

Willing participants: These users give agents benefit of the doubt initially. Poor orchestration decisions or irrelevant responses quickly erode this goodwill.

Skeptical users: These users expect failure and are watching for it. Transparent limitations and graceful error handling matter more here than perfect performance.

Forced users: Some users must use agents due to organizational policy. Users resent friction and compare every interaction to the human alternative. Excellence matters more here because you don't have voluntary adoption.

What Are Users Actually Trying to Accomplish?

With generative orchestration, you're not mapping specific intents. You're understanding underlying goals so you can describe capabilities in ways that match user thinking.

The Language Users Actually Use

This is the most critical research for generative agent design. You need to know how users naturally express needs, because that's what the orchestrator will interpret.

Poor approach: Assume users will use formal corporate language "I need to initiate the benefits enrollment process."

> **Reality**: Users use natural, varied language – "How do I sign up for insurance?", "I need to get health coverage," "When can I enroll in benefits?", "What are my insurance options?", "I want to add my family to my health plan."

All of these express the same core need, but in varied ways. Your action descriptions must account for this variation.

Primary, Secondary, and Emotional Goals

Users often have multiple layers of goals:

- **Primary**: The stated reason for interaction – "I need to enroll in benefits."

- **Secondary**: The underlying need they may not articulate – "I need to make a confident decision about coverage for my family."

- **Emotional**: How they want to feel during and after – "I want to feel like I made a smart choice and didn't miss anything."

Understanding all three layers helps you design capabilities that serve complete needs, not just stated requests. Example: benefit enrollment agent.

- **Primary goal served**: Collect enrollment selections and submit to HR system.

- **Secondary goal served**: Provide decision support through plan comparison and personalized recommendations.

- **Emotional goal served**: Confirmation that selections are appropriate, explanation of next steps, assurance nothing was missed.

The agent needs capabilities for all three layers. Action descriptions should reflect this completeness.

Context-Dependent Goals

How users express goals shifts based on situation. The same person might interact with your agent very differently at different times:

- Week one of employment: "What's the remote work policy?" (exploring what's possible)

- Month three: "Can I work from home on Fridays?" (planning specific arrangements)

- Before vacation: "How do I submit time off?" (immediate need)

- During system migration: "Why can't I access my benefits info?" (troubleshooting)

Your capability descriptions need to account for these contextual variations. The orchestrator can interpret them if you've provided semantic guidance about when capabilities apply. Here's how to design for context systematically:

Identifying Contextual Patterns

User context typically falls into five categories that affect how they express needs:

- **Temporal context: where are they in the journey?**

  New/onboarding: Exploratory, seeking overview ("what benefits do we get?")

  Established/routine: Specific, executing known processes ("submit my expense report")

  Transitional/change: Triggered by life events ("I'm getting married, what do I do?")

- **Urgency context: How time-sensitive is their need?**

  Planning/non-urgent: Thoughtful exploration ("I'm thinking about taking vacation in June")

  Immediate: Action focused, present tense ("I need to submit PTO for next week")

  Crisis/emergency: Problem-focused, frustrated ("why can't I access my benefits?")

- **Knowledge context:** What do they already know?

  Novice: Broad questions, basic terminology ("what is PTO?")

Intermediate: Specific questions, some domain knowledge ("which plan should I choose?")

Expert: Technical questions, advanced terminology ("can I donate PTO to another employee?")

- **Emotional context: What's their state of mind?**

  Confident/proactive: Clear requests, direct ("I want to enroll in benefits")

  Uncertain/cautious: Tentative, seeking reassurance ("Should I choose the PPO?")

  Frustrated/stressed: Problem-focused, emotional ("This doesn't work," "I've tried everything.")

- **Task context: What else is happening?**

  Focused/single task: Complete attention, detailed questions, thorough exploration

  Multitasking/distracted: Quick questions, abbreviated ("Quick question:")

  Interrupted/returning: References previous conversations ("I was asking about…")

These contextual variations don't require complex programming in your descriptions. The orchestrator's semantic understanding handles much of this naturally; however, your descriptions need to

- **Include varied example phrases** that reflect different contexts

- **Set clear boundaries** between exploration and execution

- **Distinguish between related but different needs**

Quick recap: Understanding your users

- Direct users interact with agents, indirect beneficiaries experience downstream value from those interactions.

- User language varies by technical sophistication, but generative orchestration handles this naturally.

- Context shapes how users express needs: Temporal, urgency, knowledge, emotion, and task contexts all affect user requests.

- Design for direct users determines orchestration decisions; measuring indirect beneficiaries proves business value.

Setting Your Agent's Foundation: Agent Instructions

You've identified who will use your agent, how they naturally express their needs, and what contexts shape their interactions. This user understanding provides the raw material for design decisions. But before writing individual tool descriptions or configuring knowledge sources, you need to establish something more fundamental: your agent's core identity and behavioral foundation.

Think of this as setting the stage before the actors perform. Individual capabilities – tools, knowledge sources, topics – are the specific things your agent can do. But how should the agent behave while doing them? What personality should it project? What boundaries should it respect? How should it communicate when things go wrong?

These are foundational decisions that shape interactions, regardless of which specific capability the orchestrator selects. An HR onboarding agent should maintain consistent helpfulness whether it's retrieving policy information, submitting an equipment request, or explaining why it can't help with a particular question.

This foundation gets established through **agent instructions** – high-level guidance that shapes the agent's overall behavior, personality, and decision-making approach. System instructions sit above individual capability descriptions in the instructions hierarchy. They're the first thing the orchestrator considers when interpreting requests and formulating responses.

Getting agent instructions right is crucial because they create the user's first and lasting impression of your agent. Poor system instructions create agents that feel robotic, inconsistent, or unhelpful even when individual capabilities work perfectly. Strong system instructions create agents that feel like trusted colleagues: knowledgeable, reliable, and genuinely helpful.

Understanding the Instruction Hierarchy

Before we explore how to write effective system instructions, it's important to understand how different levels of instruction work together in Copilot Studio. The orchestrator doesn't treat all instructions equally; there's a clear hierarchy that determines which guidance takes precedence.

- **Agent instructions provide the highest-level guidance**: These define who the agent is, how it should behave generally, and what global rules it must follow. Agent instructions apply to every interaction, regardless of which capability is being used. They set personality, tone, ethical boundaries, and broad behavioral patterns.

- **Capability descriptions provide specific guidance about individual tools, knowledge sources, and topics**: These are the "when to use" criteria, example phrases, and boundaries for specific capabilities. Capability descriptions tell the orchestrator when to invoke particular functions and how to use them appropriately.

The orchestrator considers all levels together, but agent instructions have **foundational priority**. If your agent instructions say:

```
"never provide medical advice"
```

and a tool description says

```
"help users understand their health benefits",
```

the orchestrator should retrieve benefits information while carefully avoiding any statement that could be construed as medical guidance. The agent-level boundary constrains how the specific capability gets used.

Once you've identified who experiences value and how that value flows, the next challenge is **translating intent into reliable agent behavior**.

This requires separating *what is globally true* about the agent from what is *situational and capability-specific*. Many times this collapses into a single block of instructions, which quickly becomes brittle, inconsistent, and difficult to govern as agents grow in scope.

Figure 7-2 below introduces a simple but critical hierarchy. It distinguishes **agent-level instructions**, which define identity, boundaries, and behavioral norms from **capability descriptions**, which specify when and how particular tools, knowledge, or actions should be used. This separation allows agents to remain consistent and trustworthy while still supporting multiple tasks and workflows.

Figure 7-2. *Hierarchy of agent instructions and capability descriptions*

Understanding this hierarchy helps you decide what belongs in agent-level instructions versus capability descriptions. Agent instructions handle global concerns: personality, boundaries, ethical guidelines, and behavioral patterns that apply universally. Capability descriptions handle specific concerns; when this particular function applies and how to use it.

Let's explore how to craft system instructions that establish the right foundation for your agent.

Defining Your Agent's Identity and Purpose

The first and most important element of agent instructions is establishing who your agent is and what it's meant to accomplish. This is to create a clear identity that helps the orchestrator make consistent decisions.

Identity statements answer fundamental questions:

- What roles does this agent serve?

- Who does it help?

- What's the primary purpose?

- What makes it valuable?

For the HR onboarding agent, a strong identity statement might be:

"You are an HR onboarding assistant designed to help new employees navigate their first 90 days at the company. Your purpose is to make onboarding smooth, informative, and welcoming by providing timely information, guiding employees through required processes, and connected them with the right resources and people when needed."

Notice what this identity statement accomplishes:

- **Defines the role clearly**: "HR onboarding assistant" immediately scopes the domain and sets expectations about what kind of help the agent provides.

- **Identifies the primary audience**: "New employees" clarifies who the agent serves, which affect language choices, assumptions about prior knowledge, and the types of questions to expect.

- **Articulates the time frame**: "First 90 days" create a natural boundary. Questions about advanced career development or long-term policies might be acknowledged but redirected.

- **Establishes the purpose**: "Make onboarding smooth, informative, and welcoming" sets behavioral tone. The agent must be more than functional, it should actively work to reduce new employee stress and uncertainty.

- **Defines value through actions**: "Providing timely information, guiding through process, connecting to resources" clarifies how the agent creates value; not by doing everything itself, but by being helpful in specific ways.

This identity statement becomes the lens through which the orchestrator interprets every subsequent instruction and capability description. When someone asks a question or makes a request, the orchestrator's first consideration is: *"Given I'm an HR onboarding assistant helping new employees through their first 90 days, how should I respond to this?"*

Weak identity statements miss these elements. Consider this alternative:

```
"You are an HR chatbot that answers questions about company policies and
helps with onboarding tasks"
```

This tells the orchestrator what the agent does, but not who it is or why. There's no personality, no clear audience focus, no sense of purpose beyond generic function. The orchestrator has less guidance about how to prioritize competing concerns or how to behave when faced with ambiguous requests.

Figure 7-3 below contrasts a weak identity statement with a strong one, highlighting what effective agent identity framing actually requires.

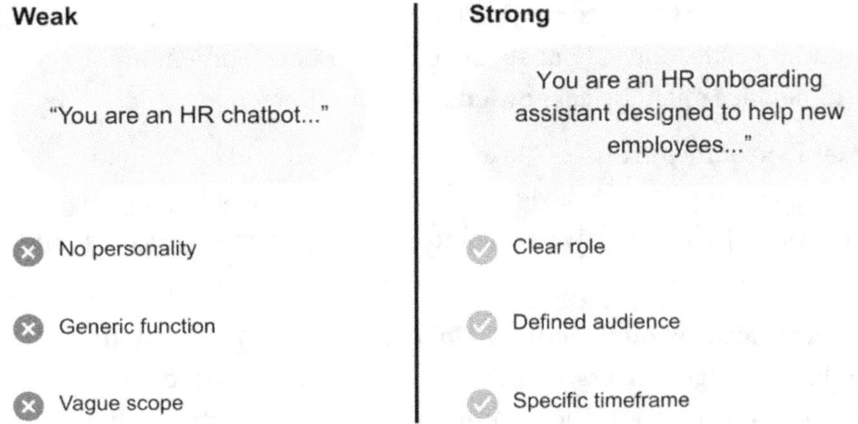

Figure 7-3. *Weak vs. strong agent identity statements*

Identity statements should be concise but complete – typically 2–4 sentences that establish role, audience, purpose, and approach. Longer statements risk diluting focus, shorter statements miss critical framing.

Establishing Behavioral Guidelines

With identity established, the next layer of system instructions defines how your agent should behave in specific situations. These guidelines create consistency across diverse interactions and help the orchestrator make appropriate decisions when facing ambiguity or edge cases.

Communication style and tone

One of the most impactful behavioral guidelines addresses how the agent communicates – the language it uses, the personality it projects, and the relationship it establishes with users.

For the HR onboarding agent:

```
"Communicate in a friendly, professional tone that balances warmth with
credibility. Use clear, jargon-free language unless technical terms are
specifically relevant to the user's role. When explaining processes, break
complex information into digestible steps. When users seem uncertain or
overwhelmed, offer reassurance and additional context."
```

This guidance accomplishes several things:

- **Sets clear tone expectation**: "Friendly, professional" with "warmth" and "credibility" gives the orchestrator a personality target. Responses shouldn't be cold and bureaucratic but also shouldn't be overly casual or inappropriately informal.

- **Addresses language complexity**: "Clear, jargon-free language unless technical terms are specifically relevant" helps the orchestrator adapt to context. Don't use "PRO accrual pro-ration" when "how vacation days are calculated" works better; unless the user is HR staff who understand and use that terminology.

- **Provides structural guidance**: "Break complex information into digestible steps" tells the orchestrator how to present information, not just what information to present.

- **Enables empathy**: "When users seem uncertain or overwhelmed, offer reassurance" gives the orchestrator permission and guidance for responding to emotional context, not just factual questions.

Communication guidelines are particularly important because they affect every single response your agent generates. Whether retrieving knowledge, confirming a tool invocation, or explaining why it can't help, the agent should maintain consistent tone and approach.

Handling Uncertainty and Limitations

Another critical behavioral guideline addresses what happens when the agent doesn't know something, can't help, or encounters ambiguous requests.

```
"When you don't have information to answer a question, be honest about
limitations while offering alternatives. Say what you can't do and suggest
what might help instead. If a request is ambiguous, ask clarifying
questions rather than making assumptions. If something requires human
judgment or is outside your scope, explain why and suggest who the user
should contact."
```

This guidance prevents common failure patterns:

Avoids fake confidence: Without this guidance, agents sometimes fabricate information or over-extrapolate from limited knowledge. Explicit instruction to "be honest about limitations" helps the orchestrator recognize and acknowledge uncertainty.

Maintains ambiguity appropriately: "Ask clarifying questions rather than making assumptions" prevents the agent from triggering wrong capabilities based on misinterpreted requests. Better to ask "Are you asking about requesting new equipment or troubleshooting equipment problems?" than to launch into the wrong workflow.

Enables graceful escalation: "Explain why and suggest who to contact" turns limitations into appropriate handoffs. The agent can't provide legal advice about an employment contract, but it can explain that limitation and direct the user to the legal department or HR business partner.

Confirmation and Safety Patterns

For agents that perform actions with business consequences (submitting requests, updating records, triggering workflows) behavioral guidelines should establish when and how to seek confirmation; below, we provide this to our HR onboarding agent:

```
"Before submitting any request that has business consequences (equipment
orders, time off submissions, benefits enrollment), summarize what you're
about to do and ask for explicit confirmation.
```

```
Present the summary in clear terms: 'I'm about to submit an equipment
request for a Surface Pro, to be delivered to your home address [address].
This will require manager approval. Should I proceed?'. Wait for
affirmative confirmation before taking action."
```

This pattern accomplishes several goals:

Prevents accidental actions: Users might mention something conversationally that the orchestrator interprets as an action request. Confirmation catches these misunderstandings before they cause problems.

Builds trust: Seeing exactly what the agent is about to do and having control over whether it happens reassures users that the agent isn't acting unpredictably or beyond their control.

Creates documentation: The confirmation exchange provides a clear record of what was requested and approved, which matters for audit trails and dispute resolution.

Enables correction: Users might realize they made a mistake or forgot something when they see the summary. "Wait, I meant to include a second monitor too" is much better discovered before submission than after.

Confirmation patterns should be calibrated to risk and reversibility. Retrieving information doesn't need confirmation. Submitting an expense report with an audit trail might need confirmation. Submitting a resignation notice definitely needs multiple confirmations.

Boundary and Scope Clarity

Agent instructions should explicitly state **what the agent will not do**, establishing clear boundaries that prevent capability scope creep and protect both users and the organization, like in this example below:

```
"You do not provide medical advice, legal advice, or financial planning
recommendations. When questions touch these areas, acknowledge the
question's importance while clearly explaining you can't advise on it.
Direct users to appropriate resources instead.

You do not make exceptions to company policies or approve requests that
require manager or HR review. When asked to bypass normal processes,
explain why those processes exist and help users work through proper
channels.

You do not access or discuss employee records, performance reviews, or
confidential information beyond what's necessary for onboarding processes."
```

These boundaries serve multiple purposes:

Prevents unauthorized actions: making clear the agent can't bypass approval processes or make exceptions aids in preventing users from trying to use the agent to circumvent controls.

Protects privacy and confidentiality: stating data access boundaries helps prevent inadvertent information disclosure and sets clear expectations about what the agent can and cannot discuss.

Guides orchestrator decisions: when requests fall into these boundary areas, the orchestrator has clear guidance about how to respond rather than attempting for fulfill requests it shouldn't.

Boundary statements work best when paired with helpful alternatives. Don't just say what the agent can't do; explain what users should do instead. `"I can't provide medical advice about your health condition, but I can help you understand your health insurance coverage and connect you with the employee assistance program that provides access to healthcare professionals"` maintains helpfulness while respecting boundaries.

Quick recap: Agent instructions foundation

- Agent instructions sit above capability descriptions in the hierarchy, constraining how all capabilities work.

- Strong identity statements define role, audience, time frame, and purpose in 2–4 sentences.

- Behavioral guidelines cover communication style, handling uncertainty, confirmation patterns, and boundaries.

- Clear boundaries prevent scope creep and protect both users and organization.

- Agent instructions create consistent personality across all interactions, regardless of which capability is used.

Writing Effective Descriptions That Guide Orchestration

Keep descriptions concise and focused. Copilot Studio limits tool descriptions to 1024 characters. Aim for 300–500 characters: well below the limit while remaining clear and comprehensive.

Why shorter is better:

- **Easier for orchestrator to process** key signals

- **More maintainable** as capabilities evolve

- **Forces clarity and focus** on essential information

- **Leaves room for iteration** without hitting limits

Example: Remote work policy action

```
RemoteWorkPolicyEnquiry action - Retrieves remote work policy information
including eligibility, requirements, and approval process.

Use when users ask about remote work policies, eligibility, or
requirements.


Example phrases:
"What's the remote work policy?"
"Can I work from home?"
"Am I eligible for remote work?"
"Tell me about working remotely"

Do NOT use for:
- Submitting requests (use RemoteWorkRequest action)
- VPN/technical issues (use ITSupport action)
**Character count: 385 / 1024 (38% of limit)**
```

Topics can have slightly more detail since they describe multi-turn workflows, but aim for 400–600 characters to maintain clarity.

```
Example: Benefits enrollment topic
```

BenefitsEnrollment topic - Guides employees through complete benefits enrollment including health, dental, and vision plan selection.

Trigger when users explicitly want to enroll or have decided on plans and are ready to submit.

Example phrases: "I want to enroll in benefits" "I'm ready to sign up for insurance" "Enroll me in the PPO plan" This topic guides through plan selection, collects dependent information, calculates costs, and submits enrollment.

Do NOT trigger for: - Questions about benefits (use generative answers) - Comparing plans (use comparison action) - Checking status (use status action)

Deep Dive: Building an Effective Action Description

Let's walk through designing action and topic description for a common enterprise scenario: employees requesting IT equipment. We'll show the thinking process, common mistakes, and best practices.

The Scenario

Your organization needs an agent to help employees request IT equipment like laptops, monitors, keyboards, and accessories. The request requires manager approval and routes through IT procurement.

Figure 7-4 below shows the step-by-step process used to develop agent descriptions in practice, highlighting how problem understanding, scope definition, and example selection work together before any instructions are finalized.

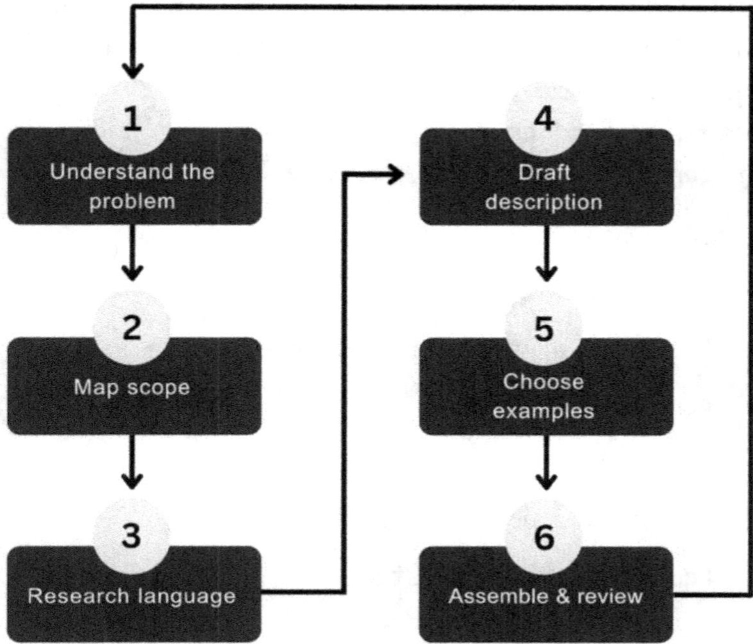

Figure 7-4. *A six-step process for crafting clear, effective agent descriptions*

Step one: Understand what problem you're solving

Before writing any description, clarify the underlying need.

Questions to answer:

- What pain point does this solve for users?

- What business goal does this serve?

- How will you know if it's working?

For IT equipment requests:

> **User pain point**: "I don't know how to request equipment, the process is unclear, my requests get lost."

> **Business goal**: "Standardize equipment request, ensure proper approval, create audit trail."

> **Success looks like**: "Faster processing, fewer incomplete requests, clear tracking."

Understanding the problem shapes your description. If the pain point is "unclear process," your description needs process clarity. If it's "requests get lost," your description needs to emphasize tracking.

Step two: Map what this does versus what it doesn't

List what this capability should handle, and what it should not handle.

```
This action handles:
```

- New equipment requests

- Equipment upgrades or replacements

- Accessory requests

```
This action does not handle:
```

- Equipment problems or repairs

- Equipment policy questions

- Tracking existing requests

Common mistake: trying to make one action do everything related to a domain. Instead, create focused tools with clear boundaries that point to alternatives. Clear scope prevents the orchestrator from selecting this action when a different capability would serve the user better.

Step two: Research actual user language

Review how users currently express this need. From support tickets, emails, and conversations:

Actual phrases employees use:

- "I need a new laptop."

- "Can I get a second monitor?"

- "How do I request a keyboard?"

- "I want to order equipment."

- "My role changed, I need better equipment."

- "Request IT gear."

Notice the variation:

- Direct need: "I need..."

- Permission seeking: "Can I get...?"

- Process questions: "How do I request...?"

- Commands: "Request"

- Context-based: "My role changed..."

A common mistake is using formal, corporate language instead of natural language. The orchestrator matches semantic meaning, but your examples should reflect how people actually communicate.

Step three: Draft the basic description

Start drafting the core capability statement. The statement should cover the following:

- Problem

- Define when to use it

- Select diverse example phrases

- Define clear boundaries

Attempt one: too vague

```
ITEquipmentRequest action - Requests IT equipment
```

The problem is that the description doesn't explain what happens or the outcome

Attempt two: Too detailed

```
ITEquipmentRequest action.- Initiates a comprehensive IT equipment
procurement workflow that collects detailed specifications, validates
against company standards, routes thorugh multi-level approval chains based
on cost thresholds and equipment categories, integrates with procuement
systems, and generates tracking numbers.
```

The problem is that the description is too detailed. It's using 345 characters just for capability statement. Overwhelming technical detail that describes the implementation instead of the purpose.

Attempt 3: Just right

```
ITEquipmentRequest action - Guides users through requesting IT equipment
with manager approval and procurement routing.
```

This example has clear purpose, mentions key steps (approval, routing), it's concise (95 characters), focuses on user experience, not technical implementation.

It follows a good practice pattern: **[ActionName]** action – **[Verb]** users through **[purpose]** with **[key outcome/process]**.

Examples:

- "Guides users through requesting IT equipment with manager approval"

- "Helps users submit expense reports with automatic category validation"

- "Walks users through benefits enrollment with plan comparison support"

Step four: Define when to use it

Describe the situations where this action is appropriate.

Attempt 1: too broad

```
Use when users need IT equipment.
```

The problem here is this can match too many unrelated scenarios. "My laptop is broken" is about equipment but shouldn't trigger this action.

Attempt 2: too restrictive

```
Use only when users explicitly say "I want to request IT equipment" and
have determined exact specifications including model number and SKUs
```

The problem with this approach is that it is too narrow. It misses natural variations. Users rarely know model numbers up front.

Attempt 3: well-scoped

```
Use when users want to request, order, or ask about requesting IT equipment
or accessories
```

This covers variations (request, order, ask about requesting) without being too broad. Clear intent focus (85 characters)

Good practice pattern: "Use when users **[want to/need to/ask about]** **[core action]** **[domain]**

Examples:

- "Use when users want to request, order, or ask about requesting IT equipment."

- "Use when users need to submit or inquire about submitting expense reports."

- "Use when users want to enroll, sign up, or learn about enrolling in benefits."

Step five: Choose example phrases strategically

Select 4–6 phrases representing different linguistic patterns

Attempt one: too similar

- `"I need a laptop"`
- `"I need a new laptop"`
- `"I need to get a laptop"`
- `"I need to request a laptop"`
- `"I would like a laptop"`

The problem with these phrases is that they are all variations of "I need a laptop." It wastes character count without adding diversity.

Attempt two: wrong example

- `"My computer broke"`
- `"What equipment policy do we have?"`
- `"Where is my laptop order?"`

These should not trigger this action. They're good examples of what **not** to match.

Attempt three: well-chosen diversity

- `"I need a new laptop"` (direct need)
- `"Can I get a second monitor?"` (permission-seeking)
- `"How do I request equipment?"` (process question)
- `"Order a keyboard and mouse"` (command form)
- `"I need better equipment for my role"` (context-based)

This works because each phrase represents the genuinely different ways that users express their need. It covers different linguistic patterns (135 characters for 5 phrases).

Some good practices:

Choose phrases that represent

1. Direct need – "I need X"

2. Permission seeking – "Can I get X?"

3. Process inquiry – "How do I [action]?"

4. Command – "[Action] X"

5. Context-based – "Situation + need"

Step six: Define clear boundaries

Specify what this action should NOT handle and point to correct alternatives.

Attempt one: vague boundaries

```
Do not use for other IT stuff
```

The problem is that this is unhelpful. It doesn't guide the orchestrator toward better choices.

Attempt two: exhaustive list

```
Do NOT use for: equipment repairs, equipment troubleshooting, equipment
returns, equipment transfers, equipment disposal, equipment upgrades,
equipment warranty questions, equipment policy questions, equipment budget
questions, equipment approval status, equipment tracking
```

The problem this time is that there are **too many boundaries** (300+ characters); there are unclear priorities.

Attempt three: focused boundaries with alternatives

Do NOT use for:

- Equipment problems or repairs (use ITSupport action)

- Equipment policy questions (use ITPolicy action)

- Tracking existing requests (use CheckRequestStatus action)

This approach works best because it covers the most common mismatches (155 characters). It points to the correct alternatives and helps you identify comprehensive capability coverage.

Good practices:

Include 2–4 boundaries that

1. **Address common confusion**: What related needs might the orchestrator confuse with this?

2. **Point to alternatives**: Where should those requests go instead?

3. **Use clear language**: Describe the boundary case clearly

Step seven: Assemble and review

Put all components together:

```
ITEquipmentRequest tool - Guides users through requesting IT equipment with
manager approval and procurement routing.

Use when users want to request, order, or ask about requesting IT equipment
or accessories.

Example phrases:

"I need a new laptop"
"Can I get a second monitor?"
"How do I request equipment?"
"Order a keyboard and mouse"
"I need better equipment for my role"

Do NOT use for:
- Equipment problems or repairs (use ITSupport action)
- Equipment policy questions (use ITPolicy action)
- Tracking existing requests (use CheckRequestStatus)
```

The capability statement is clear and concise (under 120 characters), the use case is well-scoped without being restrictive (under 100 characters). Example phrases represent different contexts (need, permission, process, command, context); boundaries are set to prevent common mismatches. The total length is well under 50% of the limit, there is no redundant information, it's easy to scan and read, and finally, it is **focused on user needs**, not technical implementation.

Some common mistakes at this stage:

- "This looks good, ship it": It is better to test against realistic user requests before deploying (we'll cover this in more detail soon).

- "It's under the character limit, let's add more examples": Stay well under the limit for future iteration room.

- "I wrote it once, it's done": Plan to iterate based on real usage patterns.

Quick recap: Writing effective tool descriptions

- Start by understanding the problem, not the solution.

- Map clear scope boundaries: what this tool does vs. doesn't handle.

- Research actual user language from support tickets, email, conversations, and interviews.

- Keep descriptions concise (300–500 characters) with clear purpose statements.

- Choose 4–6 example phrases representing different linguistic patterns (direct need, permission, process, command, and context).

- Define 2–4 clear boundaries that point to alternative capabilities.

- Plan to iterate based on real usage patterns.

Designing Your Agent's Capability Portfolio

You now understand how to write effective tool descriptions: clear purpose statements, strategic example phrases, well-defined boundaries. The ITEquipmentRequest tool description you've crafted guides the orchestrator toward appropriate decisions when users need to request equipment. Tool descriptions alone don't create a complete agent. They're one piece of a larger capability portfolio that determines what your agent can actually do. The orchestrator needs more than just tools to serve user needs effectively, it needs knowledge sources to answer questions, topics to guide multi-step workflows, and various types of tools to connect with external systems and perform computations.

Consider the HR onboarding agent. When a new employee asks "What's the remote work policy?", they're not trying to trigger a workflow; they want information. A tool isn't the right capability here. The agent needs access to policy knowledge it can retrieve and present conversationally.

When that same employee later says "I want to enroll in benefits," they need a structured process that collects information, validates choices, and submits to HR systems. Now, you need a topic that coordinates multiple steps, possibly calling tools along the way. When the benefits enrollment needs to check whether they're in the enrollment window, the agent might need a tool that queries the HR system in real time to verify eligibility dates.

Knowledge, tools, and topics work together to create complete agent capabilities. The orchestrator selects from this entire portfolio based on what it interprets the user needs. Your job is to design a portfolio where

- Each capability type serves its appropriate purpose

- Capabilities complement, rather than compete with each other

- The orchestrator has clear signals about when to use what

- The complete portfolio covers user needs identified in your stakeholder analysis

Getting the portfolio right (choosing which capabilities to build and in what form) is as important as writing good descriptions and providing clear instructions.

Understanding the Four Capability Types

Before designing your agent's portfolio, you need to understand what each capability type does, and when it's appropriate.

Knowledge sources provide information the agent can retrieve and present conversationally. When users ask questions, seek explanations, or need to understand policies, procedures, or concepts, knowledge sources serve these needs. The agent searches across configured knowledge, finds relevant content, and generates natural language responses grounded in that content.

Tools enable the agent to perform actions: submitting requests, updating records, triggering workflows, performing calculations, or calling external systems. Tools execute specific functions when the orchestrator determines they're needed to fulfill user requests.

Topics provide structured, multi-turn conversations for complex processes requiring specific sequences, conditional logic, or explicit conversational control. When you need to guarantee certain questions get asked in order, or when business logic dictates conversation flow, topics give you that control.

Prompts (a specialized tool type) use generative AI to perform tasks like analysis, summarization, classification, or code execution. When you need the agent to reason about information, transform content, or perform computations beyond simple data retrieval, prompts provide that intelligence.

The boundaries between these types aren't always obvious. A benefits enrollment could be built as a topic (structured dialog) or as a tool called by the orchestrator (flexible invocation). Understanding when each approach serves better is the craft of portfolio design.

Knowledge Sources: The Foundation of Conversational Q&A

Knowledge sources are often the first capability teams configure when building an agent, and it's easy to see why. Most organizations have vast repositories of information: policy documents, procedure guides, training materials, FAQ pages. The promise of an agent that can answer questions from this existing knowledge is compelling and seems straightforward.

However, here's where teams often stumble: they treat knowledge sources like traditional FAQ systems, expecting users to ask questions that match predefined answers. This misses the transformative power of semantic understanding that makes modern AI agents genuinely useful.

Let's start by understanding what's actually happening when your agent uses knowledge sources, because this understanding helps to shape everything about how you should structure your content.

How knowledge actually works in Copilot Studio

When you add knowledge sources like SharePoint sites, OneDrive folders, websites, upload documents, Copilot Studio **processes the content into searchable chunks**.

When users ask questions, the orchestrator performs semantic search across these chunks, identifies the most relevant content, and generates responses grounded in that content.

When a user asks a question, something sophisticated happens behind the scenes. The orchestrator doesn't look for keyword matches or predefined question-answer pairs. Instead, it performs semantic search across your knowledge chunks, identifying content that's conceptually related to the user's question, even if the exact words differ. It then uses this relevant content as grounding material, generating a natural language response that draws from – and cites – your authoritative sources.

This is fundamentally different from keyword matching or FAQ lookup. The agent understands meaning, not just word matching. A user asking "What happens if I quit before my vacation days are used?" can be answered from a document section about "unused PTO at termination" even if those words never appear in the question.

Understanding this distinction is crucial because it changes how you should structure and write your knowledge content. You're not creating a list of anticipated questions with prescribed answers. You're creating a knowledge base that AI can search semantically and draw upon to construct answers to questions you might never have anticipated.

With this mental model in place, let's explore the practical choices you'll face when configuring knowledge sources.

Choosing your knowledge sources

Copilot Studio supports several knowledge source types, each with distinct characteristics that affect how you'll maintain content, how security is handled, and how current the information stays. Choosing the right knowledge source type shapes your ongoing maintenance burden and determines whether your agent stays current as information evolves.

Let's walk through each option, exploring not just what they are but when you'd choose one over another.

SharePoint sites and document libraries represent the most common choice for enterprise knowledge, and for good reason. When you connect your agent to a SharePoint site or document library, the agent automatically syncs with the content. As documents are updated, added, or removed in SharePoint, your agent's knowledge stays current without requiring manual intervention.

This automatic synchronization is powerful but comes with an important consideration: the agent indexes what it has permission to access based on how you configured authentication. You can set the agent to respect user permissions, meaning it will only surface knowledge that the current user has rights to view in SharePoint. This security-aware knowledge retrieval is critical when your knowledge base contains sensitive or role-specific information.

SharePoint excels when your knowledge is collaborative; when multiple people contribute to and maintain documentation, when content requires version control and approval workflows, and when different audience need access to different subsets of information. The HR onboarding agent we've been discussing would benefit from SharePoint knowledge sources because HR policies are living documents, maintained by multiple people, with some content restricted to specific roles.

OneDrive folders provide similar functionality to SharePoint but at an individual level. When you connect to a OneDrive folder, the agent syncs with files in that folder and respects the same update and authentication patterns as SharePoint.

OneDrive makes sense when knowledge ownership is clearer – perhaps a department head maintains a set of reference documents, or a subject matter expert curates resources for a specific domain. It's also useful when you're starting small, testing an agent with a focused knowledge set before expanding to broader SharePoint sites.

The key distinction isn't technical capability – both SharePoint and OneDrive provide similar features. The distinction is organizational: SharePoint suggests collaborative, enterprise-scale knowledge management, while OneDrive suggests individual or small-team content ownership.

Public websites and URLs allow your agent to index content from websites, making this approach suitable when your knowledge is already published online. Perhaps you have extensive product documentation on a public site, or technical guides that live on a corporate intranet. Rather than duplicating this content elsewhere, you can point your agent directly to the web-based sources.

The agent crawls and indexes the site content, much as a search engine would. This works well for relatively stable, published content where the web presence is the authoritative source. However, you're depending on the website's structure and format. If the site reorganizes or if important information is behind interactive elements the crawler can't access, your agent's knowledge may develop gaps.

Public websites work best when you're extending an agent beyond internal knowledge; adding external reference materials, industry standards, or product documentation that exists publicly. They're less suitable as your primary knowledge sources for internal policies and procedures that change frequently.

Uploaded files represent the most straightforward approach: you directly upload PDF, Word, or other document files to Copilot Studio. The platform processes these files just as it would content from other sources, chunking and indexing them for semantic search.

This approach is simple and gives you complete control, but it comes with a significant maintenance burden. Unlike SharePoint or OneDrive, uploaded files don't sync automatically. When a policy document changes, you must remember to download the updated version and re-upload it. For agents with extensive knowledge bases or frequently changing information, this manual process becomes unsustainable.

Uploaded files work best for relatively static reference materials; perhaps industry regulations that change annually, or foundational training content that remains stable. They're also useful during initial agent development when you're testing with a small set of documents before connecting to organizational knowledge systems.

Dataverse tables provide a fundamentally different approach to knowledge. Rather than strong information in documents, you're treating structured data in Dataverse as a knowledge source. This is powerful when your "knowledge" is actually data – product catalogs with specifications, service records with details, or customer information that needs to be surfaced conversationally.

A support agent might query Dataverse tables to answer questions about order status, product availability, or service history. Rather than writing documentation that describes how to look up this information, you're making the data itself directly queryable by the agent.

Dataverse knowledge sources bridge the gap between traditional knowledge (documents and policies) and operational data. They're less common for employee-facing agents like HR onboarding, but crucial for customer service or operational support agents that need real-time access to business data.

Now that we understand what knowledge sources are available, we need to address a more subtle challenge: even with the right knowledge source type, how you organize and write your content dramatically affects whether users get helpful, complete answers or frustrating, partial information.

Structuring content for semantic retrieval

You've chosen your knowledge source type – perhaps SharePoint for your HR policy documents. Now comes the critical part: how should you organize and structure the actual content so the agent can retrieve and present it effectively?

The way you structure content directly affects how the AI chunks it for semantic search, which sections get retrieved together, and whether users receive complete, coherent answers or fragmented, confusing snippets.

Let's start with the fundamental challenge: when your agent searches semantically across knowledge sources, it's not retrieving entire documents. It's retrieving chunks: portions of documents that the system determined are semantically relevant to the user's question. These chunks need to be coherent on their own, contain sufficient context, and relate to the user's actual need.

This chunking reality creates a design problem: how do you structure documents so that meaningful chunks align with how users ask questions, and so that retrieved chunks contain enough context to be genuinely useful?

Document Structure Principles

The foundation of effective knowledge structure is using clear, descriptive headings throughout your documents. The chunking process respects document structure, using headings as signals about where topics begin and end. A well-organized document with clear heading hierarchy helps the orchestrator understand topic boundaries and retrieve focused, relevant sections.

But "clear headings" means more than just proper formatting. It means headings that describe content in the same language users would use to ask about that content. Consider a section of your HR policy document about working remotely. Which heading better serves semantic retrieval?

```
"Section 4.2.2: Flexible Work Arrangements, subsection A"
```

Or

```
"Who can work remotely and how to request approval?"
```

The second heading does something important: it mirrors the question a user would likely ask. When someone asks, "Can I work from home?", the orchestrator can recognize the semantic connection between the question and the heading, making it more likely the right section gets retrieved. The first heading might be proper corporate documentation style, but it does nothing to help the AI understand what the section actually addresses.

This principle extends beyond just headings to how you organize related information. Keep content about a single topic together in coherent sections rather than scattering it across multiple places. If your remote work policy mentions eligibility in one document, requirements in another, and the approval process in a third document, users might receive incomplete answers because the orchestrator retrieves chunks from only one or two sources.

This doesn't mean cramming everything into one single document though! That creates its own problems. It means being thoughtful about what constitutes a "topic" from the user's perspective and keeping that topic's information together. A section about remote work eligibility should include who's eligible, what makes someone eligible, and any exceptions or special cases; all the information a user needs to understand if they qualify. These pieces belong together because they collectively answer a single user question.

Another structural consideration: avoid overly nested document hierarchies. Three levels of headings maximum provide sufficient structure without creating problematic nesting. If you find yourself needing deep nesting to organize content, that's often a signal the document is trying to cover too much and might benefit from being split into focused, topic-specific documents.

With these structural principles in mind, let's turn to a less obvious but equally important consideration: how you actually write the content within those well-structured sections.

Content Style for AI Retrieval

The writing style of your knowledge content matters as much as its structure. Remember, the AI is searching semantically and generating responses grounded in your content. The clearer and more explicit your writing, the better the agent can understand, retrieve, and present that information accurately.

Be explicit rather than implicit. AI handles natural language remarkably well, but explicit statements work better than implied meaning or corporate euphemisms. "Employees can work remotely up to 3 days per week with manager approval" is clearer and more retrievable than "Remote work is generally flexible within reasonable limits subject to business needs and management discretion."

This doesn't mean dumbing down your content or removing important nuance. It means leading with clear statements and adding necessary context and exceptions afterward. "Employees can work remotely up to 3 days per week with manager approval. Some roles may have different arrangements based on business needs; check with your manager if you're unsure" gives users a clear baseline while acknowledging exceptions exist.

Use consistent terminology throughout your knowledge base. If you call something "paid time off" in one document and "vacation days" in another and "PTO" in a third, users asking questions with any of these terms should get consistent, complete information. Inconsistent terminology can fragment knowledge retrieval, where different terms pull different chunks that together would form a complete answer.

The solution isn't to avoid synonyms; natural variation in language is normal and the AI handles it reasonably well. The solution is to be consistent within documents and explicitly acknowledge when you're using different terms for the same thing. "Paid time off (PTO), sometimes called vacation days, includes..." creates that explicit connection.

Provide complete answers within sections. When documenting policies or procedures, include the complete picture in each section rather than spreading information across multiple places with cross-references. A section about benefits enrollment should mention eligibility criteria, timing windows, required information, the submission process, and what happens next; not just "employees can enroll in benefits during open enrollment, see section 7 for eligibility and section 12 for the enrollment process."

Those cross-references made sense in traditional document design where readers flipped through pages sequentially. With semantic retrieval, the orchestrator might retrieve only one section, leaving users with partial information and no awareness that more details exist elsewhere.

Again, this is a balance.

You don't want massive sections that repeat identical information in multiple places, this creates maintenance problems and potential inconsistencies; but, you do want each section to be somewhat self-contained, or at least as much as practical, providing enough information that a user reading just that chunk would have a useful, actionable answer.

Let's look at a concrete example to see how these principles work in practice.

Example: Poorly Versus Well-Structured Knowledge

Imagine your organization has information about remote work scattered across several documents. Here's how it might look with poor structure:

```
Document 1: "HR Policies Overview"
Section 2.4: General Policies
```

"The company supports various flexible work arrangements including
remote work.
Employees interested in remote work should consult the detailed policy
documentation for specific requirements and procedures."

Document 2: "Remote Work Detailed Policy"
Section 1: Eligibility
"Eligibility for remote work is determined based on role requirements,
performance history, and manager discretion. See Manager Responsibilities
guide for approval procedures."

Document 3: "Manager Responsibilities"
Section 5: Various Duties
"...managers are responsible for reviewing remote work requests,
considering operational needs, employee performance, and role suitability
before making approval decisions. The approval process requires submission
of Form RW-1..."

When a user asks "Can I work remotely?", what happens? The orchestrator might
retrieve the overview from Document 1, which essentially says "maybe, look elsewhere
for details." Even if it retrieves eligibility criteria from Document 2, those criteria are
vague and redirect to yet another document. The approval process is buried in a section
about general manager duties in a third document. The user receives fragmented,
incomplete information requiring multiple follow-up questions.

Now consider a better structure:

Document: "Remote Work Policy and Procedures"

Who Can Work Remotely

You can work remotely if you meet these criteria:
            - You've been with the company for 90+ days
            - Your role is designated as remote-eligible (check with your
              manager if unsure)
            - You have consistent good performance (no active
              performance plans)
            - Your manager approves based on team and business needs
            - You have an appropriate home office setup with reliable internet

Some roles cannot work remotely due to facility access requirements or equipment needs. Ask your manager if you're unsure whether your role qualifies.

How Much Remote Work Is Allowed

You can work remotely up to 3 days per week with manager approval. Your manager determines the specific arrangement based on your role, team needs, and business requirements.
Some teams may have different arrangements. Your manager can explain what applies to your specific situation.

How to Request Remote Work Approval

To request remote work arrangements:
1. Discuss your desired schedule with your manager, explaining how you'll maintain productivity and collaboration
2. Submit a Remote Work Request through the HR portal
3. Complete the Home Office Safety Checklist
4. Wait for manager approval (usually within 5 business days)
5. Once approved, your schedule is documented in the HR system
Your manager may ask for a trial period before committing to a permanent arrangement.

Equipment and Support for Remote Work

When working remotely, you'll receive:
- Laptop and necessary peripherals (monitor, keyboard, mouse if needed)
- VPN access to company systems
- Microsoft Teams and collaboration tools
- IT support during business hours via helpdesk

You're responsible for maintaining a quiet, professional workspace with reliable high-speed internet (minimum 25Mbps).

Now when users ask, they get complete, actionable information. "Can I work remotely?" retrieves the eligibility section with clear criteria. "How do I request remote work?" retrieves the step-by-step process. "What equipment do I get?" retrieves the equipment section. Each section stands on its own while connecting to a broader, coherent policy.

Notice several patterns in the better structure:

- **Heading phrases as question**: "Who can work remotely?" mirrors how users actually ask about eligibility. This semantic alignment helps the orchestrator connect user questions to relevant content.

- **Complete information in each section**: The eligibility section doesn't just say "ask your manager"; it provides specific criteria, acknowledges exceptions, and helps users self-assess before needing to ask follow-up questions.

- **Clear, explicit statements**: "You can work remotely up to 3 days per week" is unambiguous. Users know the baseline policy even while understanding their specific situation might vary.

- **Consistent document scope**: All remote work information lives in one place. Users don't bounce between policies, manager guides, and process documents to piece together a complete picture.

- **Contextual information included**: Each section includes enough context to make sense independently. The "How to Request" section doesn't assume you've read the eligibility section first – it's useful even if retrieved in isolation.

This restructuring does require rethinking how organizations traditionally write policy documents. Corporate policies often prioritize legal precision, cross-referencing, and formal structure over natural language and semantic clarity. Building effective agent knowledge sources sometimes means translating existing policies into more agent-friendly formats while maintaining the same core information and requirements.

From Answering Questions to Taking Action

You now understand how to design knowledge sources that help your agent answer questions effectively: structuring content for semantic retrieval, choosing appropriate source types, and configuring behavior to balance security with accessibility. Your HR onboarding agent can explain remote work policies, describe benefits options, and clarify organizational procedures by drawing from well-structured SharePoint documentation.

However, answering questions, no matter how well, represents only half of what makes agents genuinely valuable.

When that employee finishes reading about benefits and says "I want to enroll in the PPO plan," something needs to happen beyond information retrieval. The agent needs to collect enrollment details, validate selections against eligibility rules, submit the enrollment to HR systems, and confirm the transaction. Knowledge sources explain what's possible; tools make it happen.

Quick recap: Knowledge sources for semantic retrieval

- Knowledge sources undergo semantic chunking, not keyword matching; design content accordingly.

- Choose source types based on maintenance needs:

  - SharePoint/OneDrive sync automatically

  - Uploaded files require manual updates

- Structure content with clear, question-like headings that mirror how users naturally ask.

- Write explicitly rather than implicitly; use consistent terminology; provide complete answers within sections.

- Keep related information together so retrieved chunks contain sufficient context.

- Avoid deep nesting (max 3 heading levels) and cross-referencing to other documents.

Tools: Enabling Agent Capabilities

Tools are how your agent performs actions beyond retrieving and presenting information. While knowledge answers questions, tools execute functions: submitting requests, updating records, triggering workflows, performing calculations, calling external APIs.

In Copilot Studio, "tools" is the umbrella term for various capability types that perform actions. Understanding the different tool types helps you choose the right approach for each capability.

Tool Types in Copilot Studio

When you add a tool in Copilot Studio, you're presented with six distinct options, each serving different integration and execution needs. Let's explore what each type does and when you'd choose one over another.

Prompt tools use generative AI to analyze, transform, or reason about information without calling external systems. When you need your agent to summarize text, classify content, extract insights, or perform analysis that requires AI reasoning rather than database lookups, prompt tools provide that intelligence. These tools can also execute code through the code interpreter capability, enabling mathematical calculations, data transformations, or programmatic logic.

Agent flows connect your agent to Power Automate workflows, allowing orchestration of multi-step processes across multiple systems. When your capability requires coordinating actions across different services, implementing complex business logic, or executing established workflows that already exist as Power Automate flows, agent flows provide that integration. These are the workhorses of enterprise integration, leveraging Power Platform's extensive connector ecosystem.

Custom connectors extend beyond Power Platform's standard connector library when you need to integrate with proprietary systems, internal APIs, or services that don't have pre-built connectors. If your organization has custom applications, legacy systems, or specialized services that need agent integration, custom connectors provide the bridge.

REST API tools offer a lightweight alternative to custom connectors when you need direct API integration without the overhead of building a full connector. When you have well-documented REST APIs and want quick integration, REST API tools provide straightforward connectivity.

Model Context Protocol (MCP) tools represent an emerging standard for AI-agent-to-service communication. MCP servers expose tools and resources that agents can discover and use dynamically. This approach works well when integrated with services that already implement MCP or when building integration patterns that multiple agents will share.

Computer use (in preview at time of writing) enables agents to directly interact with web and desktop applications through a controlled browser or desktop environment. This experimental capability allows agents to navigate user interfaces, fill forms, and interact with applications as a human would, useful for legacy systems without APIs or for workflows requiring visual interface interaction.

Let's explore the most common tool types in depth, understanding not just their technical characteristics but also the practical decisions that determine when each approach serves your needs best.

Prompt Tools: AI-Powered Reasoning and Analysis

Prompt tools represent a fundamentally different approach to agent capabilities. Rather than calling external systems or databases, they use generative AI to process information, make judgments, or perform transformations that require reasoning rather than retrieval.

When Prompt Tools Excel

Prompt tools shine when your capability needs intelligence rather than integration. Consider these scenarios:

Analysis and categorization: A support agent receives unstructured feedback from customers. A prompt tool can analyze sentiment, categorize issues by department, extract key concerns, and identify urgency level. All tasks requiring interpretation rather than database queries.

Content transformation: An HR agent needs to convert policy documents written in formal legal language into plain-language explanations for new employees. A prompt tool can rewrite content while preserving meaning, adjusting tone and complexity appropriately.

Pattern recognition: A procurement agent reviews expense reports to identify potential policy violations or unusual patterns. Rather than rigid rule-checking, a prompt tool can recognize contextual anomalies that merit human review.

Code execution and calculations: Through the code interpreter capability, prompt tools can execute Python code to perform complex calculations, data analysis, statistical operations, or algorithmic processing that goes beyond what simple formulas can handle.

Designing Effective Prompt Tools

Creating prompt tools requires a different mindset than designing integration-based tools. You're instructing an AI how to think about a problem rather than specifying exact steps to execute.

Start with clear objective: what specific reasoning or transformation does this tool need to perform? `"Analyze customer feedback"` is too vague. `"Identify the primary issue category, sentiment (positive/neutral/negative), and whether immediate response is needed based on tone and content"` provides better guidance.

Context and constraints: the prompt tool needs to understand boundaries and expectations. Without clear constraints, AI reasoning can wander into areas outside your intended scope or make assumptions that don't align with organizational policies.

For an expense analysis tool, effective context setting looks like:

```
"You are analyzing expense reports for policy compliance. Company policy
allows: meals up to $75 per person for client meetings, hotels up to
$300/night in major cities ($200/night elsewhere), ground transportation
including rideshare and taxis, and economy airfare for domestic travel
(business class allowed for international flights over 6 hours). Identify
expenses that exceed these limits or fall into unexpected categories. Flag
potential issues but do not make final approval decisions; those require
human judgment."
```

This context gives the AI the reference framework it needs while making clear where its authority ends. The tool can identify issues but explicitly cannot approve or reject expenses.

Include examples of expected reasoning: just as tool descriptions benefit from example phrases showing varied user language, prompt tools benefit from example scenarios that demonstrate the reasoning you expect.

Consider including examples like:

- "Example: 'dinner with Northwind traders team - $520 for 8 people' > analysis: within policy (under $75 per person). Client meeting clearly stated. No issues identified."

- "Example: 'Hotel stay - $450/night in New York City' > Analysis: exceeds policy limit for major cities. Requires justification or approval exception"

These examples serve as reasoning templates. The AI learns not just what to evaluate but how to think about edge cases and how to communicate its analysis clearly.

Define output structure: specify the format you need rather than leaving it open-ended. Structured output integrates more easily with subsequent workflow steps and ensures consistent, parseable respsonses.

"Provide your analysis in this format:
- Compliance status: [compliant/ require review/ policy violation]
- Issue (if any): [brief notification of the concern]
- Recommended action: [approve/ request justification/ escalate to manager]
- Reasoning: [one sentence explaining your determination]"

This structure means every response follows the same pattern, making it straightforward for your agent to present results consistently or for subsequent tools to process the analysis programmatically.

Handle uncertainty gracefully: AI reasoning works with probabilities, not certainties. Your prompt tool design should acknowledge this reality and guide the AI toward appropriate behavior when confidence is low.

"If the expense category is ambiguous or you cannot determine compliance from the information provided, set status to 'Requires review' and not what additional information would help make a determinations. Never guess or make assumptions when key details are missing."

This instruction prevents the tool from fabricating reasoning when it lacks sufficient information. Better to flag uncertainty than to provide confident but incorrect analysis.

Code Interpreter Considerations

The code interpreter is a specialized prompt tool that lets your agent run sandboxed Python code in isolation. This makes it possible to do calculations, change data shapes, or run statistical tests that go beyond simple formulas. Let's take a look at when to use the code interpreter and some good practices in using it:

When the code interpreter is the right choice: use it when the task needs real computation, not just text changes or lookups. Good examples are

- Statistical tests, such as checking if the number of support tickets this week is much higher than normal

- Financial forecasts, such as working out the total cost of a purchase plan over six months

- Cleaning and reshaping data that arrives in different formats, such as short CSV tables or bullet lists

- Optimization tasks, such as finding the lowest-cost travel option that still follows policy rules

Security and sandbox limits: The code runs in a protected area. It cannot reach the Internet, cannot save files, and can use only a fixed list of libraries (at the time of writing: pandas, numpy, scipy, sympy, matplotlib, and a few others). Write these limits directly into the prompt:

```
"You are in a secure sandbox. You may use only these libraries: pandas,
numpy, scipy, statsmodels, sympy, matplotlib, seaborn, networkx, pulp. Do
not try to use the internet, read or write files, or install new packages.
If the task needs a library that is not listed, answer 'External library
required' and suggest a different way to do the work."
```

Clean the input data first: data from users is often messy. Tell the model to fix common problems before it starts the main work:

```
"Remove currency symbols, commas, and extra spaces from money values, then
change them to numbers (float). Treat empty cells as NaN. If more than 20
% of the rows cannot be read correctly, answer 'Data quality too low' and
list the rows that caused problems."
```

Keep the code fast: Code that takes too long will stop. Guide the model to stay quick:

"Use pandas vectorised operations when possible. Do not write loops that run more than 10 000 times. If the data has more than 500 rows, take a random sample of 30 % (keep the same mix of categories) and add a note: 'Result is based on a sample; the full result may be different'."

Make the results easy to understand: give the answer in two parts so anyone can follow it:

"Return the answer in two sections:

1. A JSON block with the exact numbers (for example: total_cost, p_value, risk_score).

2. One short paragraph in plain English that a manager can read without technical knowledge. Include any assumptions and the confidence level."

Add simple tests: put a few known cases in the system prompt. The model must check them first:

"Before you give the final answer, run these tests:

Test 1: 'Dinner, 6 people, $420' → cost per person $70 → compliant.

Test 2: 'Hotel in New York, $450 per night' → higher than $300 limit → policy_violation.

If a test fails, show the failure message and give a corrected code piece."

Keep track of changes: treat the prompt as code. Give it a version name (e.g., expense_analyzer_v1.4) and store it in the same solution as the agent. If a new model version changes how numbers are rounded, you can go back to the old prompt quickly.

Figure 7-5 below shows a complete, example-driven instruction layout for a code interpreter style agent. Rather than relying on a single block of text, the instructions are deliberately decomposed into role definition, task constraints, input handling, output format and validation; making the agent's responsibilities explicit and testable.

Role & Objective
What: Define who the AI is and its one main job
Why: Gives the model a clear identity and focus
How: "You are ExpenseAssistant, an AI that runs Python code to check expense items against company policy"

Task description
What: Explain the exact job in one sentence
Why: Prevents the model from doing extra or wrong work
How: "For each expense item, write and run code to check policy limits and return a result"

Input handling
What: List accepted formats and cleaning rules
Why: User data is messy - this makes it safe to use
How: "
- Accept: free text, bullet list, or CSV block
- Convert to Pandas DataFramewith columns: date, item, category, amount, currency, notes
- Clean rules:
    - Remove $,£, commas from amount
    - Change amount to float
    - Empty cells - NaN
    - If >20% row fail, return 'Data error'"

Output format (JSON)
What: Defines exact JSON structure
Why: Makes it easy to read and use in other tools
How: "
```
{
  'result': [any numbers or summary],
  'explanation': [one plain-English sentence],
  'confidence': [high | medium | low],
  'code_used': [code snippet],
  'warnings': 'text or null'
}
```
"

Reasoning examples
What: Show real input - expected JSON
Why: Teaches the model how to think and format
How: "
- Input: 'Sales: Jan $1200, Feb $1500, Mar $1100'
- {'result': {'total': 3800, 'avg': 1266.67},
    'explanation': 'Sum of three months...',
    'confidence': 'high'}"

Unit tests (run before final answer)
What: Add 2 - 3 small tests the model must pass
Why: Catches mistakes before the user sees them
How: "
- Test 1: 'Cost: $75, $120' - results.total = 195
- Test 2: 'Empty row' - confidence = 'low'

Figure 7-5. *A structured instruction template for a code-interpreter*

Validating Your Design: Evaluation and Testing

Designing an agent is as much about validating your assumptions as it is about defining capabilities or shaping conversations. Once you understand what the agent should do and how users are likely to phrase their requests, the next question becomes: does the system actually behave the way we think it will? Evaluation is the discipline that answers this. It gives you a structured way to examine the agent's reasoning before users experience it.

It would be natural to think of evaluations as a late-stage activity; something performed once the agent is "finished." In reality, evaluation begins during design. Every capability boundary you draw, every action description you write, and every knowledge source you curate embodies a prediction about how the orchestrator will interpret user needs. Those predictions must be tested early, and repeatedly.

At design time, the goal is not to measure performance in the statistical sense; it is to surface blind spots, ambiguities, and orchestration behaviors you did not anticipate. You are validating the mental model you have constructed for the agent, and refining it based on evidence.

Evaluations begin at design time   Although Copilot Studio provides powerful evaluation tooling, the principles of evaluation begin during design.

You define the scenarios, the expected behavior and the linguistic patterns your agent must understand **before** you build anything.

In Chapter 8, we'll explore how Copilot runs evaluations, but the thinking that underpins them starts here.

Building Test Sets That Represent Real Behavior

The first step is to create a set of prompts that represent how people will actually interact with the agent. Copilot Studio offers several ways to build these evaluation sets, each with a different purpose.

One of the quickest places to start is with AI-generated test prompts. The system can generate a handful of representative questions based on your capabilities and agent description. These are useful for stress-testing the basics: does the orchestrator recognize the capability? Does it retrieve the right knowledge? Does it attempt to take an action where it should not? These prompts are only a starting point, however. They often vary in quality, and because they are generated without context of your organization or your users' language, they require review. Some will be irrelevant, some too generic, and some will need refining before they are useful. But, they are an efficient entry point in the early stages of design.

A second source of evaluation prompts comes from your own exploratory testing. As you work through your agent manually, posing questions, trying different phrasings, pushing the boundaries, Copilot Studio can automatically turn those inputs into test cases. This is particularly valuable because these prompts reflect your immediate, human understanding of how a request might be expressed. Often, the most revealing orchestration failures happen during this exploratory phase, when you are testing the edges of what the agent can do. Capturing these as formal test cases ensures they remain part of your evaluation suite as the design matures.

The most valuable prompts, however, are the ones you add manually. These are the hard cases; nuanced, high-risk, or pivotal scenarios that deserve explicit attention. A privacy-related HR question; a safety scenario where the agent must decline; an ambiguous IT request that could trigger several different capabilities. These prompts reflect the edge conditions of your design: the situations where you most need the agent to behave predictably. A small number of carefully chosen examples usually does more to strengthen the design than a much larger volume of unreviewed ones. Quality beats quantity here.

Across these methods, the intention is the same: assemble a set of questions that truly represent your users, not idealized "sample conversations," but the messy, informal, condensed phrases people use in real environments.

Defining the Acceptance Criteria

Before you evaluate a single prompt, you have to decide what "good" looks like. Each scenario is tied to an acceptance criterion; a short statement describing the standard you expect the agent to meet. In some situations, that criterion is accuracy: the information must be factually correct and grounded in approved sources. In others, the priority might be relevance, personalization, or the ability to abstain. Some scenarios carry safety considerations, others require privacy-preserving behavior.

These criteria shape everything that follows. They determine what the expected response should contain, which test method is used to evaluate it. Together, these elements anchor the evaluation in reality.

The expected response is not always a verbatim paragraph for the agent to repeat. In many cases, it simply contains the essential facts or semantics that the answer must express. For example, for an HR benefits that agent asked "What is my premium this year?"; the expected response may contain nothing more than "$450 per month"; the detail that must appear for the answer to be considered correct. In privacy scenarios, the expected response may simply be "I cannot disclose that information." In safety scenarios, it might be "I'm not able to provide medical advice."

The expected response defines the boundaries of acceptable behavior, not the wording.

Choosing How to Evaluate the Agent's Answer

Copilot Studio provides several evaluation methods that determine what counts as a "pass."

The most flexible method and the one used frequently is *General Quality*. Instead of comparing the response to an expected answer, the model judges the quality of the reply across four dimensions: how complete the answer is, how grounded it is in available information, how relevant it is to the user's intent, and whether the agent appropriately abstains when the question is out of scope. This method works well for broader informational questions where many valid phrasings exist.

Where precision matters, personalized responses, privacy, compliance, or safety, the *Similarity* method is more appropriate. Here, the agent's answer is compared semantically to the expected response you defined. The phrasing can vary, but the meaning must match. This approach gives you a consistent way to ensure critical details are expressed correctly.

A stricter variant, *Text Match*, is useful only when specific wording or identifiers must appear, for example, code, plan names, or key numerical values.

These methods are not about judging prose. They are about confirming that the agent behaves in alignment with the design, the policies, and the acceptance criteria you defined earlier.

Running Evaluations and Learning from Failure

Running an evaluation produces a detailed report: a pass/fail result for each test case, an overall score, and a breakdown of where the agent struggled. You can export these results into your design artifacts, allowing you to track progress over time or share findings with stakeholders.

The value of evaluation lies not in the score itself but in the analysis that follows. Each failure points to something concrete: a capability boundary that needs tightening, an action description that needs clearer disambiguation, a knowledge source that must be structured differently, or a prompt that reveals a phrasing pattern you did not anticipate. Evaluation is a feedback mechanism, a source of insight into what the agent misunderstood and why.

This is the point where design and evaluation start to loop. You refine the description, adjust the knowledge, add new prompts, tighten the criteria, and test again. Each cycle reduced the risk of unexpected behavior in production.

Connecting Design-Time Evaluation to Real-World Performance

Design-time evaluation prepares the agent for its first interaction with users. It establishes a baseline for correctness and consistency. Once the agent is deployed, production monitoring takes over, showing you what users actually ask, which answers land well, which do not, and where the agent struggles under real conditions.

The two phases are inseparable.

Design-time evaluation shapes the agent's initial behavior.

Production monitoring helps you refine it over time

The work you do here, defining criteria, crafting evaluation sets, and understanding failure patterns, sets the foundation for everything that follows.

Linking Evaluation Design Back to Stakeholders, Requirements, and Value

When you reach the point of designing evaluation test sets, you are not starting from nothing. You are building on a foundation laid much earlier in the process. Evaluation is not an isolated technical step; it is where the decisions made in the opportunity framing and value clarity stages become concrete, testable, and accountable.

By the time you arrive here in Chapter 7, you have already identified the people who matter, the work they struggle with, the value they expect, and the outcomes the organization is trying to improve. Through the conversations in Chapter 3, you uncovered the friction points that shape demand for an agent, the expectations stakeholders hold for its usefulness, and the risks they are unwilling to accept. Those insights were not academic; they form the backbone of your evaluation plan.

The scenarios you choose to test should reflect the scenarios stakeholders told you mattered most. If frontline employees said that waiting for policy answers slows their work, then your evaluation set must include prompts that reflect the natural language they use when asking for those answers, not the neat, formal phrasing we imagine in our heads. If managers emphasized accuracy and compliance, your acceptance criteria must reflect that, with test methods calibrated to assess groundedness and factual correctness. If the HR director expressed concerns about inconsistent interpretations of eligibility rules, then you should have boundary cases designed to stress-test those distinctions.

Evaluations, in other words, becomes the **operationalization of value clarity**. It is where qualitative insight turns into behavioral expectation; where "this matters" becomes "this must work reliably." With this grounding established, we can now turn to the practical question: how to construct evaluation sets that reliably validate the agent's behavior before it reaches users.

Let's walk through evaluation step by step, using the HR onboarding agent as an example.

Step One: Create Test Sets That Represent Real Usage

A strong design-time test set does three things. It reflects the real scenarios that matter most to users, it captures the language people naturally use when expressing those needs, and it deliberately probes the boundaries where your capabilities could be confused or misapplied. When a test set does these three things, the results it produces begin to resemble real-world performance. This is what makes evaluation valuable: it gives you evidence about behavior, not just correctness.

Four ways to build test sets

Copilot Studio provides multiple approaches for creating test cases, each suited to different situations:

- **Generate test cases automatically**: Copilot Studio can create ten test questions based on your agent's configured capabilities; topics, tools and knowledge sources. This option provides quick initial coverage: "What's PTO?", "How do I request a laptop?", "Tell me about benefits options."

Use auto-generation when

- Starting evaluation for the first time and need baseline test coverage

- Adding a new capability and want immediate test cases

- Exploring what types of questions the system considers relevant

Auto-generated questions provide starting points but lack the linguistic variety and edge cases that manual test creation offers. Use them to establish initial coverage, then supplement with more targeted test cases.

- **Import from CSV or spreadsheet**: Upload a file containing questions collected from real user interactions; support tickets, email requests, slack messages, Teams conversations. This grounds your test set in actual user language rather than assumed phrasings.

Your import file should include columns for

- **Question**: the user's request or query

- **Test method**: How to evaluate the response (covered in the next section)

- **Expected response (optional)**: For similarity-based testing

For the HR onboarding agent, import a CSV containing 30+ phrases gathered during user research:

```
"How do I sign up for insurance?"
"need laptop"
"Can I work from home on Fridays?"
"What's the PTO policy?"
"I'm getting married - what do I do about benefits?"
```

Importing real user language ensures tests reflect how people actually communicate, not how you imagine they'll communicate.

- **Pull from test chat history**: If you've been testing your agent manually, Copilot Studio can extract questions from those test conversations and convert them into test cases. This captures the exploratory testing you've already done and makes it repeatable.

  Use chat history extraction when

  - You've conducted extensive manual testing during development

  - Stakeholders have tested the agent and you want to formalize their scenarios

  - You want to preserve edge cases discovered during interactive testing

- **Add cases manually**: For specific scenarios that automated generation or imports might miss, add individual test cases directly in the interface. This allows precise control over test case phrasing, test methods, and coverage of edge cases.

  Add manual test cases for

  - Boundary scenarios between related capabilities

  - Deliberately ambiguous requests that could match multiple capabilities

  - Edge cases with unusual phrasing, typos, or abbreviated language

  - Context-dependent requests where the same words require different responses

Structuring Test Cases

Regardless of how you generate initial test cases, organize them to cover three validation dimensions that test different aspects of orchestration quality:

Positive cases verify correct capabilities trigger for expected requests:

```
"What's the remote work policy?" > should retrieve knowledge about
remote work
"I need a new laptop" > should trigger equipment request tool
"Enroll me in benefits" > should start benefits enrollment topic
```

For the HR onboarding agent, positive cases confirm the agent handles the core use cases you designed for. Aim for 60–70% of your test set to be positive cases representing the most common user needs.

Boundary cases validate that related but different requests trigger appropriate alternatives:

```
"My laptop is broken" > should trigger IT support, not equipment request
"Where's my equipment order" > should trigger order tracking, not
new request
"What benefits do we offer?" > should retrieve knowledge, not start
enrollment
```

Boundary cases are a direct reflection of your capability design. The "Do NOT use for…" guidance you wrote when defining each tool is put to the test here. If your boundaries are well-defined, boundary cases should behave cleanly. If the orchestrator mixes capabilities, it is often because the design needs tightening, not because the model failed. You should allocate 20–30% of test cases to boundaries.

Edge cases confirm handling of unusual language, ambiguity, or unexpected contexts:

```
"PTO" > abbreviated, lacks context, but should retrieve PTO information
"I need a laptop but mine still works" > contradictory statement requiring
clarification
"Remote work?" > extremely terse, needs interpretation as
information request
```

Edge cases test for robustness; does the agent handle imperfect user language gracefully? These represent 10–20% of test cases but reveal failure modes that erode user trust when they occur in production.

Step Two: Configure Test Methods

Each test case uses a test method that determines how Copilot Studio evaluates whether the agent's response is acceptable. The test method defines what "passing" means for that specific question.

Three Available Test Methods

Quality method evaluates whether responses meet general quality standards: relevance and completeness, without comparing to a specific, expected answer. This method asks: "did the agent provide a helpful, relevant response to the question?"

Quality evaluation works by assessing

- **Relevance**: Does the response address what the user actually asked?

- **Completeness**: Does the response provide sufficient information to be useful?

Use the quality method when

- The exact wording of responses doesn't matter, only that they're helpful

- Questions can be answered correctly in multiple ways

- You want to test general agent competence rather than specific outputs

- Knowledge retrieval questions where many valid responses exist

For the HR onboarding scenario, questions like "what's the remote work policy?", quality method confirms the agent retrieves relevant policy information and presents it completely, without requiring specific phrasing.

Similarity method compares the agent's actual response to an expected response you provide, evaluating whether they have the same meaning even if worded differently. This method asks "did the agent say essentially what we expected it to say?"

Similarity evaluation assesses semantic equivalence; the agent's response must convey the same core information as the expected response, but exact wording doesn't need to match.

Use similarity method when

- Specific information must be included in responses

- You want to verify the agent provides particular details consistently

- Certain facts or policy points must be communicated

- Testing that refinements haven't changed what the agent tells users

For a test case "how many PTO days do new employees get?", similarity method verifies the agent's response aligns with your expected response: "new employees receive 21 days PTO in their first year." The agent might say "you'll get 21 days PTO during your first year" (different wording, same meaning) and still pass.

The third method, *Text Match*, is the strictest. It requires the agent's response to contain a specific phrase, keyword, or value exactly as written. Unlike Similarity method, which tolerates changes in wording as long as the meaning is preserved, **Text Match is literal**. It is used sparingly, but when required, it provides an unambiguous way to test for information that must appear in particular form.

Most generative interactions are not suited to strict matching, but some scenarios genuinely require it. Codes, identifiers, fixed labels, or mandatory keywords in safety-critical or compliance-critical situations often need exact reproduction. For example, a policy might require that the phrase "21 days PTO" appear precisely, or that an employee be shown a specific code during onboarding. In those circumstances, Text Match allows you to confirm that the agent includes the required language every time, without risking semantic drift.

Because Text Match leaves no room for interpretation, it should be used only when exact wording matters. For everything else, Similarity and Quality methods allow the agent the flexibility that generative systems are designed for.

Step Three: Run Evaluations and Interpret Results

With test sets created and test methods configured, execute evaluations to generate performance data showing how your agent handles the test scenarios.

Running bulk evaluations

Clicking "Evaluate" on a test set will run all test cases. Copilot Studio processes each question through your agent, captures responses, applies the configured test message and generates a pass/fail result. However, evaluation is not a pass/fail moment, it is an iterative cycle. You should expect the first run to surface gaps, misinterpretations, or unexpected behaviors. That is the point.

Each evaluation highlights where the design needs attention; whether in capability descriptions, knowledge structuring, or acceptance criteria, so that you can refine it and test again. Over a few cycles, the agent becomes more predictable, more trustworthy, and better aligned with the value you set out to deliver.

Understanding Evaluation Results

When you run an evaluation, Copilot Studio shows a pass rate for the test set, along with a detailed view of how each question performed. You can drill into individual results or export into Excel or CSV. The export includes both the expected and actual responses, the test method users, the model's explanation of why a case passed or failed, and any errors encountered. This makes it straightforward to sort, filter, and analyze patterns, especially when you are looking for the types of failures that repeat across capabilities or phrasing variations.

Closing

Regardless of how they are generated, test cases should collectively represent the three dimensions of behavior you care most about: the typical scenarios users will encounter day-to-day, the boundary conditions where capabilities might compete for relevance, and the linguistic or contextual edge cases that expose brittleness. Together, these dimensions give you a rounded picture of how the agent behaves.

Design-time evaluation brings the agent as close as possible to the behavior you intended. It gives you structured evidence that the orchestrator interprets language correctly, that boundaries between capabilities hold, and that the scenarios which matter most to stakeholders are handled with consistency. It closes the design loop.

But, it does not close the journey.

To this point in the book, we have focused on framing opportunities, building value foundations, and shaping solutions, the first three stages of the Value by Design approach. These stages give you and organizations the clarity, structure, and design discipline needed to create agents that are capable, safe, and genuinely useful.

With this chapter, we reach the end of Stage 3.

What comes next is fundamentally different.

Stage 4 – **Value in Motion** – is about what happens after the agent is released into the real world. It is about how agents behave when people rely on them, when usage patterns shift, when policies change, when unexpected questions appear, and when value must be proven rather than anticipated. It is the moment where design gives way to operations, and where the organization must take responsibility for sustaining performance, trust, and alignment over time.

Evaluation tells you whether the agent meets the behavior you designed. Telemetry tells you whether it meets the behavior the organization needs.

The next chapter opens this final phase of the framework. It explores how telemetry, monitoring, and improvement loops give you a living picture of how the agent performs (day by day), conversation by conversation. It shows how insights surface, how issues are identified, how value is measured, and how continuous improvement becomes part of the operating model rather than an occasional exercise.

This is where value becomes durable.

This is where agents become part of how the organization works.

This is where design intent meets real-world truth.

With that, we turn to **Chapter 8** and begin the final stage of the Value by Design journey: Value in Motion

Value in Motion

Where value is no longer predicted but proven.

There is a moment in every AI project when the design work is done, the agent is built, and the team steps back. For a brief second, it feels as if the journey is complete. The capabilities behave as expected. The evaluation sets pass. The agent is ready.

But this is the moment where most stories end far too early. In reality, this is the point where the work truly begins.

Up to now, the Value by Design framework has focused on the thinking, alignment, decisions, and craft that go into making agents that are useful, safe, and grounded in organizational purpose. Stage One helped you frame the opportunity; Stage Two built the foundations of value; Stage Three shaped a solution that people would want to use.

With Stage Four, the entire orientation shifts.

This stage focuses on **running the agent** and ensuring it continues to deliver value long after launch.

It asks a different set of questions:

- How does the agent behave when real people depend on it?

- What patterns emerge when hundreds or thousands of interactions accumulate?

- Where does value appear, and where does it leak away?

- How do you evolve an agent when the organization changes around it?

- And how do you sustain trust, quality, and alignment over time?

If the first three stages built the promise of value, Stage Four is where that value becomes **observable, measurable, and resilient.**

This is the stage where

- Telemetry replaces assumption

- Evidence replaces optimism

- Improvement becomes continuous

- And agents become part of the operating fabric of the organization

Most importantly, this stage reveals a truth that sits at the center of the Value by Design philosophy:

Value is not created at launch

Value is created in motion

It is created through every interaction, every refinement, every insight surfaced by monitoring, every small improvement made by a team that cares about what the agent is becoming. It is created through stewardship, thoughtful, persistent, evidence-driven stewardship, not through one-off delivery.

This final stage is where organizations differentiate themselves – not in their ability to build an agent, but in their ability to **sustain and grow its impact.**

Welcome to Stage Four: **Value in Motion** – the operating world of AI agents. A world where design evolves into practice, where value becomes durable, and where the work of the organization and the work of the agent move forward together.

CHAPTER 8

Telemetry, Monitoring, and Improvement Loops

Every agent behaves perfectly in isolation. It responds to clean prompts, follows the patterns you designed for it, and performs exactly as expected. In a controlled environment, behavior is predictable because the inputs are predictable. Evaluation gives you confidence that the agent can perform the work it was designed to do.

However, the moment real users begin interacting with it, the conditions change.

The prompts become messier; the requests vary in detail, tone, and intent. The workflows you anticipated merge with ones you didn't. People ask for things in ways no test set can fully anticipate, and the agent's behavior becomes something that can only be understood through what it does in motion, not what it did in isolation.

This is where telemetry matters. Telemetry is the mechanism through which organizations learn the truth about their agents. It reveals how design decisions hold up under real conditions, how often the agent makes the right choices, where it struggles, and how its behavior evolves as usage grows. Telemetry is the bridge between design-time confidence and operational reality.

Telemetry As the Source of Truth

Telemetry gives you the **observational data** you need to understand how an agent functions once it meets the realities of organizational life (shown in Figure 8-1).

It reveals patterns of use, moments of friction, and areas where people either depend on, or attempt to use the agent in ways you did not anticipate. It also brings to light the signals that indicate strong performance, emerging risk, or opportunities for refinement.

© Steve Jeffery 2026
S. Jeffery, *Value by Design with Microsoft Copilot Studio,* https://doi.org/10.1007/979-8-8688-2613-9_8

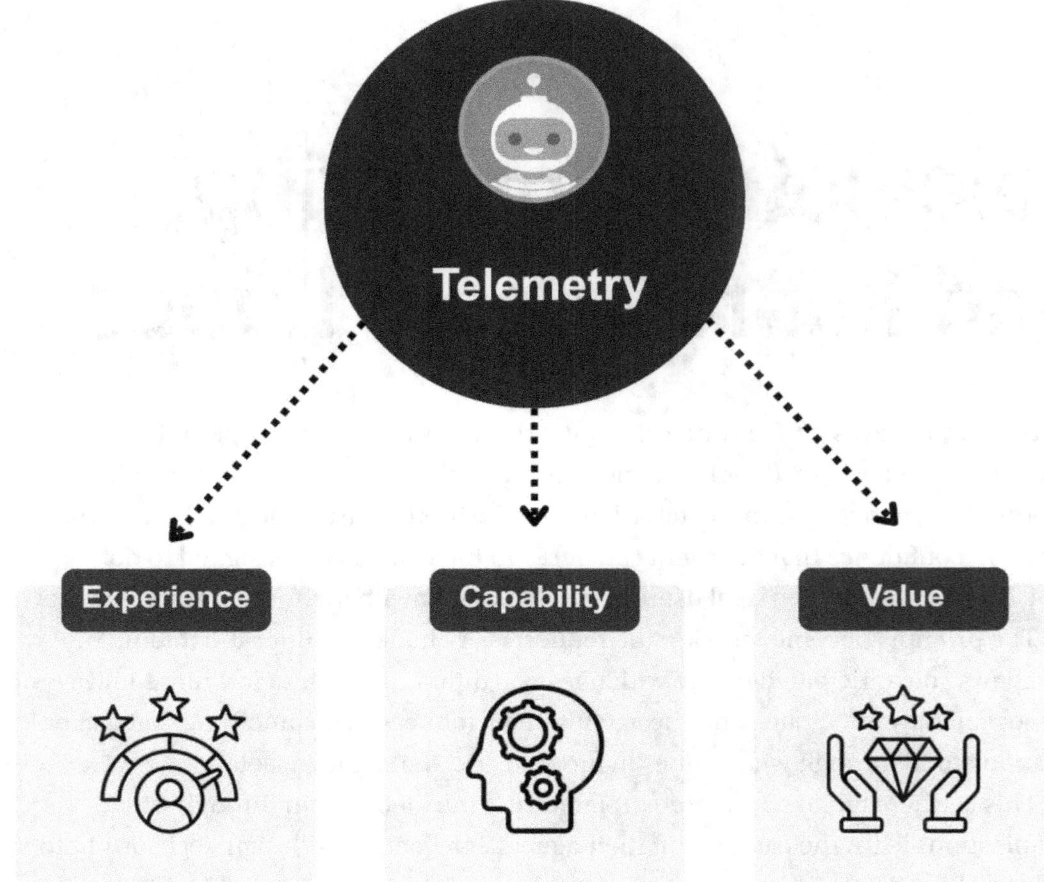

Figure 8-1. *Telemetry across experience, capability, and value*

Telemetry is not a single stream of data. It operates across distinct layers, each revealing a different truth about how an agent behaves once it enters real work. Together, these layers show how interactions, internal decisions, and outcomes connect; and where value begins to form as work moves through the system.

Together, they create a full picture of how work flows through the system and where value emerges. Let's look at the first layer of telemetry: experience.

Experience Telemetry: Understanding How People Engage

The first layer capture how people interact with the agent. Every question and request tells you something about real usage. This includes[1]

- The volume and timing of interactions

- The topics that attract the most questions

- The queries that appear most frequently

- The questions that appear unexpectedly

- The points where users abandon a conversation

- The moment where they seek help, escalate, or try again

These signals reveal the shape of demand.

They show which scenarios occur in daily work, which ones generate uncertainty, and which ones drive people to rely on the agent more heavily. Experience telemetry also highlights the gaps.

Unanswered questions, unclear phrasings, and patterns of repeated attempts often indicate where users are struggling or where the agent is not interpreting intent as expected. These signals help to identify opportunities for knowledge expansion, capability adjustments, or improvements to phrasing and guidance.

Experience telemetry becomes essential for understanding how the agent is being used as intended, when it is performing a role you may not have originally designed for.

The second layer observes the internal decision the agent makes.

Capability Telemetry: Understanding How the Agent Behaves

Here, telemetry is showing which capabilities the orchestrator activates, how often they succeed, and where capability boundaries need attention.

Key capability signals include[2]

- Which capabilities were triggered[3]

---

[1] https://learn.microsoft.com/en-us/microsoft-copilot-studio/analytics-bot
[2] https://learn.microsoft.com/en-us/microsoft-copilot-studio/analytics
[3] https://learn.microsoft.com/en-us/microsoft-copilot-studio/actions

- How often the agent selected the correct capability

- Where the agent attempted to use the wrong one

- Success and failure rates for specific tools

- Unexpected sequences or interruptions

- Moments where guardrails intervened

- Decline behavior for safety, privacy, or accuracy reasons

Capability telemetry offers insight into the agent's internal reasoning. It shows you your action descriptions, boundaries, use cases, and knowledge structures shape orchestration decisions. When capability signals drift from expected patterns, it often indicates that the design needs refinement or that user behavior has changed in ways the agent is not yet handling effectively.

This layer forms the foundation for safe and predictable agent behavior. It helps areas where controlled adjustments can strengthen stability and reduce risk.

Value Telemetry: Understanding Whether Outcomes Emerge

The third layer focuses on outcomes.

It answers the question that sits at the center of Value by Design: Is the agent creating meaningful organizational value?

Outcome signals include

- Evidence of time saved

- Improvements in decision speed or clarity

- Increased throughput

- Error reductions

- Compliance improvements

- Reduced administrative burden

- Patterns of self-service adoption

- Indicators of user confidence

- Behavioral changes that align with desired ways of working

These signals map directly to your success architecture from Chapter 4. They show whether the organization is moving toward the outcomes that shaped the opportunity, the requirements and the design. Value telemetry makes the work measurable and visible. It allows teams to track value over time and understand how the agent's presence changes the flow of daily work.

How to Interpret Telemetry Across Three Layers

Telemetry only becomes useful when it is interpreted through the same lenses that shaped the opportunity:

- The value outcomes

- The performance expectations

- The risks that matter

- The behaviors the organization hoped to influence

With this grounding, telemetry reduces to activity counts and surface-level measurements that reveal very little.

Reading telemetry well is a skill. It begins with understanding what you were trying to achieve in the first place.

Before exploring any dashboard, return to the foundations you set earlier:

- What value was this agent expected to create?

- What performance conditions mattered most?

- Which risks required active monitoring?

- Which behaviors were a priority to influence or shift?

- What assumptions underpinned your design?

These questions frame the way you interpret any telemetry signal. They ensure you look for evidence of progress, not artifacts of activity.

Understanding What the Data Is Showing You

Good telemetry reading starts by asking: *"What behavior does this signal represent?"*

A spike in unanswered queries may reflect missing knowledge, but it may also reflect a change in organizational policy, a seasonal surge, or users attempting to treat the agent as something it is not.

A sudden increase in escalations may indicate confusion, or it may be evidence that the agent is correctly declining unsafe or uncertain requests. A drop in capability success may reflect technical issues, or it may be signaling a shift in how users describe their needs.

The skill here lies in recognizing that each metric expresses a behavioral truth about one of three things:

- How people work

- How the agent interprets that work

- How value flows (or fails to flow) through the system

Reading telemetry is, at its heart, reading how the organization works.

Looking for Alignment or Misalignment with Value Benefits

The agent you're building is designed to encourage behavior your organization wants more of, or less of, and thresholds it needs to protect. When you read telemetry through the value lens (operational, strategic, and transformational), signals begin to reveal whether the agent is reinforcing the organizations goals or drifting away from them.

Telemetry only becomes meaningful when it is interpreted through intent. The same signal can indicate progress, risk, or opportunity depending on the value lens you apply. Reading telemetry through operational, strategic, and transformational perspectives helps teams distinguish activity from impact, and recognize whether the agent is reinforcing the outcomes it was designed to support.

	Experience	**Capability**	**Value**
Operational	Where do users hesitate or repeat steps?	Are workflows executing smoothly?	Is effort actually being reduced?
Strategic	Are users confident in guidance?	Are decisions handled consistently?	Are outcomes predictable and reliable?
Transformational	Are expectations changing?	Is scope of use expanding?	Is trust and reliance increasing?

Figure 8-2. *Interpreting telemetry through operational, strategic, and transformational value lenses*

Operational value – reading for flow and effort

Operational value becomes visible when you watch how work moves through the agent. Telemetry at this level answers a practical question:

"Is the agent making everyday work easier or harder?"

Signals that touch operational value often reveal

- How smoothly users move through interactions

- Where hesitation or uncertainty appears

- Where repeated effort occurs

- Where expectations and behavior diverge

You are reading for **flow**.

Anywhere the flow strengthens, operational value rises. Anywhere the flow slows, repeats, or stops, operational value is losing momentum.

So, your mindset and focus needs to be about noticing patterns that indicate either friction or clarity; looking for the small movements that either give people confidence or erode it:

Ask yourself

- Where are people relying on the agent?

- Where are they shifting away from it?

- Does the process look effortful?

- Does the process convey smoothness?

The answers point directly to operational benefits such as time saved, productivity improvements, and better access to information.

Strategic value – reading for consistency and quality

Strategic value emerges when the agent helps people perform work with greater clarity, coordination, or reliability. Telemetry at this level surfaces the agent's judgment, the internal choices, pathways, and interpretations that shape outcomes.

The guiding question here is

"Is this agent supporting decisions and workflows in a consistent and reliable way?"

Signals at this level help you see

- Whether the agent interprets similar situations consistently

- Whether outcomes align with organizational rules or expectations

- Whether workflows progress smoothly or fracture under variation

- Whether guidance supports confident decision-making

You are reading for **coherence**.

Coherence strengthens strategic value. Loss of coherence weakens trust in decision support, process reliability, and accuracy.

Ask yourself

- Do the agent's choices reflect the patterns we designed?

- Do users move through tasks with clarity and confidence?

- Are there signs the agent is interpreting the world differently than intended?

- Does behavior support the strategic outcomes we defined?

This reveals where the agent strengthens or pressures strategic value benefits, such as improved accuracy and reduced operational risk

Transformational value – reading for trust and behavioral change

Transformation value appears when the agent (or agents) reshape how the organization operates. Telemetry here is subtle. Usage and adoption shows not just whether the agent is being used, but whether it is becoming a part of how people think, decide, and collaborate.

The guiding question becomes

"Is this agent changing the way the organization works?"

Signals at this level reveal

- Shifts in reliance

- Changes in workflow patterns

- New behaviors emerging in response to the agent

- Adoption beyond the original scope

- Expectations rising as trust grows

You are reading for movement.

Movement in how people approach tasks, seek knowledge, or coordinate work. Movement in the organization's willingness to rely on the agent for more meaningful tasks.

Ask yourself

- Where is trust forming?

- Where do people choose the agent before older methods?

- Where are new expectations emerging?

- What does this tell us about how the organization works now?

This is where transformational value appears: higher satisfaction, empowerment, reduced operational burden and new opportunities for redesign.

Monitoring the Patterns That Matter

Once telemetry begins to flow, the most important skill is learning to recognize the patterns that reveal movement; movement toward the outcomes the organization values, or movement away from them.

Monitoring is not about scanning dashboards for anomalies, it is about developing an awareness of the signals that indicate that something significant is happening inside your workflows, your capabilities, or your organization.

These patterns are not tied to a specific domain or scenario. They are observable across any agent, because they emerge from how people behave and how systems respond.

The purpose of monitoring is simple: to notice when behavior is changing in ways that influence value (Figure 8-3).

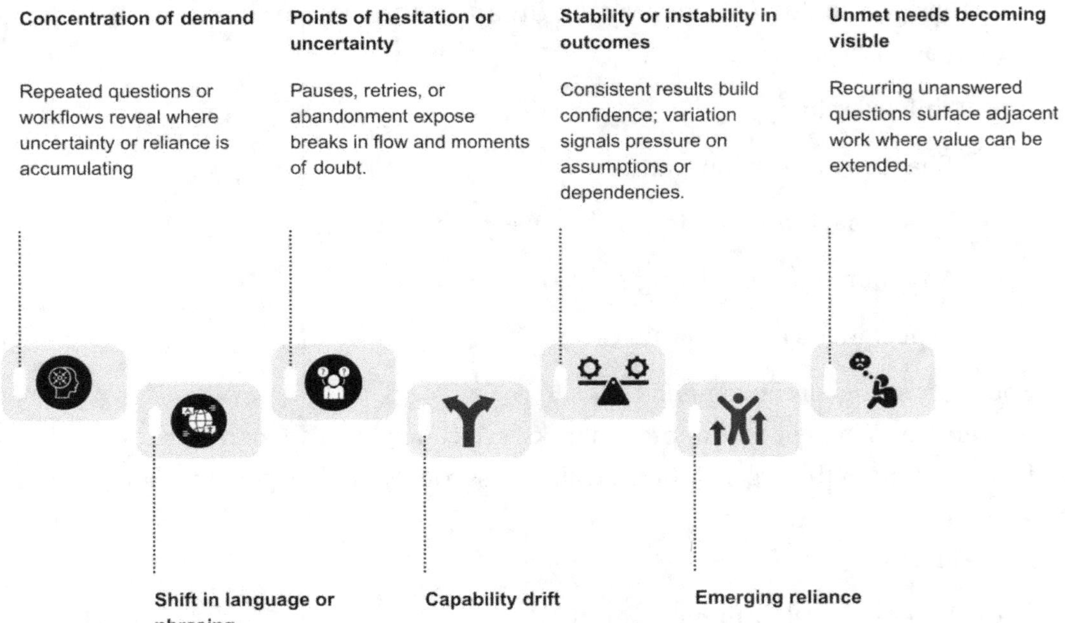

Figure 8-3. *Common telemetry patterns that signal changes in behavior and value*

Certain signals appear again and again once an agent is in use. They are not tied to a specific domain or implementation but emerge from how people behave and how systems respond. Recognizing these patterns helps you move beyond individual metrics and develop an instinct for noticing when something meaningful is changing in how work flows, decisions are made, or value is forming.

Pattern 1: Concentration of Demand

You begin to notice certain themes appearing repeatedly: *specific questions, certain workflows, or recurring tasks.* This concentration can indicate genuine organizational demand that may not have been fully captured during opportunity framing. In Copilot Studio, these questions are grouped into themes[4] with metrics such as total questions, answer rate, and reactions, which makes concentrated demand very visible. This concentration can often reveal demand that was not fully captured during opportunity framing.

Example (HR onboarding): The agent begins receiving a steady flow of questions about one specific topic: equipment setup. The same theme appears across new hires, phrased in slightly different ways.

Where it appears in telemetry[5]:

- **Themes/knowledge section**: Clusters of equipment-related questions (e.g., a suggested "Device setup" theme with high question volume and answer rate metrics).

- **Analytics > overview/effectiveness**: High volume of questions in that theme or topic over the selected period

- **Tools/tools analytics**: The IT setup topic or tools triggered more frequently than others

Concentration of demand signals where users feel uncertainty and seek clarity. It often reflects moments where operational value can increase quickly, strengthen operational flow, documentation and topic design, and to focus refinements on the themes that carry the most load for your agent.

Which value outcomes it touches

- **Time saved**: New hires resolve setup tasks faster

- **Experience**: Fewer emails and tickets to HR/IT

- **Empowerment**: New hired feel more capable on day 1

---

[4] https://learn.microsoft.com/en-us/microsoft-copilot-studio/analytics-themes
[5] https://learn.microsoft.com/en-us/microsoft-copilot-studio/analytics-overview

Pattern 2: Shifts in Language or Phrasing

Users begin changing the way they ask questions. Simple requests evolve into more natural, conversational, or expectation-driven phrasing. Themes and transcripts make these shifts visible over time by grouping similar questions and letting you drill into raw conversation data.

Example (HR onboarding): Users of the HR onboarding agent initially ask, "where can I find the onboarding guide?". Over time, phrasing shifts to "walk me through onboarding," or "what should I do first?", signaling that new hires now expect guided assistance, not document retrieval.

Where it appears in telemetry:

- **Usage analytics**: Transcripts showing new conversational patterns

- **Unanswered questions**: Clusters of new phrasing or unfamiliar synonyms

- **Topic triggers**: Increased use of guidance or workflow topics rather than lookups

Language shifts indicate the agent is becoming a trusted part of the process. They show rising expectations and emerging behaviors that may require expanded guidance or re-aligned capability boundaries.

Which value outcomes it touches:

- **Access to knowledge**: Fewer requests for documents, more direct answer

- **Experience**: Smoother onboarding conversations

- **Accuracy**: Clearer guidance reduces misunderstanding

Pattern 3: Points of Hesitation or Uncertainty

Users pause, retry, ask follow-up questions, or abandon a step in the workflow. Topic-level analytics and conversation outcomes together reveal where these points of hesitation cluster in your flows.

Example (HR onboarding): The majority of tasks in the HR onboarding agent proceed smoothly, but new hires repeatedly struggle with the "benefits enrollment" step. They ask clarification questions or abandon the workflow before finishing.

Where it appears in telemetry:

- **Topic analytics:** The topic analytics pane for "benefits enrollment" shows lower completion rates and higher drop-off at a specific node.

- **Conversation outcomes:** More sessions related to benefits end as "abandoned" or escalate to a human channel.

- **Transcripts/themes:** Downloaded transcripts and theme drill-downs show repeated questions about eligibility, deadlines, or options.

Hesitation shows where users need clearer guidance or where a step is more complex than the design accounted for. It signals a break in operational flow and potential risk to compliance if critical steps are not completed reliably.

Which value outcomes it touches

- **Compliance:** Benefits enrollment is time-sensitive and policy-driven.

- **User satisfaction:** Clarity and reassurance reduce frustration.

- **Error reduction:** Better guidance prevents omissions and incorrect choices.

Pattern 4: Capability Drift

The agent begins selecting capabilities in unexpected ways, responding with the wrong action or relying too heavily on fallback behavior. Tool and knowledge source analytics are designed to reveal exactly these shifts in how the orchestrator is using your actions.

Example (HR onboarding): The agent uses the "policy lookup" capability when new hires ask "how do I request parental leave?", even though this query should trigger a "task guidance" topic that walks them through the process.

Where it appears in telemetry

- **Tool use:** Tool analytics show unexpected usage patterns, for example, policy-lookup tools being invoked more often than task guidance tools for certain themes.

- **Topic/knowledge source use:** The knowledge section shows queries routed to content-only sources instead of workflow topics.

- **Evaluation results/transcripts**: Test sets and transcripts reveal that specific prompts consistently lead to the wrong capabilities.

Capability drift shows where boundaries need refinement, descriptions need tightening, or user phrasing reflects genuine shifts in organizational language. Drift affects reliability and the sense of coherence in the agent's behavior, especially when actions have policy or compliance implications.

Which value outcomes it touches

- **Improved accuracy**: Correct actions must align with intent.

- **Decision quality**: Users rely on consistent, appropriate guidance.

- **Operational efficiency**: Fewer manual escalations to HR to "fix" misrouted tasks.

Pattern 5: Stability or Instability in Outcomes

Over time, telemetry reveals whether the agent delivers consistent results. Conversation outcomes, topic completion metrics, and tool success rates make stability, or the loss of it, visible.

Example (HR onboarding): For several weeks, the agent supports "mandatory training registration" successfully. Suddenly, success rates vary. Some users complete the workflow, others get stuck at step 2 or are handed off to HR.

Where it appears in telemetry:

- **Conversation outcomes**: The share of "resolved" drops and "unresolved" (or escalated) outcomes escalate for sessions that involved training registration.

- **Topic analysis**: Completion metrics for the training topic show more drop-offs or error paths over the same period.

- **Tool use/errors**: The tools used for enrollment start to show a higher error rate or failed runs.

Instability is often the earliest warning that a design assumption no longer reflects reality. Perhaps, a backend system changed, content was updated, or users are approaching the task differently. Stability under change is central to user trust and to strategic value.

Which outcomes it touches:

- **Compliance**: Training completion rates and deadlines must be met.

- **Decision speed**: Unstable paths slow progress.

- **Experience**: Consistency is a cornerstone of confidence in the agent.

Pattern 6: Emerging Reliance

Users begin turning to the agent for tasks beyond the initial scope. Adoption metrics and themes are helpful there: they show when daily and monthly active users grow, and when new questions types start to cluster.

Example (HR onboarding): New hires start using the agent to understand internal career growth paths, seek mentorship resources, or explore learning portals, none of which were part of the original onboarding design.

Where it appears in telemetry:

- **Active users**: Daily and monthly active users trend upward even after the initial onboarding period.

- **Themes**: New themes appear around "career development" or "mentoring," or existing themes show a growing share of questions in these areas.

- **Conversation outcomes**: These sessions increasingly end as resolved without escalation, indicating the agent is handling the new demand effectively.

Emerging reliance reveals where the organization is ready for deeper support. It is also a sign that the agent is broadening from a task tool into a trusted advisor for early-career employees, which may drive decisions about scope and investment.

Which value outcomes it touches:

- **Empowerment**: Users explore independently instead of waiting for HR.

- **Satisfaction**: The agent becomes a go-to resource, not a one-time utility.

- **Reduced operational burden**: HR teams see fewer repetitive enquiries.

Pattern 7: Unmet Needs Becoming Visible

As users build confidence in the agent, they begin expressing needs it does not yet cover. Analytics for unanswered questions, combined with themes and cost-savings calculations, make these unmet needs visible and measurable.

Example (HR onboarding): New hires consistently ask "how do I get software access?" or "who approves my system permissions?", even though software provisioning was never part of the agent's scope.

Where it appears in telemetry:

- **Unanswered questions/generated answer rate**: The agent shows a recurring cluster of access-related questions it could not answer or resolve.

- **Themes**: An access-related theme appears with low answer rate but high question volume.

- **Savings/custom analytics**: When you model the time currently spent resolving access issues manually, potential savings from extending the agent become visible.

Unmet needs offer insight into adjacent workflows where value can be extended. They show where the organization expects the agent to play a more integrated role in the onboarding journey and where additional topics or tools could unlock measurable time and cost savings.

Which value outcomes it touches:

- **Faster onboarding**: Fewer delays related to the system and software access

- **Reduced operational costs**: Fewer IT-HR interventions for routing provisioning questions

- **Access to knowledge**: A more unified, "one place to ask" user experience

Improvement Loops: Creating the Rhythm That Keeps Agents Aligned with Value

Telemetry is telling you what is happening. Patterns show you where behavior is shifting. Improvement loops turn those observations into action.

An improvement loop is the operational rhythm that keeps an agent aligned with the outcomes it was designed to achieve. It is a disciplined proactive that turns signals into decisions, and decisions into refinements. In mature organizations, this rhythm becomes part of agent life cycle rather than ad hoc activity triggered only when something breaks, or someone asks a question about the agent's performance.

Microsoft Copilot Studio provides the foundational signals needed to support this rhythm:

- **Usage analytics** reveal adoption, engagement, and patterns of user behavior.

- **Conversation outcomes** indicate which sessions succeed, which fail, and where flows break or succeed.

- **Topic analytics** show how capabilities perform, which steps produce friction, and where flows break or succeed.

- **Themes and unanswered questions** uncover new demand or unmet needs.

- **Tool and knowledge source analytics** reveal how actions behave and where drift or failure emerges.

- **Savings and effort-avoidance metrics** provide evidence of operational value.

When viewed together, these signals create the conditions for a predictable improvement loop.

Improvement Loops As a Practice

An improvement loop is a way of maintaining alignment between real-world behavior and organizational intent. It rests on five movements:

1. **Observe: Identify where behavior is changing**

   The loop begins with noticing. Telemetry reveals how people are interacting with the agent, how the agent is responding, and how outcomes shift over time.
   Sources for this step include

   a. Themes and unanswered questions to see what new demand is emerging

   b. Topic analytics to identify friction, drop-offs, or unexpected interactions

   c. Conversation outcomes to monitor where tasks resolve, escalate, or fail

   Observation is continuous. Clarity comes from seeing where signals converge into meaningful patterns.

2. **Interpret: Understand what the signals mean**

   Interpretation tries to link behavior to value. A drop in completion rates may reflect a system issue or dependency. A rise in unanswered queries may indicate new expectations. A recurring escalation may show where guidance lacks clarity.
   Interpretation involves

   a. Reviewing transcripts for context and intent

   b. Analyzing how often capabilities were selected correctly or incorrectly

   c. Checking tool success/failure logs if actions are involved

   This step is focusing on "what does the behavior represent?" The answers determine whether action is needed.

3. **Prioritize: Decide what to act on first**

   Not every signal warrants immediate change. Prioritization anchors decisions in value outcomes and risk tolerances defined earlier in the design process.
   Telemetry that touches any of the areas below should be addressed before lower-value opportunities:

   a. Compliance or policy accuracy

   b. High-volume workflows

    c. Onboarding or customer-facing outcomes

    d. Safety or privacy constraints

Copilot Studio's analytics dashboard helps teams identify which themes carry the highest volume and where value or effort-avoidance metrics indicate the greatest impact. Prioritization is where organizational goals, telemetry, and design meet.

4. **Refine: Make targeted improvements**

Refinements may involve

    a. Updating topic phrasing or adding clarifying variations

    b. Expanding or tightening capability boundaries

    c. Restructuring workflow steps based on drop-off telemetry

    d. Updating knowledge sources to address unanswered clusters

    e. Adjusting instructions or prompt patterns inside actions

Each refinement is grounded not in guesswork but in clear signals from telemetry, supported by analytics that show exactly where the experience or capability requires improvement. The improvement loop is incremental; small changes accumulate into meaningful shifts in user confidence and outcome stability.

5. **Validate: Evaluate the agent before changes reach users**

After validation, the agent returns to production with new behaviors. Telemetry begins to flow again. New patterns and behaviors start to emerge, value continues to shift. The loop begins anew.

This rhythm creates resilience.

It ensures that agents do not degrade quietly over time or drift away from their purpose. Instead, they evolve in step with the organization, keeping pace with new expectations, language shifts, process changes, and real-world complexity.

Improvement Loops As Part of the Operating Model

In a value-driven organization, improvement loops become a routine part of the agent life cycle:

- Weekly reviews of themes and unanswered questions

- Monthly review of topic performance and capability behavior

- Quarterly checks of value outcomes and effort-avoidance metrics

- Periodic evaluation cycles to ensure continued alignment

These loops support the long-term health of the agent and reinforce responsible AI practices.

Bringing the Improvement Loop to Life: The HR Onboarding Agent

To see how an improvement loop works in practice, imagine the HR onboarding agent after its first few months in production. Adoption is strong, new hires are using it daily, and HR administrators already see fewer routine questions. As with any real agent, its behavior begins to reflect the complexity of the organization it serves.

Each week, the agent owner and platform admin meet for a short telemetry review. Their goal is simple: to understand how the agent behaves in the real world and decide whether anything needs attention.

1. **Observing the signals**

   They begin with **Themes**; the high-level clusters of user questions. Two themes stand out:

   a. Benefits have grown significantly in question volume.

   b. A new "device setup" theme has significantly emerged with unusually high activity.

   The admin opens **topic analytics** for benefits and notices a pattern: the drop-off rate at the "Select benefits package" step is noticeably higher than at any other point. Completion rates are inconsistent, and several conversation transcripts show new hires asking, "do I need to decide this today?"; a question the team had not anticipated.

226

For device setup, **tool analytics** shows that the laptop configuration instructions are being viewed far more often than expected, and unanswered questions reveal variations like "VPN not working," "Can't find Wi-Fi menu," and "where do I download software?"

None of these signals alone tells the full story.

Together, they show how real people are experiencing onboarding.

2. **Interpreting what these signals mean**

The agent owner and admin move from observation to interpretation. They ask

a. Why are new hires hesitating at the benefits step?

b. Why are setup questions appearing with so much linguistic variation?

c. What organizational behavior is driving these patterns?

Reviewing transcripts, they see that the benefits step feels high-stakes for new hires. They need more context, reassurance, and clearer guidance about deadlines. The device setup theme, meanwhile, reflects a natural difference between documented IT processes and the lived experience of configuring new equipment.

Experience telemetry shows the behavior. Capability telemetry shows the downstream effect; increased escalations to HR, reduced compliance confidence, and a slower onboarding journey.

3. **Prioritizing what to act on first**

Although both themes matter, they require different responses.

The team prioritizes the **benefits enrollment step** because it directly affects compliance and onboarding timelines. Consistent completion matters to HR leadership, so this becomes the highest-value area for refinement.

Device setup is important, but less time-critical. It becomes a secondary enhancement area, to be addressed after the benefits refinements are validated.

Prioritization is grounded in value, not in volume.

4. **Refining the agent based on telemetry**

   The admin and agent owner make targeted adjustments:

   a. They update the benefits topic to include clearer explanations about deadlines and eligibility.

   b. They add clarifying questions that anticipate confusion: "would you like help understanding the difference between plans?"

   c. They expand the knowledge source with a short, friendly overview authored by HR.

   d. They add synonym variations to help the agent recognize phrasings such as "do I have to choose today?" or "what happens if I wait?"

   Each change is small, but each directly addresses a behavior that telemetry illuminated.

5. **Validating refinements through evaluation**

   Before releasing updates to production, the team moves into a controlled testing phase.

   They open Evaluation test sets:

   a. They add new test cases using the exact phrasing that appeared in transcripts ("Do I need to choose benefits today?", "VPN not working," "How do I set up my laptop?").

   b. They run similarity tests for benefits explanations to ensure that responses contain the key information, even with varied wording.

   c. They run quality tests to confirm the agent handles ambiguous queries with helpful, safety-aligned responses.

   d. They compare results to previous evaluations run to verify that the agent's improvements do not degrade performance elsewhere.

   Only when the test set passes consistently does the team publish the updated agent.

6. **Returning to observation – closing the loop**

Over the following two weeks, telemetry reflects the impact:

- Benefits drop-offs shrink noticeably.

- Device setup questions become more consistent, with fewer escalations.

- Conversation outcomes show more sessions ending with "resolved – confirmed."

- HR administrators report fewer urgent messages from new hires.

The loop begins again with new patterns, new signals, and new opportunities.

Improvement loops mark a quiet but important shift in how an organization works with agents. Early in the journey, much of the effort goes into design, evaluation, and launch. But once an agent enters the real world, the center of gravity moves. The work becomes less about creation and more about stewardship, watching how the organization responds, noticing where value is emerging, and refining the agent so it stays aligned with the behavior it supports.

Telemetry gives teams the visibility they need to protect value, to ensure that decisions remain accurate, and to maintain trust in the moments that matter. It also reveals new possibilities: the themes that grow naturally, the unexpected questions that surface, the early signs that an agent has become part of how people navigate their work.

When improvement loops become routine, the organization develops a kind of muscle memory. Agents no longer drift quietly away from their purpose, nor do they stagnate once deployed. They evolve in step with the people they serve. Each refinement, each evaluation run, and each telemetry review helps the agent reflect the organization more faithfully; its processes, its language, its priorities, and its values.

This is what maturity looks like in the agentic era: not a perfect launch, but a steady rhythm of observing, understanding, adjusting, and validating. A rhythm ensures agents continue to create the value they were designed for; operational, strategic, and transformational.

As this rhythm takes hold, something else becomes possible.

Teams gain the evidence, confidence, and clarity needed to tell the story of their agents: where value is appearing, how behaviors are shifting, what burdens have been eased, and which outcomes have moved.

This brings us to the next part of the journey; one that is often overlooked but essential to sustaining momentum.

If telemetry shows how value emerges, communicating value is how you make it visible. It is how you build trust with stakeholders, strengthen sponsorship, and ensure that the work of design, evaluation, and improvement leads to lasting organizational impact.

Quick recap:

- Telemetry tells you what is happening; evaluations tell you why.

- Improvement loops turn agents into learning systems rather than static assets.

- Monitoring is not about catching failures; it is about understanding behavior, patterns, and opportunities.

- The agent owner and CoE form the backbone of continuous improvement.

In the next chapter, we turn to the craft of telling that story; communicating value with confidence.

CHAPTER 9

Communicating Value with Confidence

Organizations rarely change because of dashboards. They change because of stories. Stories that reveal what is happening, why it matters, and what it makes possible next.

Agents, even the most thoughtfully designed can stall if people cannot see the progress taking place around them. As with any meaningful transformation, value must be communicated, not assumed.

Communicating value must not be an afterthought. It is a vital mechanism that turns early success into sustained momentum. It provides leaders with the clarity they need to support further investment. It helps operational teams understand the difference the agent is making in their day-to-day work. It reassures risk and compliance teams that the system is behaving responsibly; and it creates confidence in the wider organization that the agent is not just a proof of concept but an asset that changes the way work flows.

This chapter gives you a practical, accessible approach to telling the story of your agent; drawing on evidence, shaped by insight, and grounded in the value architecture you developed earlier in the journey. This is about providing clarity, coherence, and purpose: explaining what changed, why it matters, and how it contributes to the organization's goals.

The Architecture of a Value Story

Effective stories follow a structure; not because structure makes them rigid but because it makes them understandable. Leaders and operational teams alike make sense of change through narrative shape. They look for context, movement, and consequence.

To support this, let's introduce a straightforward narrative model for communicating the impact of an agent:

The value arc: context ➤ change ➤ consequence

© Steve Jeffery 2026
S. Jeffery, *Value by Design with Microsoft Copilot Studio*, https://doi.org/10.1007/979-8-8688-2613-9_9

This is a simple, durable storytelling pattern. It works for a one-minute update, a leadership briefing, a written case study or quarterly review. It also aligns directly with the value by design philosophy: value is established in context, delivered through change, and realized through consequence.

Before we dive deeper into the value arc, there is one essential principle: **Every story must be rooted in the specific value benefits the agent was designed to deliver.**

Earlier in the journey, you identified the **value benefits**; time saved, improved accuracy, better access to knowledge, and so on. These benefits provide *anchors* of the narrative. They ensure that your story does not float in abstraction but remains grounded in the intended purpose of the agent.

However, value does not emerge all at once. Agents mature, adoption spreads, behaviors change, governance strengthens. Because of this, value unfolds across three horizons (we covered these earlier, this is a refresher):

Operational value – immediate and visible

Cycle times, accuracy improvements, reduced manual effort: these appear early and give the story momentum.

Strategic value – achieved through consistent use over time

Higher-quality decisions, better customer experience, improved compliance, and more stable business processes. These benefits require sustained adoption, refinement and alignment.

Transformational value – the long arc

The organization begins operating in a fundamentally different way:

- New workflows become possible

- Roles evolve

- Innovation accelerates

- Knowledge moves more freely

- The culture shifts toward data-driven, agent-supported work

Transformational value cannot be claimed early in an agent's life. It is something that emerges through episodes, moments of progress, insight, challenge, and expansion.

This means the value story is never "one and done." It is a series of chapters. Each one moves the organization forward. Each one reveals a different facet of the value the agent is capable of delivering.

And this is where the value arc shines. It provides a structure that works not just once but *every time you need to tell the next episode.*

Before exploring each element of the value arc in detail, it is useful to see how they come together in practice. The following example is not a retrospective success story, nor a polished case study. It is a snapshot in time: one episode in the life of an agent that is still maturing.

Read it not as a claim of full transformation, but as an illustration of how context, change, and consequence can be woven together to communicate credibly. The intent is to show how evidence, insight, and narrative combine to help an organization understand what has improved, why it matters, and what becomes possible next.

A Worked Example: The HR Onboarding Agent

To make the value arc concrete, let's return to the HR onboarding agent that has appeared throughout this book. At this point in its life cycle, the agent has been live for six months. It is stable, adopted across multiple regions, and has moved beyond initial proof-of-concept.

Context: Why This Mattered

Before the agent was introduced, onboarding created friction for several groups at once. New hires struggled to find accurate, role-specific information and frequently relied on informal channels for answers. HR administrators spent a significant portion of their time responding to repetitive questions, while leaders had limited visibility into whether mandatory steps were being completed consistently and on time.

The immediate priority was operation: reduce friction and manual effort during onboarding. The longer-term concern was strategic: ensure compliance, consistency, and confidence as hiring volumes increased.

Change: What the Agent Enabled

With the agent in place, new hires could access answers and guidance at the moment they needed it, without waiting for human response. Routine HR queries were handled through self-service, and the agent guided users through mandatory steps in the correct sequence.

Over time, patterns of use began to shift. Managers increasingly relied on the agent's summaries to understand onboarding progress. HR teams adjusted their workflows, spending less time responding to questions and more time improving onboarding content and experience.

The most significant change was not a single feature, but a behavioral shift: onboarding became a guided flow rather than a fragmented set of handoffs.

Consequence: What Difference It Made

Operationally, average time to find onboarding information dropped from 45 minutes to under 5 minutes, and routine HR inquiry volume decreased by more than 60%. Strategically, onboarding completion rates stabilized across regions, and leaders gained confidence that compliance requirements were being met consistently.

Perhaps most importantly, the organization began to treat onboarding as a designed experience rather than an administrative task. That shift opened the door to broader conversations about role readiness, early productivity, and long-term employee experience – signals of transformational value beginning to emerge.

This story is not the final chapter. It is one episode in a longer arc, providing credible evidence of progress while pointing clearly toward what becomes necessary next.

Now, let's step back from the example and how it works.

The story you have just read follows the same structure you will use repeatedly as an agent evolves. Context sets direction and relevance. Change describes what shifted in real terms. Consequence explains why those shifts matter; now, and over time. The power of the value arc lies not in the example itself but in its repeatability.

What follows breaks down each element of the value arc in turn, highlighting what to include, what to emphasize, and how to adapt the story depending on audience and value horizon.

Context: Why This Mattered (Breaking Down the Value Arc)

Every value story begins by reminding the audience what problem the agent set out to solve. This is not a retelling of the design process; it is a concise framing that anchors the narrative in purpose. Whose work was affected? What friction existed? What risks were present? What outcomes mattered most?

Good context brings the audience back to the moment when the work began. It reconnects them to the constraints, pressures, and opportunities that shaped the initiative.

When telling the context of an agent's story, it is often helpful to echo the value horizon relevant to the audience. For example:

- **Operational teams resonate strongly with immediate value**: Reduced handoffs, fewer errors, faster answers

- **Senior leaders listen for strategic value**: Stability, decision clarity, reduced risk, customer impact

- **Transformation and innovation leaders look for signals that point toward long-term change**: New capabilities emerging, new behaviors taking hold, new opportunities appearing

This ensures that the context does not simply describe where the value journey began, but why this particular kind of value mattered right now.

Change: What the Agent Enabled

Change describes what actually shifted once the agent was introduced. It focuses on behaviors, not features. Rather than listing capabilities, it explains how work now flows differently. New hires can complete tasks without waiting for HR. Managers receive decision-ready information rather than raw data. Customers get consistent guidance at the exact moment they need it.

Change is the movement visible in telemetry and outcomes: the signals that show real usage, the stability of workflows, the decision paths that are now clearer and faster.

Change is rarely uniform. In the early stages, change tends to cluster around **operational improvements**; work becomes smoother, faster, more predictable. But over time, change begins to include emergent behaviors: people trusting the agent more, using it in new scenarios, or reorganizing their workflow around it.

These emerging signs are often the early signals of **strategic value** taking shape. For example:

When managers begin to rely on an agent's summaries to prepare for decisions, they are not just saving time, they are improving the quality of judgment. This is strategic value.

Later still, you may see signs of transformational change:

Policies or processes being redesigned because the agent unlocked a simpler path; teams reorganizing around new flows; capability spreading beyond the original use case.

Consequence: What Difference It Made

The final stage of the value arc is consequence, the meaning behind the movement. This is where metrics and narrative intersect: time saved becomes operational efficiency; a reduction in escalations becomes improved experience; a rise in successful outcomes becomes strategic clarity; and increase in adoption becomes a sign of trust and emerging transformation.

Consequence connects the story to the value drivers from earlier chapters. It shows that the work did not only improve a process but advanced outcomes that matter to the organization: effectiveness, empowerment, transparency, compliance, stability.

A good value story does not end with a number but with a sentence that explains why the number matters.

Consequence is where timing matters most. Every agent produces operational consequences early; that is expected. But, strategic and transformational consequences often take months or quarters to surface in measurable ways.

Because of this, value storytelling is less like writing a book and more like producing a series. Each episode contributes to an unfolding arc. Each update reinforces momentum, each consequence builds credibility and anticipation for the next phase.

To help audience understand the timing, frame consequences across horizons.

> **Operational consequence**: What difference is being felt right now?
>
> **Strategic consequence**: What difference is becoming possible because patterns are stabilizing?
>
> **Transformational consequence**: What longer-term opportunities are emerging; not claimed prematurely, but recognized thoughtfully?

Anchoring consequences in this way avoids overstating early results while still celebrating genuine progress.

Finding the Story You Need to Tell

Different audiences care about different kinds of value. Executives look for strategic alignment and risk reduction. Operational teams look for smoother flow and increased capacity. End users look for clarity and trust. A single story rarely serves all needs; instead, the underlying narrative must be shaped to match the audience.

Broadly, organizations tend to recognize three kinds of value stories:

The Efficiency Story

These stories focus on smoother processes, fewer bottlenecks, and reduced manual effort. They resonate with leaders who oversee operations and service teams. Efficiency stories are often grounded in telemetry showing reduced escalations, increased self-service, or measurable time saved.

The Quality Story

These stories speak to accuracy, consistency, and confidence in decision-making. They matter to risk managers, compliance teams, and leaders responsible for regulated processes. Quality stories draw on data showing improved outcomes, fewer errors, and greater predictability.

The Transformation Story

These stories capture changes in behavior and culture; when an agent becomes part of how work happens rather than an optional tool. They rely on adoption signals, language shifts, reliance patterns, and new opportunities that emerge over time.

Most agents contribute to all three forms of value but the strongest stories choose one as the center of gravity. The others then provide balance and depth without diluting the message.

Turning Telemetry into Narrative

Telemetry provides the evidence needed for a value story. However, evidence is not the story itself. Data describes what happened; narrative explains why it matters.

The improvement patterns from chapter eight offer a natural bridge from signals to narrative. Each pattern contains the seeds of a compelling story:

- **Concentration of demand becomes**: "This is where people needed help the most."

- **Shifts in language become**: "Users began to trust the agent for guidance."

- **Points of hesitation become**: "We found friction, and removed it."

- **Capability drift becomes**: "We strengthened the agent's judgment."

- **Emerging reliance becomes**: "People began using the agent in new ways."

- **Unmet needs become**: "A new opportunity became visible."

Connecting telemetry patterns to your value story reinforces that the narrative is grounded in real usage, not in theory.

Using Generative AI to Shape the Narrative

Generative AI is particularly effective at transforming evidence into narrative. It can

- Summarize insights in plain language

- Rewrite technical observations for non-technical leaders

- Propose variations of the Value Arc based on different audiences

- Draft multiple story lengths: executive summary, presentation script, long-form reports

- Help refine tone, clarity, and emphasis

It is not a substitute for judgment; it is an amplifier. It accelerates the process of shaping the story so that teams can focus on insight, accuracy and intent.

A Practical Example: Prompting for a Value Story

One of the most effective ways to use generative AI in value communication is to treat it as a narrative-shaping partner rather than a source of truth. The quality of the output depends heavily on the quality of the prompt; particularly how clearly evidence, intent, and audience are defined.

The following example illustrates a prompt designed to transform telemetry and observations into a value story structured around the value arc:

```
You are helping me communicate the value of an AI agent to a senior
leadership audience.

The agent supports HR onboarding. It has been live for six months.
```

Context:
```
Before the agent, new hires struggled to find accurate onboarding
information. HR teams handled a high volume of repetitive queries, and
leaders lacked consistent visibility into onboarding completion and
compliance.
```

Change:
```
The agent now provides guided onboarding support, handles routine HR
questions through self-service, and summarizes onboarding progress for
managers. Adoption is stable across multiple regions.
```

Evidence:
```
• Average time to find onboarding information reduced from 45 minutes to
  under 5 minutes
• Routine HR inquiries reduced by over 60%
• Onboarding completion rates are now consistent across regions
```

Intent:
```
Write a concise value story using the structure context > change >
consequence.
Emphasize credibility and progress, not full transformation.
Avoid hype and avoid claiming long-term cultural change.
```

Audience:
```
Senior leaders interested in operation stability, compliance confidence and
readiness to scale.
```

Used well, prompts like this allow teams to generate multiple versions of the same story: a one-paragraph leadership update, a slide narrative, or a longer written summary; all grounded in the same evidence and intent.

Building Value Communication Assets

A well-told story is rarely a single artifact. Most organizations benefit from a small set of communication assets that allow messages to cascade naturally.

A one-slide value summary distills the Value Arc into an executive-friendly snapshot: context at the top, change in the middle, consequence at the bottom. A process illustration can show how workflows now flow with more predictability. A short narrative paragraph can be used in leadership updates. Telemetry snapshots can provide quantified confidence without overwhelming the audience.

Figure 9-1 below shows how these assets come together in practice. It is not a dashboard for analysis, but a communication artifact: a concise snapshot designed to support storytelling. The intent is to give leaders and stakeholders a shared view of progress at a glance, combining evidence, interpretation, and confidence without requiring deep technical explanation.

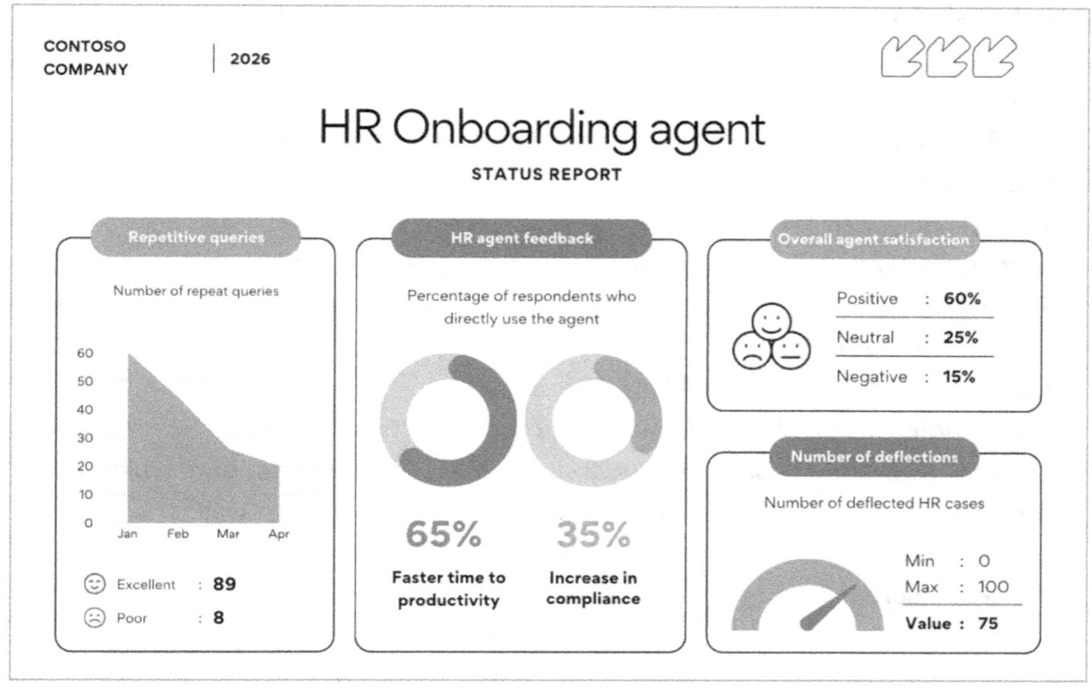

Figure 9-1. *Value communication snapshot illustrating operational metrics, human feedback, and adoption signals*

Each element reinforces a different aspect of the value story: operational signals, human experience, and emerging trust, allowing the narrative to be adapted depending on audience while remaining grounded in the same underlying evidence.

These assets allow teams to tailor the message without reinventing the story each time.

Storytelling Across Different Audiences

The strongest value communicators adapt their narrative to different audiences while keeping the underlying structure intact.

With executives, the emphasis is on consequence: strategic alignment, risk reduction, organization readiness. With operational managers, the story centers on the experience of their teams and the efficiency or reliability gains they can feel in daily work. With end users, stories highlight clarity, speed, and trust. With technical teams, stories emphasize stability, telemetry patterns, and improvement loops.

Before shaping the message, take a moment to identify the audience using four simple questions:

Who is the audience?

Are they executives, operational leaders, practitioners, technical specialists, or frontline users? Each group holds a different mental model of value.

What do they need to know?

Executives need clarity and consequence; managers need evidence of flow and stability; technical teams need signals that the system behaves correctly; end users need confidence and simplicity.

How invested or impacted are they?

Some audiences care because their work changes immediately. Others care because the outcomes affect their goals, KPIs, or accountability. Some have minimal day-to-day involvement but high influence over whether the agent continues to scale.

What influence do they hold?

A stakeholder's influence often determines how much detail or precision your story needs. A frontline user may have high interest and low influence, whereas a risk assurance leader may have high influence even with limited direct contact with the agent. Knowing this helps you tailor emphasis, not content.

With this understanding in hand, the story becomes more intentional.

The story is the same. Its emphasis changes depending on who needs to understand it.

Audience analysis does not alter the underlying value arc; it simply sharpens it, ensuring that each group receives a version of the story that feels relevant, timely, and aligned to their concerns. The agent does not succeed through a single narrative but through a sequence of well-aimed ones.

Quick recap:

- A good value story is not a list of features; it is a narrative of change anchored in outcomes.

- The value arc (context ➤ change ➤ consequence) helps different audiences understand different horizons of value.

- Operational, strategic, and transformational value are not competing stories; they are chapters of the same story.

- What you communicate shapes how your organization perceives progress.

Communicating value is an act of leadership. You turn evidence into shared understanding, and shared understanding into momentum. It aligns teams around the outcomes that matter. It helps people recognize not only what has improved, but why that improvement creates new possibilities. And it ensures that the value delivered through design does not remain hidden inside telemetry dashboards.

When you tell the story of your agent clearly; when you bring context, change, and consequence into focus; you give the organization a way to see itself differently. You illuminate how work is shifting, how decisions are improving, how confidence is growing, and how people are empowered to do more than before.

And in doing so, you prepare the ground for the next and final stage of the journey: understanding how agents reshape roles, responsibilities, and the operating model itself.

The New Workforce and the Platform Operating Model

Every major technological shift reconfigures the relationship between people, processes, and performance. Each era leaves behind one operating model and ushers in another.

Spreadsheets rewired finance; cloud computing rewired product delivery, mobile connectivity rewired customer expectations overnight.

Low-code platforms such as Microsoft Power Platform introduced another shift over the past decade, softening long-standing boundaries by enabling employees to design apps, automate processes, and create the solutions they needed themselves. This was the moment when the separation between "the business" and "the system" first began to dissolve.

Agents represent the next of these structural shifts, extending that progression rather than replacing it. But they introduce one major difference: agents do not simply support work or accelerate workflows; they participate in work. They interpret goals, respond to context, engage with systems, and collaborate with people. What low-code began (bringing users closer to the systems they depend on), agents now amplify by becoming active contributors in those systems, shaping decisions and coordinating work alongside their human counterparts.

Many organizations are still framing AI in terms of efficiency or automation. The real question though, the "frontier firm" question, is this:

If intelligent systems now perform parts of our work, how should the system around that work be redesigned?

We are moving from technology that supports work to technology that *co-creates* it. This shift demands new mental models, new skills, and new structures. It demands an

S. Jeffery, *Value by Design with Microsoft Copilot Studio*, https://doi.org/10.1007/979-8-8688-2613-9_10

operating model capable of absorbing continuous intelligence, shifting from workflows to learning systems, from handoffs to orchestration, from rigid controls to adaptive governance.

What emerges is not simply a new way of delivering technology but a different kind of operating model.

In an agent-enabled organization, the operating model is no longer organized around static workflows, fixed roles, or predefined handoffs. Instead, it is organized around outcomes, intent, and learning. Humans define direction and constraints. Agents interpret, coordinate, and execute within those boundaries. Performance is assessed not by activity completed, but by the reliability, quality, and experience of end-to-end outcomes.

This is a platform-operating model: one in which the systems of work, governance, measurement, and improvement are designed to evolve continuously. The platform becomes the coordination layer between people, agents, policy, and value creation, absorbing change without requiring constant structural design.

A platform-operating model does not imply a single centralized team controlling all work, nor does it mean uncoordinated local experimentation. In practice, it requires a clear split of responsibilities: shared platforms, standards, and guardrails at the organizational level, with authority and accountability for outcomes remaining close to the work.

Central functions provide the foundation: common capabilities, governance principles, telemetry, and safety boundaries. Business teams design and evolve how agents are applied within those boundaries, aligned to their outcomes and operating realities. The model works because ownership is explicit.

Humans + Agents: A New Division of Labor

For the most part of three decades, "digital worker" or "virtual worker" was a metaphor; a convenient way to describe software that supported human effort. It referred to tools that helped people do their jobs: automated forms, workflow engines, CRM systems, and productivity apps. These systems followed fixed rules, relied on users to drive the process, and could not adapt on their own. They were "workers" in name only.

Agents change this. They retrieve knowledge, interpret policies, take actions, and coordinate across systems with growing autonomy. They are not tools watched over by humans; they are *participants* in work.

This forces a reassessment of who (or what) does what inside a modern organization.

The most significant shift is not automation. It is a restructuring of the cognitive responsibilities within the organization.

Humans now concentrate on defining what needs to happen, and why. These are tasks anchored in intent: setting strategic direction, shaping policies, assessing risk, and making judgments that depend on human context, care, and discretion. Agents increasingly take on the how: interpreting instructions, searching across knowledge domains, proposing next steps, executing routines, and coordinating the micro-decisions that keep operations flowing.

This redistribution does not diminish human contribution. It elevates it. The elevation of human contribution also carries responsibility. When agents act on behalf of the organization, accountability does not shift to the system. It remains with the people who define intent, set boundaries, and own outcomes.

When errors occur, the questions shift to "how was the system designed to make that decision possible?" rather than assigning blame. Accountability moves away from individual execution and toward ownership of design choices, escalation paths, and controls.

It frees practitioners from the pull of administration and repetition and moves their attention upward; toward system design, exception analysis, continuous improvement and the higher-order reasoning that automation alone cannot reach.

The inverse is also true. When organizations introduce agents without redesigning the surrounding system, the result is rarely transformation. Instead, existing inefficiencies are amplified. Agents accelerate broken processes, humans lose clarity over accountability, and trust erodes as decisions become harder to explain or challenge.

In these environments, people do not feel augmented; they feel displaced from understanding. The issue is not agent capability but the absence of clear boundaries, ownership, and intent. Without deliberate design, intelligence becomes noise rather than leverage.

Evolving Roles and Responsibilities: Designing for Augmentation

AI does not eliminate roles; it reshapes them. The most visible and immediate impact of agents is felt at the level of the practitioner. This is where work is performed, where tasks accumulate, where exceptions appear, and where time is consumed by the friction of everyday operations. Once practitioners experience a shift, the effects cascade upward: managers begin coordinating differently, leaders redefine organizational expectations, and ultimately the organization itself reshapes how it creates value.

Practitioner: The Front Line of Transformation

Practitioners are the first to feel the reconfiguration of work because they are the closest to its texture. They are the ones searching for information, moving between systems, and coordinating between teams. These activities consume time not because they require deep expertise but because they are necessary scaffolding; the tissue that holds processes together.

Agents change this dynamic. They become the new operational substrate, performing the activities that previously consumed human attention: retrieving context, interpreting rules, drafting, summarizing, reconciling, coordinating steps, monitoring for changes, and surfacing uncertainties.

What shifts for practitioners:

The practitioner's role evolves from performing work to shaping the conditions under which work is performed.

Practitioners now

- **Shape intent**: Expressing what the agent needs to achieve rather than performing every step themselves

- **Review and refine agent output**: Adding judgment where nuance is required

- **Design and tune workflows**: Adjusting instructions and handovers as they uncover exceptions or opportunities

- **Focus on high-judgment cases**: Spending more time on decision where context and experience matter

- **Become stewards of improvement loops**: Identifying where agent struggles and how it must adapt

In other words, practitioners become the designers, supervisors, and improvers of their own digital workforce.

This does not distance them from the work. It places them at the center of how the work works.

Managers: Orchestrating Human–Agent Collaboration

As practitioners shift upward into roles of interpretation, validation, and improvement, managers experience an equally significant shift. Their responsibilities extend beyond coordinating human effort to orchestrating a blended ecosystem of humans and agents. What actually changes is the manager's relationship to capacity, outcomes, and accountability.

This transition is rarely smooth at first. Roles may temporarily overlap, metrics may lag reality, and teams may struggle to recalibrate expectations as agent support increases unevenly across processes. These are not signs of failure but signals that the operating model is being rewired while work continues.

The role of management during this phase is not to eliminate friction but to contain it: providing clarity, protecting focus, and ensuring that short-term disruption does not obscure long-term gains.

Managers have always been responsible for ensuring their teams can deliver what the organization requires. With agents taking on portions of operational load, two things shift:

1. Managers inherit a team with a different capacity profile.

    Teams can move faster, respond sooner, and handle higher volumes because agents absorb repetitive work. Managers don't run the agents, but they benefit from what agents enable.

    The change they feel is

    a. Fewer bottlenecks

    b. Fewer delays

    c. Fewer blockers caused by mundane tasks

    d. More time available for their people to engage in judgment, relationship-building, and improvement

2. Managers shift from supervising activity to enabling effectiveness.

    Their focus can now move toward

    a. Clarifying expectations

    b. Removing organizational barriers

   c. Supporting higher-value practitioner work

   d. Aligning the teams purpose with what agents now make possible

Managers become the enablers of uplift. If practitioners are climbing into more skilled, system-shaping roles, managers ensure they have the clarity, support, and bandwidth to do so. They keep teams pointed at outcomes rather than drowning in tasks.

3.   Managers don't manage the agents; they manage the environment in which agents are effective.

This is a crucial distinction. Managers influence agent effectiveness indirectly through

   a. Ensuring good practice is followed

   b. Helping resolve escalations

   c. Shaping culture and trust around human–agent collaboration

   d. Aligning workloads and expectations across the team

   e. Ensuring teams adopt continuous improvement practices

All of this fits naturally within the managers remit today. It simply occurs in a context where the team's baseline capacity and capability have changed. They remain focused on people, performance, well-being, clarity, and outcomes, not operational mechanics.

Leaders: From Process Efficiency to Organizational Design

When practitioners work differently, and managers enable new kinds of performance, leaders face the challenge of aligning the organization around this new division of labor.

Leaders do not design the systems agents operate. They design the organization that can support and scale them.

This includes

- Defining where agents create value

- Establishing decision-making frameworks

- Ensuring fairness, transparency, and responsibility

- Aligning incentives to outcomes rather than activity

- Ensuring that structures, roles, and governance keep pace with new capabilities

Leaders help the organization let go of old assumptions:

- That value equals effort

- That productivity equals visible activity

- That expertise is measured in volume rather than impact

Responsibility in an agent-enabled organization does not mean tighter control over execution. It means explicit ownership of the system within which execution occurs.

Leaders are accountable for defining the boundaries within which agents operate, the escalation paths when judgment is required, and the principles by which trade-offs are made visible and contestable. They do not approve every decision; they design the conditions under which good decisions can be made consistently.

This is a shift from managing behavior to stewarding systems. Accountability moves upstream, from individual actions to organizational design choices.

In an agent-enabled organization, leaders focus on direction, clarity, capability, and culture; the scaffolding within which human and agent contributions combine sustainably.

The Organization: A Shift in How Value Is Produced

Once these layers align, practitioners reshaping work, managers enabling effectiveness, leaders updating organizational models, the whole organization begins to change shape.

Three structural shifts emerge:

1. End-to-end outcomes become the unit of performance.

   The value lens shifts upward; what matters is flow, reliability, and experience, not individual task completion.

2. Continuous improvement becomes the operating norm.

   Agents create the conditions for ongoing refinement because exceptions become visible, patterns accumulate, and improvements can be applied incrementally.

3.   Human contribution rises in value, not volume.

Judgment, empathy, negotiation, creativity, interpretation, and reasoning expand as operational burden decreases.

The organization becomes designed for scalability, clarity, and adaptability; not because AI replaces work but because it redistributes work in a way that enables humans to operate closer to their strengths.

Increased capacity does not eliminate the need for workforce decisions; it changes their nature. As agents absorb repeatable work, organizations must make deliberate choices about where released capacity is reinvested: deeper expertise, faster response, improved experience, or new forms of value creation.

Without explicit reinvestment decisions, capacity gains dissipate. With them, organizations convert efficiency into resilience, adaptability, and sustained performance rather than short-term cost reduction.

A Final Reflection on the System We Are Choosing to Build

As humans and agent begin to work together, the organization is no longer defined solely by the people it employs but by the capabilities it cultivates. Agents do not replace human contribution; they *reorganize* it. They remove friction, lift operational load, and create a foundation of consistency that allows human judgment and creativity to matter more, not less.

The future of work is not one where humans step aside. It is one where humans step into roles that make full use of their strengths: interpretation, empathy, ethical reasoning, design, exploration, because agents take responsibility for the repeatable, the structured, and the predictable.

The real transformation therefore is not technological. It is organizational.

It requires

- Clarity or purpose

- Responsible boundaries

- Redesigned roles

- New forms of accountability

- Coherent operating models

- Leadership that understands value as a system, not an activity

The frontier firms leading this shift are not the ones with the most advanced agents. They are the ones with the clearest sense of how humans and agents create value together.

This is the heart of the new platform model: an organization that evolves continuously, learns from its own work, and treats improvement not as a project but as a constant source of advantage.

Chapter 10 ends here not because the transformation is complete but because it is the point where the organization must now take responsibility for what it becomes.

Value by Design: A New Way Forward

Throughout this book, we have taken a journey: from identifying opportunities to designing agents that serve real human and organizational needs to building systems that are safe, responsible, scalable, and ready for continuous improvement.

We began with a simple claim:

Value is not created by technology, it is created by design.

Design of systems, design of work, design of roles, design of governance, design of intent.

By the final chapter, that statement becomes literal. The real promise of agents is not automation. It is the chance to re-design how value is produced in a way that is more humane, more strategic, and more scalable than anything else available in prior generations of technology.

The transformation ahead is not something done to the organization. It is something done **by** them – with clarity, discipline, and imagination.

You now have

- The frameworks to identify real opportunities

- The tools to shape solutions that work for people

- The methods to design for impact

- The operating principles to sustain value over time

This book has one final invitation:

Do not wait for the future of work to arrive.

Design the future of work you want to lead.

When humans and agents work together by design, with clarity of intent, responsibility, and purpose, organizations unlock a form of value that is both scalable and profoundly human.

This is the moment of opportunity, and value by design is the vehicle.

The question facing organizations is no longer whether agents will become part of how work is done. That is already underway. The real question is whether the surrounding system is being redesigned with the same care as the technology itself.

Those who treat agents as tools will see incremental gains. Those who treat them as participants in work will be forced to redesign roles, accountability, and value measurement. Only the latter will experience sustained advantage.

Thank you for reading.

Index

I, J, K

L

M, N

GPSR Compliance
The European Union's (EU) General Product Safety Regulation (GPSR) is a set
of rules that requires consumer products to be safe and our obligations to
ensure this.

If you have any concerns about our products, you can contact us on

ProductSafety@springernature.com

In case Publisher is established outside the EU, the EU authorized
representative is:

Springer Nature Customer Service Center GmbH
Europaplatz 3
69115 Heidelberg, Germany